DATE DUE

Nov 12 69			
Jan26'70			
Jun 8 70			

HORATIO GREENOUGH

The First American Sculptor

HORATIO GREENOUGH by Hiram Powers, 1838.
(Courtesy of the Boston Museum of Fine Arts.)

Horatio Greenough

THE FIRST AMERICAN SCULPTOR

By

NATHALIA WRIGHT

Philadelphia . University of Pennsylvania Press

Published in Great Britain, India, and Pakistan
by the Oxford University Press
London, Bombay, and Karachi.

Library of Congress Catalog Card Number: 62–11261

7324

Printed in The United States of America

To

EVELYN BLIGHT SANDS

ALICE THORNDIKE

MERCEDES HUNTINGTON

MARY CURTIS

and the memory of

BEATRICE BLAKE NICKERSON

and

MARGUERITE WAGNIÈRE HORTON

Grandnieces of Horatio Greenough

Acknowledgments

My interest in Horatio Greenough was aroused during a year of study in the Department of American Civilization at Yale University in 1948–49. When in 1951 I began searching for biographical material about him, I applied to his collateral descendants, his children having died without issue. His brother Henry's granddaughters Mrs. Beatrice B. Nickerson and Miss Alice Thorndike and great-grandsons David and Fred Richardson generously allowed me to read family documents and see family pictures in their possession and to have copies of these items made. Subsequently, granddaughters of Greenough's sisters and of his brother Richard—Miss Mary Curtis, Mrs. Marguerite W. Horton of La Tour de Peilz, Switzerland, Mrs. Mercedes Huntington of Florence, and Mrs. N. Evelyn Sands of Cannes—furnished me with further family background; and Mrs. Horton made available to me the drawings and sculpture by Greenough and the other items associated with him in her possession. Without the aid of these representatives of the Greenough family this book could not have been written.

For the use of other indispensable materials I am indebted to the owners and administrators of many manuscript, book, and art collections. I have drawn most extensively on the resources of the Massachusetts Historical Society in Boston, whose librarian, Mr. Stephen Riley, was of unfailing assistance. I have also depended heavily on material in the Houghton Library at Harvard University, where Miss Carolyn Jakeman was consistently helpful, and in the National Archives, Washington, where Mr. Francis J. Heppner performed an invaluable service in locating the separately filed group of Greenough letters pertaining to his statue of Washington. The other principal collections which I have used are those of the Boston Athenaeum, the Boston Public Library, the Harvard Archives, the Library of Congress, the Maryland Historical Society in Baltimore, the New-York Historical Society, the New York Public Library, the Historical Society of Pennsylvania in Philadelphia, Yale University; and, in Florence, the Biblioteca Nazionale Centrale, the Biblioteca del Risorgimento, and the Gabinetto Vieusseux. For information by correspondence I am particularly obliged to Mr. David McKibbin of the Boston Athenaeum, Mr. Richard B. K. McLanathan of the Boston Museum of Fine Arts, and Mrs. H. W. Howell of the Frick Art Reference Library, New York.

To many other individuals I am deeply indebted for particular services: Mrs. Clara L. Dentler of Florence, who supplied me with the Greenough references in the material she used in her manuscript biography of Hiram Powers and who generally facilitated my investigations in Florence; Sign. Elio Tontulli of Florence for guidance in that city; Prof. James F. Beard of Clark University, who supplied me with the Greenough references in the papers of James Fenimore Cooper, which he is editing; Prof. Thomas Brumbaugh of Emory University, Mr. John Coolidge of the Fogg Art Museum of Harvard University, Prof. LeRoy P. Graf of the University of Tennessee, Mr. Francis Haber, formerly of the Maryland Historical Society, Miss Helen McCormack of the Gibbes Art Gallery in Charleston, S.C., Mr. Harold Small of the University of California Press for assistance in locating Greenough's sculpture; Mr. John D. Hatch of Lenox, Mass., for making Greenough's Roman sketchbook available to me; Dr. Helga Heintze of the Deutsches Archaelogisches Institut in Rome, Mr. Sigurd Schultze of Thorvaldsens Museum in Copenhagen, Mr. Dietrich von Bothmer of the Metropolitan Museum in New York, R. M. Mme. de Valon,

Supérieure du Couvent des Dames du Sacré-Coeur à la Trinité des Monts in Rome, for the identification of some of Greenough's sketches; Mr. Robert Martens and Mr. Alan L. Campbell, American vice consuls in Naples in 1953 and 1956 respectively, for copies of the documents in the Neapolitan Archives relative to Greenough; Sign. Guliano Valieri of Florence for copies of the documents in the Florentine public records relative to the studio which Greenough built there; my mother, Mrs. Elizabeth M. Wright, for assistance in assembling the photographs for this volume. To still other individuals I have acknowledged my indebtedness in footnotes to the text.

Early in my study of Greenough I was financially assisted by a grant from the American Philosophical Society (in the summer of 1952) and by a Fellowship from the John Simon Guggenheim Foundation (in 1953–54). I used the grant for research in Boston, Cambridge, and Washington. Enabled by the Fellowship, I gathered material in various places in this country and in Italy. From the administrators of the University of Tennessee Emperor Memorial Fund I have received financial assistance in having the manuscript typed and in providing the photographs for reproduction in this volume.

Valuable suggestions about revising the manuscript have come from Prof. James M. Fitch of Columbia University and Prof. Norman H. Pearson of Yale University; and advice about bibliographical matters from Prof. Richard B. Davis of the University of Tennessee. Miss Eleanor Goehring of the University of Tennessee Library helped me secure rare books. I was assisted in preparing the manuscript by Mrs. W. L. Norton, Knoxville, Tenn.

I have permission to print herewith unpublished material in the possession of or under the jurisdiction of the Academy of Fine Arts, Florence; the American Academy of Arts and Letters; the Art and Reference Library, Office of the Architect of the

Capitol, Washington, D.C.; the Biblioteca Nazionale Centrale, Florence; Georgetown University; Haverford College; the Historical Society of Pennsylvania; the Longfellow House, Cambridge, Mass.; McLean Hospital, Somerville, Mass.; the Maine Historical Society; the National Academy of Design; the New York Public Library; Mr. Henry G. Nickerson, Dedham, Mass.; the Ralph Waldo Emerson Memorial Association; and Mr. David Richardson, Washington, D. C.

I have permission to reproduce herewith photographs of sculpture in the possession of the Boston Museum of Fine Arts; Mrs. William Burnham, Brookline, Mass.; Mrs. Louis Curtis, Brookline, Mass.; Miss Mary Curtis, Hamilton, Mass.; Mrs. Grover Cleveland Edwards, Inman, S. C.; Mr. Gerald Horrigan, Quincy Adams, Mass.; the Mary Buie Museum, Oxford, Miss.; the National Collection of Fine Arts, Washington, D. C.; Mrs. Sumner A. Parker, Baltimore; the Pennsylvania Academy of the Fine Arts, Philadelphia; Dr. George C. Shattuck, Brookline, Mass.; the Somerset Club, Boston; Mrs. Florence Cole Vincent, Catskill, N. Y.

I have permission both to quote from unpublished material and to reproduce sculpture, drawings or paintings in the possession of the Boston Athenaeum, the Boston Public Library, Harvard University, the Maryland Historical Society, the Massachusetts Historical Society, the New York Historical Society, Miss Alice Thorndike of Manchester, Mass., the Valentine Museum in Richmond, Va., and Yale University.

I have permission to quote from printed material copyrighted by Charles Scribner's Sons, Columbia University Press, Harvard University Press, Houghton Mifflin Co., Little Brown & Co., Longmans, Green & Co., and the Ralph Waldo Emerson Memorial Association.

For photographic work I am in debt especially to George

Cushing, Boston, Mrs. Lou Spears, Maryville, Tenn., De Violette Bernhardt, of Spartanburg, S.C., the Barry Studio, Catskill, N.Y., Jack Engeman, Baltimore, Laurence Curtis, Brookline, Mass., William Charles, Beverley, Mass., Gerald Forbes, Oxford, Miss., Kerschner, Newport, R.I., H. B. Allison, Boston, and to others as indicated in the illustrations.

I am also obliged to other owners of Greenough letters and sculpture for allowing me to have copies of these items made for study, though they have not been quoted or reproduced. The names of most of these owners appear in the index to this volume.

To all these individuals, institutions, societies, and publishing houses, and to all others who have helped make this account of Greenough's life possible, I take pleasure in expressing my gratitude. I only wish I could have made it a better account.

Maryville, Tennessee N. W.

CONTENTS

ILLUSTRATIONS

Elizabeth Todhunter Thomas.
Evan Philip Thomas. 1837.
Drawing of the rejected design for the group for the east front of the Capitol. 1837. (?)
The Rescue. 1837–1851.
Venus. 1837–*c*1841.
Abdiel. 1838–1839.
St. John and the Angel. 1838–*c*1841.
John Warren. *c*1838–1839.
Memorial to George and Mary Gibbs. *c*1839–1842.
Lucifer. 1841–1842.
Christ. *c*1845–1846.
Arno. *c*1838.
St. Bernard Dog. *c*1844.
Drawings for Artist Whose Lamp is Being Refilled, 1847–1849. Samson and Delilah group, *c*1847 (not executed). Ada Reviczky, 1840–1841?. Equestrian Washington, *c*1851 (not executed).
Drawings for Electra, Orestes, and Pylades relief (?), *c*1847 (not executed). The Genius of Poesy, 1850?. David, *c*1844.
Castor and Pollux. *c*1847–1851.
The Genius of Italy. 1850.
Bacchante and Young Faun. *c*1850.
Homer. 1847–1851?
Nude figure from Roman sketchbook. Lake Nemi; the Colonna Castle on the left. 1826.
Draft of letter to Washington Allston, October 1831.
David playing to Saul.
Helios restraining Phaeton from mounting the sun chariot. 1832?
Athena interposing between Achilles and Agamemnon. 1832?
Nude model, 1830. Hospital patients, *c*1835. Thigh muscles, 1832.
Joseph Russell? Louisa Ingersoll Gore? 1836?
Four portraits.
Four *cappriciosi*.

Part I

1

Boston Boy : 1805-1825

Greenoughs and Benders

"I WAS BORN AND BROUGHT UP," wrote Horatio Greenough in the last year of his life, "in a town 'full of notions,' and being of an obstinate temper, which is congenital, I have retained very many of these notions intact."[1] He was born in Boston on September 6, 1805, into a family which on his father's side had lived there for a century and a half and on his mother's, there or nearby for half a century. To some of the principal moral and political convictions for which this city—stronghold of Puritanism and cradle of the Revolution—was famous he was indeed heir. Yet the temper of the time in which Greenough was born—the early national period—was rather venturesome than obstinate. This temper, reflected in the recent history of his family and soon to make Boston the center of a widespread cultural and intellectual revival, he also inherited and retained.

His father was David Greenough, who, eschewing the shipbuilding, instrument-making, and mercantile callings of his forbears, became one of the first large-scale real-estate dealers and builders in Boston. During the economically unstable years following the War of 1812 he invested too rapidly in a variety of enterprises and became bankrupt. Within a few more years, however, he re-established himself, and his estate eventually proved valuable. During the first period of his prosperity, largely as a sign of it, portraits of him and his wife were painted by Gilbert Stuart.[2]

Though apparently not a designer of buildings, David Greenough was associated with some notable architectural projects carried out in Boston during the early years of his career. He owned several lots and built two of the houses on Colonnade Row—the fashionable residential block for which Charles Bulfinch drew the plans—erected at the lower end of Common (now Tremont) Street between 1810 and 1814.[3] There were in all nineteen adjoining brick houses, of uniform Georgian design but of varying widths, whose most distinctive feature was a series of nearly eighty sandstone columns. Though exhibiting an English influence, they were evidence, in their simplicity and their variation within a pattern, of the emergence of a native building tradition. Of perhaps even greater significance was the block of fourteen buildings with fronts of hammered stone which David Greenough and another merchant put up in 1818 on newly opened Brattle Street, in the business district of the city. It was Boston's first stone block,[4] evidence not only of the increasing use of a new material but of the beginning of a new, more monumental tradition in building.

On Horatio Greenough his father's professional activities seem to have exerted a vital influence. Presumably they heightened his sense of form in general, particularly of architectural form. They must also have fostered his consciousness of a rapidly growing nation and his desire to be employed on a monumental public task. Some of them, moreover, involved the use of the type of material which he pioneered in using in his profession as sculptor.

Personally, David Greenough was remembered for his practical and indulgent nature. Apparently he had few intellectual allegiances. An "honest and benevolent man," Horatio described him at his death, "who had heard the Gospel preached during a long life in silence"; "the man on earth whom I esteemed and loved the most & who was rather a companion, than a governor of my youth."[5]

Greenough's mother was Elizabeth Bender, a native of Marlborough, Massachusetts, the daughter of a merchant turned carpenter and the sister of lawyers. (One of them wrote a prize-winning essay while at Harvard and owned a sizable collection of books at the time of his early death.) Of a volatile disposition, she was noted for her interest in gardening and in reading, wrote poetry over a period of many years, and liked to speculate about religion (in her poem "Transcendentalism" she pronounced this movement "impious").[6] Of art she was said to have had neither knowledge nor appreciation. According to her daughter-in-law Frances B. Greenough, she tended "always to look on the dark side" and was "with the best intentions . . . subject to jealousies and suspicions" which made her "a thorn to herself, and those about her."[7] Probably from her Greenough derived his tendency both to enthusiasm and to self-pity. In his opinion, she was "a good mother," a "gift" for which he felt indebted to his grandfather Bender.[8]

Eleven children were born to David and Elizabeth Greenough, of whom nine reached adulthood. Five had artistic and two had literary talents. John, the eldest, born in 1801, became a painter; Horatio, the next, a sculptor, architectural theorist, and writer; Henry, two years younger than Horatio, an architect, amateur painter, and writer; Louisa, an amateur painter; and Richard Saltonstall, the youngest, born in 1819, a sculptor. The only other son, Alfred, became a merchant.

Throughout David's career the Greenoughs changed places of residence frequently, following his fluctuating fortunes. When Horatio was born they lived on Green Street, in the heart of the city. From about his fifth to his fourteenth years they occupied the houses which David built on Colonnade Row, first Number

5 and then Number 1. By 1819, the year of his financial crisis, they were in the village of Jamaica Plain, on the outskirts of the city.[9] (Only here, where they rented a pew in the First Congregational Society—then Unitarian—did they evidently have any official connection with a church during Horatio's early years, though they may have attended Old South in Boston.) Five years later, when Horatio was a senior in college, they moved back to Boston, first to Number 2 Colonnade Row and then, about the time he went abroad as an art student, to Number 7 Chestnut Street.

The Statue in the Garden

As a boy Greenough exhibited his plastic talent in a variety of enterprises. He carved daggers and other objects in wood (notably three small heads), cast a pistol of lead and mounted it on a stock inlaid with lead flowers, molded a lion of butter, and cut a head in plaster in imitation of the design on a Roman coin. During a period of nearly two years he and Henry amused themselves by constructing miniature beeswax carriages and paper estates, with which they played out adventures.

The desire to produce sculpture was first aroused in him, Greenough often said, by the constant sight of a marble statue of Phocion (presumably a copy of the so-called antique work in the Vatican) which his father had placed on a mound in the family garden. Probably the date of this occurrence was the fall of 1816, when Horatio was eleven years old. He tried his hand first with chalk, then with unburnt plaster of Paris. Within a few weeks he had filled the shelves in his room with rows of miniature busts, copied from engravings, and had made a small chalk statue of William Penn from an engraving in the *Portfolio*. About the summer of 1818 he made a chalk copy of the bust of John Adams by J. B. Binon, a French sculptor living in Boston.

Colonnade Row, Boston, looking from Number 1.
(From a photograph in the Bostonian Society.)

As he copied this work the boy Greenough attracted an observer, who took him to the Boston Athenaeum and introduced him to the librarian, William S. Shaw. Shaw showed him the Athenaeum's casts, invited him to use them, and introduced him to other Boston art fanciers. One of them described him as of "prepossessing appearance and talent," an "interesting, fine-looking boy";[1] it was an early testimony to the extraordinary personal impression which he made all his life. From this time, according to Henry, he began to study with purpose and system.

At this time the Athenaeum's collection of statuary—the largest in Boston—consisted chiefly of some plaster busts, a marble bas-relief of a horse from Herculaneum, and casts of the "Laocoön" and a gladiator. Four years later eleven casts of some of the antique world's masterpieces were added, among them the "Apollo Belvedere," the "Venus dei Medici," the Capitoline "Venus" and "Antinoüs," the Borghese "Warrior," the "Torso of Hercules," and the "Discobolus." Young Ralph Waldo Emerson, who noticed that they attracted Athenaeum visitors in every corner "from the tedious joys of writing and reading," said they "fed the eyes of young men like nectar."[2] Without doubt Greenough, then a college freshman, was one of those young men.

Yet from such works he could have learned little of practical value. From a carver and architect—Solomon Willard—and a tombstone-maker—Alpheus Cary—he learned much more. Willard showed him how to model in clay, after he had unsuccessfully tried to do so from directions in the *Edinburgh Encyclopaedia,* and Cary showed him how to cut marble. He thereupon executed what was presumably his first work (perhaps in his first "workshop"—a well-curb turned on its side)[3] in this material: a bust of Bacchus. It was a sprightly and classical contrast to the angels, willows, doves, and skeletons commonly produced in such shops as Cary's. In two of Willard's varied enterprises about this time his young pupil must have been especially interested: his efforts to obtain the commission (awarded later to the English Francis Chantrey) for a statue of Washington for the State House in Boston and his plan (never carried out) to carve the scene of Paul before Agrippa in the pediment of St. Paul's Church.

Eventually young Greenough met Binon, who taught him the rudiments of modeling. He was probably fourteen or fifteen at the time, living in Jamaica Plain. (Local tradition had it that his first lessons in sculpture were received in the W. G. Weld house there.)[4] He probably also heard Binon talk about the art and artists of Italy, where he had spent several years, and perhaps about some of the problems which he had discovered confronted an artist in America. He had hoped to secure the commission for a monument to Washington which Congress had resolved to erect (the commission eventually given went to Greenough), but further action about this project was delayed. So difficult did he find it to support himself by his art in Boston that he resorted to the production of fertilizer from calcined plaster and a few years later evidently left the city.

To Greenough's choice of profession his father and some of his friends at first objected, probably because of the uncertain income which it promised, but in the end his father approved it. David insisted, however, that both Horatio and John, who early proposed to become a painter, secure a college education before embarking upon their careers.

The profession which Horatio had chosen was, indeed, virtually nonexistent in America. There were no more than a dozen sculptors in the country, about half of them around Washington, and all were foreign born. John Frazee did not execute his first bust—the first in marble by an American—until 1824 or 1825. In the opinion of disillusioned John Trumbull, the painter, no sculpture would be wanted in America for a hundred years. Yet partly because of the recent introduction of stone into construction and partly because of the call for public monuments in the new nation, a whole generation of American artists was about to take up new materials and tools and give their country the reputation of having a peculiar genius for expressing itself in marble.

In this generation, born between 1800 and 1830, at least one hundred Americans and a dozen European immigrants became sculptors. Only the obscure Scottish James Thom was older than Greenough; most were more than ten years younger. Hiram Powers was the same age, but he did not begin to model until he was about twenty-four. Greenough was the first of his countrymen to enter and to pursue exclusively the new profession. He also set a precedent for more than a third of these sculptors by going to Italy for study. With most of them, however, he had little else in common. They were chiefly sons of farmers and tradesmen, many from frontier communities, who approached sculpture through wood carving or stonecutting, in their twenties or later. Whereas for many the making of statuary was not only a mechanical process but a business, which they expedited by the invention of numerous labor-saving devices, it was for Greenough supremely an art. In excellence of achievement he was one of the three or four best — with Powers, William Rimmer, and William Rinehart. In scope, however, his achievement was by far the broadest; he worked in all the major sculptural modes: portrait and ideal busts and statues, colossi, groups, and reliefs.

Had he been more provincial, like Frazee, or like Rimmer essentially naturalistic, had his aspirations been either less or greater, Greenough might never have left America. It was not necessary to do so in order to become a sculptor, but only to become the kind of sculptor he wanted to be. He aspired from the first to the creation of monumental works in the classical tradition already established in American public architecture and at the same time to eminence in an international and a historical sense. Only in Italy, best of all in Rome, could such a career be prepared for. That country possessed some of the finest marble, the most skilled workmen, and the richest collections of art in the world, and that city—on account of the presence there of the two leading contemporary sculptors, Canova and Thorvaldsen—was the capital of the contemporary world for sculptors. There, probably almost as early and as naturally as he settled upon his profession—surely by the time he was a sophomore in college—Greenough determined to go.

In so determining, moreover, he was following a tradition of foreign study which was well established among American painters—from West and Copley to Allston, Vanderlyn, and Morse. This tradition John Greenough followed by going to London shortly before Horatio went to Italy.

Classical Academies

As Henry described him, Horatio was a schoolboy who was unusually proficient in the classics, abhorred mathematics, had an excellent memory and once won a prize for learning over a thousand lines more English poetry than his competitors, delighted in games and amusements and excelled his fellows in running, jumping, and swimming, and engaged in artistic pursuits whenever possible. He was "generally robust, and of an active and sanguine temperament."[1]

All the Greenough children apparently first attended the Boston public schools. At an early age the older boys were sent to nearby private academies. In them all, the chief subjects taught were Greek and Latin. When John was thirteen and Horatio nine, they went for a year to the one in Andover.[2] Probably they stayed no longer because the intensely religious atmosphere there proved uncongenial. At least between the years 1817 and 1819 Horatio and Henry attended the secular and to some extent experimental institution at Lancaster, where they were happy under the headmastership of young George B. Emerson.[3] In 1821 Horatio entered Harvard, a year after John and two years before Henry and Alfred. For a while all the brothers were there together.

Like many of his fellow alumni, Greenough deprecated the education he received in college. "Fain would I also lay claim to the title of self-made man," he wrote late in life, jocosely explaining that Harvard in his day was "near enough self-making to satisfy any reasonable ambition."[4] At that time it was, indeed, hardly more than an academy itself. Yet broadening influences were already at work upon it, and even by its limited program Greenough as a student was stimulated.

The most important texts at Harvard in his day were the works of the Latin writers of the Augustan Age, Blair's *Lectures on Rhetoric,* Locke's *Essays,* Paley's *Evidences of Christianity* and *Natural Theology,* Stewart's *Elements of the Philosophy of the Human Mind,* Butler's *Analogy,* and the *Federalist.* Altogether they represented the neo-classical taste and the rationalistic and utilitarian thought—the conservative intellectual pattern—of the late eighteenth century. By such contemporaries of Greenough as Emerson, who graduated the year before he entered, and his classmates Frederic H. Hedge and George P. Bradford this pattern was largely rejected. To Greenough, however, it was profoundly congenial. His own thought proved to have the same basic outline.

At the same time he was also apparently influenced by such developments at Harvard as the triumph of Unitarianism, the introduction of a pragmatic methodology by teachers like Thomas Nuttall in natural history and Edward T. Channing in rhetoric, and, above all, the encouragement by President

John T. Kirkland of foreign study. During Greenough's college years there were on the faculty four young scholars—Edward Everett, George Ticknor, Joseph Cogswell, and George Bancroft—who had recently returned from Europe, all stimulated by their experience there. Cogswell, the librarian, had brought back casts and valuable drawings, some of which he lent Greenough. It was Cogswell, Greenough later said, who perhaps more than anyone else helped fix his purpose.[5]

As a college student Greenough was reported to have excelled in all subjects except mathematics and to have made himself particularly "a good classical scholar."[6] Evidently he read Italian and French by the time he was a sophomore; in anticipation of going to Italy he learned to speak Italian. (An accomplished linguist all his life, he once said he learned all the foreign languages he knew after he had retired for the night, by reading grammars and exercise books until he fell asleep.)[7] In his junior year he received one of the parts for the annual Exhibition Program, at which time he and two other students were to engage in a brief conference on the subject: "Comparison of the virtues and vices of the state of society described by Homer in the Odessey, that of the first ages of the Roman Republic, & that of the age of chivalry."[8] Family tradition apparently had it that he wrote his piece but out of diffidence wished to avoid delivering it. In his senior year he evidently took natural history.[9] Presumably he read a good deal throughout the four years. He became familiar with Shakespeare and the romantic poets and composed several sonnets himself. As a sophomore, for which time only the records are extant, he withdrew from the college library thirty-two volumes.[10] Most of them were anatomies, descriptions of Italy and Greece, lives of artists, and art histories and treatises (by Alberti, Cellini, Leonardo da Vinci, Du Fresnoy, Evelyn, and Winckelmann). Among the number were also the works of Fielding and Goldoni.

According to Henry, in fact, Horatio was chiefly occupied during his college years with private studies related to his chosen profession. He modeled busts of several contemporaries and of Washington from a Gilbert Stuart portrait, copied a bust of Napoleon, and painted a landscape. Probably the earliest preserved work of his is a group of eight drawings of animal skeletons copied presumably about this time from some of the engravings in William Cheselden's *Osteographia,* one of the books he borrowed from the Harvard library. From his sophomore year on he studied anatomy. (In these years his roommates and some of his closest friends were pre-medical students.) In this study he had the aid of one of Boston's prominent physicians, Dr. George Parkman, who each week lent him bones, preparations, and books. Parker also lent him money when he went abroad.

Most of his collegemates remembered Greenough for his serious artistic concerns. "Greenough," wrote his freshman roommate, J. N. Bellows, a decade later,

> was born a sculptor; that is, he was born with a temperament and disposition to nourish some noble design, some definite purpose for the benefit of his age. Endowed with a remarkable delicacy of character, even in boyhood, he shunned society, to devote himself to his darling pursuits. At school, at college, this was the single object before his mind—it absorbed his whole heart. He undoubtedly felt then, that he possessed a treasure which he must not tarnish with other interests.

"We well remember," wrote another friend, probably George Hillard, "his commanding figure and intellectual countenance while at college. His taste for art was strong; the inspiration was upon him."[11]

Probably Greenough appeared now as he did in manhood: handsome in features, six feet tall, strikingly well proportioned, and agile in movement. He had a "heroic figure," editor John Bigelow thought in later years, "fashioned for the triumphs of the ancient games."[12] When speaking, he was generally animated. He was a fluent and witty talker, a fact which many who knew him remarked about in connection with his personal appearance.

The Master

During his junior year in college Greenough met the painter Washington Allston and so began the association which meant more to him than any other he ever formed. Allston was fifty-five at the time, at the peak of his achievement and fame. His rooms and studio were in Boston, but he was more often seen in Cambridge, where his closest friends, the brothers Edmund T. and Richard H. Dana, lived. He customarily spent Saturday night at Edmund's house, presiding over a small circle. Here Greenough had rooms with John Howard in his senior year and was probably a frequent visitor the year before, when Howard alone was Dana's roomer. Howard's sister Elizabeth remembered how the two youths would bring anatomical preparations home to Boston at the end of the week and then return to Edmund Dana's to be there when Allston was. Others who were present on these occasions remembered the scene "on a moonlight evening of summer" when Greenough and Allston

> were the central figures of a charmed group on the piazza . . . the spiritual countenance and long silvery hair of Allston, wearing the semblance of a bard or prophet, and the tall agile figure and radiant face of his young disciple, both intent upon a genial theme.[1]

In the Allston circle Edmund Dana was called "The Master," because of the wide range of his professed knowledge, but it was Allston who supremely filled this role for Greenough. He filled, indeed, in Greenough's analysis, an even more intimate role. "Allston . . . was to me a father, in what concerned my progress of every kind," he wrote in the autobiographical account he prepared in 1833 for William Dunlap, the art historian.

He taught me first how to discriminate—how to think—how to feel. Before I knew him I felt strongly but blindly, as it were; and if I should never pass mediocrity, I should attribute it to my absence from him. So adapted did he seem to kindle and enlighten me, making me no longer myself, but, as it were, an emanation of his own soul.

"A note to Allston's life," he wrote Henry at the same time, *". . . might tell all of me which is essential."* Grateful that he had been in America at the time and had visited Allston shortly before his death in 1843, Greenough wrote Richard Dana that it seemed

as if Providence had so ordered it that I should enjoy once more the benefit of that light which had guided my youth and was about to be removed from hence.

"I knew all that I was enjoying while Allston lived," he wrote Dana on another occasion. "I can truly say that I heard him as an angel and that when far from him he exercised over me a power no other man ever did."[2]

Much of Allston's attraction for Greenough would seem to have been that of a kindred personality. Both men had social, intellectual, and aristocratic natures. To a great extent they typified the artist as gentleman. To Greenough, moreover, Allston represented the ideal artist: a follower of the greatest traditions of the past, a creator of original and unique forms, above all a votary of art, regardless of remuneration or popularity.

As Greenough's artistic character developed, it too conformed to this pattern, partly no doubt under the influence of Allston. Largely from Allston he imbibed two doctrines which were basic to his artistic philosophy: that the greatest art was more an expression of the mind than an imitation of the forms of nature, and that the masterpieces of the past were the best teachers of art. In consequence of subscribing to these doctrines he, like Allston, was at variance with some of the chief artistic fashions of his day: academic neo-classicism, romantic primitivism, literal portraiture. Probably in the beginning Greenough was specifically imitating Allston in drawing subjects from literature—notably from the Bible—and in insisting that a work of art have feeling.

About the precise esthetic qualities to be embodied in a work of art, however, the two artists differed radically, the older being committed to the newer romantic ideal and the younger to the older classical one. To Allston the human mind was the most wonderful of all phenomena, and nearly all his works are introspective, evoking an atmosphere of mystery if not fear. To Greenough, on the other hand, the human body was the perfect form. Most of his works are distinguished by repose, impersonality, and a severe simplicity, and his most ambitious ones by the nobly heroic in subject.

On Greenough's thought, too, Allston exerted a vital but limited influence. Like Allston, Greenough developed a theory of form as functional or organic. (Allston's theory was set forth in his *Lectures on Art,* prepared about 1830 but not published until after his death.) Probably in the beginning Greenough was influenced by Allston to believe that a work of art should have unity above everything else. Yet the theories of the two men were significantly different. Whereas Allston's was largely philosophic, Greenough's was stated in terms of comparative anatomy, merged to some extent with an organic conception of history, and applied to a particular art form: architecture. Ultimately Greenough, too, was borne on by new intellectual currents—farther, indeed, than Allston.

The Argument for the Obelisk

Greenough was nineteen, a college senior, when he undertook his first important artistic project. Like his two major projects, it was by nature public, colossal, and memorial, and like them it precipitated controversy. His defense of it, moreover, was an embryonic statement of his mature esthetic thought. This project was a design for the Bunker Hill Monument.

Early in 1825 the recently organized Bunker Hill Monument Association in Boston announced a public competition for the plan and perspective drawing of a 220-foot column to be erected on the site of the Revolutionary engagement on Bunker and Breed's Hills, in Charlestown, and offered a premium of $100 to the winner. (The preceding year it had authorized Solomon Willard to draw a plan for such a monument and had issued a circular soliciting subscriptions for it; but no explanation was given for the change of procedure.) By April 1, the deadline set, about fifty plans, mostly in the form of letters, had been received, though by no means all were of columns.

Greenough's letter (Number 12) was one of those which were not.[1] Disregarding all the announced specifications, he proposed a 100-foot obelisk resting on a 20-foot plinth and submitted a two-foot wooden model painted the color of granite and a drawing of a section. The shaft was to be of the proportions of one at ancient Thebes, to contain a circular staircase, and to be approached by flights of steps from each side of the lower base. At the corners of the plinth were to stand four pieces of sculpture or—if economy dictated—four large field pieces.

He designed four sculptural works for these places and affixed clay models of them to his wooden model.[2] The first three, entitled "Subjection of the Colonies," "Resistance of the Colonies," and "Discomfiture of the British Forces," depicted a nude male figure being held down by a lion, then forcing the lion down, and last seeming to embrace the animal. The fourth work, untitled in a sketch he made, depicted the man looking upward, his hands clasped, a sword resting on his leg, an eagle behind and a scroll on the ground before him. In two particulars —the upward gesture and the abandoned sword—this figure anticipated Greenough's statue of Washington for the Capitol. Representative as the lion was of the British Empire, the two figures in the first three works also suggested Hercules (by whom Greenough symbolized America on the chair of his "Washington") and the Nemean lion.

With due respect for the Monument Association's proposals, young Greenough was at pains to explain why he had not followed them. He had constructed a model, he wrote, because since it could be said "to *contain* in itself a perspective of the object, as seen from *every point* instead of *one only*" it was more easily understood. He had chosen the obelisk

as the most purely *monumental* form of structure. The column grand and beautiful as it is *in its place* (where it stands beneath the weight of a pediment & supports a long line of heavy entablature) considered as a monument seems liable to unanswerable objections. It steps forth from that *body* of which it has been made a harmonious *part* to take a situation which of all others requires *unity* of form—hence—the more completely it has been fitted to a situation so different—the greater must be the number of *useless* appendages and *unmeaning* parts when it assumes its new place and office.

Greenough's letter was permeated by the utilitarian and economic values of the society in which he lived. It reflected sentiments (about simplicity, appropriateness, and adaptation) widely held in his father's professional circle, opinions of Allston (who specifically disapproved of the design of a column), and the scholarly consensus (as Greenough presumably found in his reading about ancient art and history) that monumental columns were anomalous. Yet the architectural theory implicit in it was a manifestation of independent thought. It was written, moreover, in a bold and figurative style, which came to be characteristic of Greenough's literary composition.

Particularly were his proposals remarkable in comparison with those made by two other contestants: surveyor John G. Hales of Boston and the southern architect Robert Mills, both of whom submitted designs of a column and an obelisk. Hales expressed no preference between the two forms. Mills, by far the most experienced and best known of the contestants, urged that the obelisk be chosen, but his reasons were significantly different from Greenough's. It was, he said, an older form and better fitted for commemorative purposes by its height, strength, and plain surfaces, which could be inscribed. The details of his design were, moreover, far more elaborate than Greenough's.[3]

As judges of the contest, a Board of Artists, consisting of Gilbert Stuart, Allston, George Ticknor, Laommi Baldwin, and Daniel Webster, was appointed. These officials promptly announced themselves opposed to a column, and at their meeting on April 25 they recommended that the premium be awarded to Greenough; Stuart as chairman wrote "approved" on the model. Yet they added that they did not advise that the monument be erected according to Greenough's plan and that they were at the moment unable to give any opinion which would be satisfactory to themselves or the Association. Possibly they were troubled by the temporary presence of Dr. John C. Warren, nephew of the hero of the Bunker Hill battle, among those favoring a column and the absence of an estimate of an obelisk's cost.

Their recommendation proved unacceptable to the majority of the directors, who laid the report on the table and appointed a new committee on the design, which recommended a copy of Trajan's column. By this time, however, the sentiments of the directors had crystallized and this recommendation was voted down. A third and last committee, of which Allston, Ticknor, and Baldwin were members, was now chosen to bring in the plan and estimate of an obelisk. At this point—late in May—Greenough was asked to submit an estimate for an obelisk, and he apparently did so.[4] But in the meantime he had gone to Rome and there seem to have been no further negotiations between him and the Association.

The monument which was finally erected, under Willard's direction, was even plainer than Greenough's design, being merely a shaft. The absence of a plinth, Greenough complained to Samuel Morse in 1832, "made the shaft start sheer from the dirt like a spear of asparagus"; the obtuse rather than his proposed acute angle produced "broken-chimney-like effects"; and the whole was enclosed by "a light, elegant fence *à la Parigin*[*o*] [like a Parisian], as though the austere forms of Egypt were compatible with the decorative flummery of the Boulevards." In exasperation he concluded, "Let 'em go for dunderheads, as they are!"[5]

Nor did the Monument Association officially give Greenough credit for his part in the adoption of the form of an obelisk. Willard expressed surprise on reading in the *North American Review* of July 1830 an allusion to Greenough as the designer of the monument and declared he was unaware that his young friend had anything to do with the design then in progress. For that matter, the Association did not even acknowledge receipt of the plans of Mills, who assumed that his preferred plan had been appropriated and barbarously altered. Altogether the forecast which this organization represented for an American artist desirous of public employment was from one point of view not promising.

Nevertheless from another point of view this forecast was all that could be desired. The very existence of such an organization was evidence of a dawning popular consciousness of the uses of art. For young Greenough the whole monument project must have been one more incentive to prepare himself to receive a sculptural commission of like nature.

Now that his college course was nearly over only one thing threatened to keep him from going abroad: his father's financial inability to send him. Under these circumstances merchant Amos Lawrence lent David Greenough money for Horatio's use.[6] The work of the senior class at Harvard was not finished until July and the annual commencement not held until August, but Horatio was impatient at all unnecessary delay. He obtained permission to be absent from the final exercises and had his diploma forwarded to him.[7] About April or early May he sailed on a vessel bound for Gibraltar.

He was still in his teens, and he had hardly been out of the city of his birth; he had executed little more than toys, and he had seen no great original pieces of sculpture. Yet already the broad outlines of Greenough's character as a man and an artist were drawn. His idealism, nationalism, and classicism, his ambition and diligence, his interest in architecture and esthetic theory as well as sculpture, his sociability and his sensitivity—all were there. Eight and a half years later he wrote Allston from Italy, "My notions of men and things are just what they were when I sail'd."[8] After 1825 he spent only about three years altogether in America. Yet at the end of his life he was able to declare, in a peculiarly appropriate figure of speech,

> In . . . stopping here and there among men of different races, creeds and forms of civilization, I have become inoculated, to some extent, with the various ways of thinking of those about me, always retaining nearly the same proportion of original Yankee conviction to afterthought, that you will find of matrix to pebbles in the pudding-stone of Roxbury, Mass.[9]

2

Student Abroad and Critic at Home 1825-1828

On Holy Ground

EARLY IN MAY 1825 GREENOUGH reached Gibraltar. After waiting more than a month there to secure passage to Leghorn, he embarked about the middle of June for Marseilles in the brig *New York,* whose captain was his acquaintance, Bostonian John Apthorp. Because of an epidemic of smallpox in the city they had a quarantine of fifteen days to perform upon their arrival, and since all vessels to and from Leghorn were also quarantined Greenough's departure was delayed.

His first taste of this, his first European city, left him intoxicated but in full command of his national senses. He admired the picturesque feluccas and the stately Rue de Rome; was gratified to find he could make himself understood and became interested in the Provençal language; and sternly criticized the character of the French. (Though given to much talk about liberty, they had, he felt, only "a cant of freedom,—the noisiest of all cants.")[1] He promptly sent home sketches and promised to try to find positions for Henry and Alfred abroad. Above all, of course, he was excited by his first sight of European art. He objected to the baroque Hôtel de Ville, but he evidently liked the simple château Borély outside the city and especially admired in it an Andrea del Sarto, Bernini's "Dead Christ," a Rembrandt, an "Orizante," and a boy by Murillo.

Unwilling to wait until passage could be secured for Leghorn, Greenough finally proceeded on his journey by the more expensive land route. He passed through Genoa, where he evidently visited Palazzo Brignoli and admired the Van Dykes, and where, in a church, he came upon a statue which he thought was the most perfect he had ever seen. Observing that others, more accustomed to such objects than he, were passing it by unnoticed, he suddenly realized that his goal was infinitely farther beyond his reach than he had thought, and, after going out, beside a pile of rubbish in a palace yard, he wept. The episode was doubly revealing, showing up at the beginning of his career both his extreme ambition and his liability to an acute sense of failure. He also stopped briefly in Florence, where he paid a call on Lorenzo Bartolini, the leading Tuscan sculptor. At this time, however, he was not impressed by Bartolini's naturalistic work.

Sometime in the fall Greenough reached Rome. A few weeks later, about the first of December, another American art student arrived—the painter Robert Weir of New York. Soon afterward the two took rooms together, and during most of the next fifteen months they were close companions. A few other Americans, including some painters, passed through Rome while they were there, but most of the time they were the only ones in the city.

They lived first on the Pincian Hill—long the resort of foreigners, students, and artists—probably in the house designed and once occupied by the seventeenth-century painter Claude Lorrain and called, because of its simple Doric portico, Tèmpiétto.[2] It stood at the corner of Via Gregoriana and Via Sistina, on the Piazza della Trinitá, at the top of the Scala di Spagna. The spot was, as Weir said, "holy ground" to them.[3] Next door on one side was the former dwelling of Salvator Rosa, with its apertures in the shape of monstrous mouths, and on the other was Casa Zuccari, the family home of the sixteenth-century painters of that name. Across the piazza, next to the French church of Trinité des Monts (containing Lorrain's tomb), once lived Nicolas Poussin. Farther down Via Sistina was Thorvaldsen's apartment. A short distance along the brow of the hill was the French Academy, housed in the Villa Medici; here students of all nationalities studied free of charge from nude models and a large collection of antique casts. Just off the Piazza di Spagna, at the foot of the stairs, was the Caffè Greco, celebrated gathering place of the artists.

In all aspects of the artist life of Rome the two American youths were soon immersed. They customarily rose early, either pursued some study in their rooms or went to the French Academy and drew from the antique until breakfast. They then separated, Weir going to one of the galleries to copy and Greenough to another to draw or to his rooms, which also served as his studio. The closing hour of most galleries was three o'clock. Then came lunch. In the afternoons Horatio modeled from life some subject of his own composition. They dined at six, usually at a place which had formerly been the painting room of Pompeo Batoni. After dinner they repaired to the Caffè Greco, where they talked until seven, when the life schools opened. They attended the English school, where they studied and drew from life for two hours. (Eastlake, Gibson, Severn, the younger Westmacott, and Wyatt were the principal English artists in the city.) Then if the night was fine and the moon out, the pair joined parties going to walk among the ruins. "We lived and moved in art," Weir said; "it was our food, ready at all times, we had but to stretch out our hands and pluck what we wanted."[4]

The greatest sculptor in Rome at this time and the generally acknowledged head of the neo-classical school was the Danish Bertel Thorvaldsen. Greenough brought letters of introduction to him. That school's virtual founder and most brilliant exponent—Venetian Antonio Canova—had died only a few years earlier, however, and the followers of each master composed rival factions. Whereas the works of Canova which had established a vogue were sentimental, polished, and effeminate, those of Thorvaldsen were typically grand, rugged, and masculine. The Dane freely imitated rather than slavishly copied the antique (as most of the neo-classical shcool tended to do), and his range of imaginative subjects was broader than the Italian's.

Between these two masters Greenough was not prepared to distinguish at first, but he was not long in doing so. By May 1826, when he wrote Allston a letter chronicling his progress to that point,[5] he had taken a stand of his own, closer to Thorvaldsen but independent of both. His first contacts with artists in the city, he said, were with those whose chief merit was in "*execution*," on which account he was at first engrossed with the "*means*" of his art and led "to think more of the mechanical than the truly intellectual part." Probably these first associates of his were among the horde of minor Italians who aligned themselves with the school of Canova. Even at this time Greenough had, he said, "a strong notion that *something more* than mere drawing and composition was necessary," though the notion was a vague one. Soon, however, he met Thorvaldsen, and his views in consequence underwent "the greatest change." By a few words spoken in expressing an opinion of his work, Thorvaldsen taught him, he said, "to think for myself in my art." For Thorvaldsen's own work, he said a few years later, he had admiration often and respect always.[6]

Of Canova his opinion rapidly sank . The Italian "was clever," he thought, but "superficial & sensual in his style—& a most barefaced misrepresenter of Nature," who was destined to "fall *very low very shortly*." The Italians in general, he decided, had a narrow view of art, looked only at execution, and "*ape* instead of truly *imitating*. They *study* the *Greeks* for examples *altogether* instead of studying as the Greeks *did*." He was astonished that one artist should ever attempt to imitate another "in what *characterises* his style as *individual*."

Greenough's own artistic aims, as he now began to articulate them, were both idealistic and naturalistic and bore no particular resemblance to those of any school. His object, he wrote Allston, was to enable himself to "model the figure in all its ages from infancy to decrepitude—under any circumstances, naked–draped etc. at rest, in action," and at the same time to make himself master of his "*composition* . . . from the mere management of line as in Architecture & single statues up to the true poetry of telling a story with truth and grace." He became more interested in portraiture, partly no doubt because of Thorvaldsen's considerable achievement in this line. Above all, he hoped in the future to pay attention to what he called

> *character,* a beauty in a work of art perhaps the most gratifying of all to the intellect & which has been always most neglected—in fact none but the very first minds have seized it or discovered its principles.

He did not think of these powers as attainable separately but made a point of studying them together. The approach was one which Thorvaldsen was celebrated for teaching, but to the pupil of Allston, accustomed to regarding the work of art as a whole, it could hardly have seemed new.

In some of these views Greenough was confirmed by certain German artists in the city. Their best men, he thought, combined a "laborious investig[ation] of Nature and industrious study of the means of art" to tell beautiful stories and to convey deep sentiment. Presumably he meant the group of romantic and mystical painters called the Nazarenes, composed chiefly of Overbeck, Cornelius, Wilhelm Schadow, and Julius Schnorr von Carolsfeld. Allston had known and had strongly influenced some of them.

But it was in the works of the great masters of the past modeled after the forms of nature that Greenough found his own artistic aims supremely realized. His program of study was based equally on these works and these forms. How closely related and how important he thought the two was evident in the account of his development which he gave Dunlap a few years later. "I began to *study* art in Rome, in 1826," he wrote. Until then I had rather amused myself with clay and marble than studied. When I say, that those materials were familiar to my touch, I say all that I profited by my boyish efforts. They were rude. I lived with poets and poetry, and could not then see that my art was to be studied from folk who eat their three meals every day. I *gazed* at the Apollo and the Venus, and *learned* very little by it. It was not till I ran through all the galleries and studio[s] of Rome, and had had under my eye the genial forms of Italy that I began to feel nature's value. I had before adored her, but as a Persian does the sun, with my face to the earth. I then began to examine her.[7]

As for the practical aspect of his art, he learned most, he often said, from fellow students. Once when a friend complained that whenever he asked his master anything about the management of his clay he was told only *"what a great man was Phidias,"*[8] Greenough advised him to talk more freely with other students about such matters, observing that masters commonly preferred to talk of abstract principles and to attribute success to genius, if only to preserve their dignity.

A small sketchbook of Greenough's, which he began to keep in January 1826, constitutes a revealing record of the various aspects of his Roman studies. It also reveals to a remarkable extent the nature and the scope of his taste, essentially formed as it was at the outset of his career. Somewhat more than a third of the sketches in this book represent the work of other artists;

approximately a third consist of nudes, portraits from life, and original compositions; the remaining number include landscapes, studies of foliage, and anatomical casts. (He began to buy such casts, from which he modeled and drew; afterward, he found, he saw the antique "with a different eye.") About half the works by others which he drew were antique. Many of them—figures from the Parthenon frieze, the "Standing Discus Thrower," the "Hermes Belvedere," the Borghese "Mars," and the "Jason Hermes"—are expressions of the epic tradition of the Hellenic period of Greek sculpture. His preference for such figures is evidence of the independent nature of his classicism: the neo-classical school was more influenced by works of the later, Hellenistic period. His admiration for other traditions in antique art is reflected in his sketches of such reliefs as "Perseus Rescuing Andromeda," "Euridice between Hermes and Orpheus," and "Medea with the Daughters of Peleas," of Boethus' "Boy with Goose," and of Roman portrait busts. He drew three works by Michelangelo—Christ from the "Pietá," the "Madonna Taddei," and the "Risen Christ"—and seven by Thorvaldsen. Among the sketches which seem to be original compositions, several were inspired by the epic tradition in Greek literature (one depicts Thetis appearing to Achilles from the water, as recounted early in the *Iliad*). A few—notably a David with Goliath's head—were inspired by the Bible. A few other extant sketches of Greenough's made when he was in Italy at this time are similar in nature to those in his sketchbook.[9]

During his first five or six months in Rome Greenough modeled several works, but he put little or nothing in marble and nothing seems to have survived. Soon after his arrival he began a life-size statue of the Dead Abel. This subject, for all its unclassical character, was having something of a vogue at this time, probably because of the popularity of the poem "The Death of Abel," by the eighteenth-century Swiss Solomon

Gessler. Another episode from this poem—Eve startled by the sight of a dead bird—had just been treated by the young Irish sculptor, John Hogan, then in Rome, whom Greenough knew; he drew Hogan's statue in his sketchbook. He also drew, perhaps in connection with his statue, the detail of the death of Abel in one of the frescoes in the church of Trinité des Monts. By the spring he had finished modeling the statue. Allston, who saw it in Boston a few years later, pronounced it "a figure of great beauty and truth, and such a *first work* as I never before have seen."[10]

By May Greenough had begun another statue, of David at the moment of saying to Goliath, "Thou comest to me with a sword, and with a spear, and with a shield." On account of the great number of distinguished treatments of it, this subject was an even more ambitious one than that of the "Abel." Perhaps he was partly inspired by Michelangelo's treatment in Florence—the "grandest piece of the naked that the Christian world has seen done,"[11] he called it a few years later. He may not have finished his second statue, for he soon fell ill. During the early months of 1826 he also modeled several busts, including one of himself.[12]

He had plans for yet more ambitious works and looked forward to the composition soon of groups and bas-reliefs, as he wrote Allston and as several of his sketches suggested. He hoped to remain in Rome several years—to become "master" of his art.

Meanwhile, however, he had been too impatient to reach this goal. He often rose in the night to pursue his studies; he was more confined than Weir, did not visit so many galleries or sketch so much out of doors. In consequence his health declined. As the malarial season came on, in early June, he left Rome for a short time, evidently for the Alban Mountains. Among his sketches are one of the Greek stele in the museum of Grottaferrata and several of the lake and castle at Nemi. Weir, who remained in Rome, moved into cheaper quarters (each paid $10 a month in the ones they shared), and when Greenough returned to the city, late in the summer, he took others. Partly because he was alone, he fell into a state of depression, and soon, following an attack of indigestion, he became seriously ill, reportedly of malaria. The woman in charge of his quarters notified Weir, who moved in and cared for him. For a time his life was despaired of. A few years later when an American in Florence died of a similar ailment Greenough recalled his own experience as he wrote the news to James Fenimore Cooper:

[Mr. Dwight] had attack [*sic*] very like the one which prostrated me 4 years since but he fell into the hands of very different physicians. I don't remember any violent remedies in my case. . . . The physician said he despaired of saving his life from the first. Mine did likewise—but how different were the consequences of his despair. Thinking he could do nothing for me he let me alone and the Great Mother took care of me.[13]

Greenough's recovery was apparently slow, and eventually he was advised by his physician to try a change of air. Accordingly in January 1827 he set out for Naples,[14] taking with him a letter from the banking house of the American John Rogers in Marseilles to the branch of that house in the Italian city. He traveled with an American college professor, Romeo Elton, and an Englishman in a vettura. As the party entered Naples on January 14, Greenough gave signs of being mentally deranged. They were taken by the driver to the police and by the police to the American consul, Alexander Hammett, who arranged for Greenough to be accommodated at the Hotel Lombardia. By the provision of one of the Rogerses he was examined by two physicians, who advised that he be sent to the insane asylum at Aversa, where he would have been kept at the expense of the banker. Hammett requested authorization from the Prefect of

Police for this move. Instead of complying, however, the Prefect sent another doctor to see Greenough—the director of the similar establishment at Miano, in Abruzzo, who diagnosed his condition as temporary and recommended that he be sent for observation to Miano. Meanwhile he continued to require care at the Lombardia. On the 22nd Hammett urgently requested the Minister of Foreign Affairs to intervene and relieve his situation. By the 31st, however, he had become somewhat tranquil and both on this account and because one of his friends was soon to arrive in the city, Hammett asked that all these negotiations be suspended.

Presumably this friend was Weir, who came to Naples about this time. By February 9 the decision had apparently been made that Greenough would return to America, and Hammett on this date issued him a passport for Leghorn. Three days later he left Naples. Weir (who had meantime gone to Paestum to see the ruined Greek temples there) probably followed soon. Greenough was thought unable to voyage alone, and Weir cut short his own European sojourn to accompany him home. They sailed from Leghorn on March 29 aboard the brig *Prudent*.

It is possible that Greenough's derangement in Naples was symptomatic of a recurrence of the illness he had in Rome, but it may have been psychical in nature. When a short time before his death he was entered as a patient at McLean Asylum near Boston, it was recorded there that he had suffered an attack of "mania" in Italy "twenty years" earlier.[15] This reference being presumably to his illness in Naples, it appears that within his family, at any rate, his condition at that time was linked with the condition which at last took his life.

The precise causes of that final condition, essentially psychical as they seem to have been, can no longer be determined. Yet their general character is clear and their nearly lifelong influence on Greenough certain. A manic-depressive type, he was by nature excitable to the verge of exhaustion, while at the same time his almost obsessive ambition permitted the recoil only of deep despair. Between these extremes, the alternation was profoundly disintegrating. It is certain that from the devastating nature of his early illness and especially from the verdict passed at that time on his mental state he received a shock, and probable that from his twenty-first year he lived with the fear that the same fate might again overtake him. To this fear the temporary nervous illnesses during the course of years of other members of his family must have contributed. He also seems to have felt increasingly the pressure of two particular frustrations: the general failure of the public to understand his artistic aims and the limitation of his ability to realize these aims in his work.

Promethean Man

On his homeward voyage Greenough was seasick. To this experience and the sea air was credited his recovery at last from his lingering illness. When the *Prudent* reached Boston on May 23, 1827, he was in fair health again.

During the remaining months of 1827 he stayed with his family (then living in Jamaica Plain) and occupied himself largely by drawing and modeling, reading, and writing. He must have attended in the summer the first annual exhibition at the Athenaeum, at which Stuart's full-length "Washington at Dorchester Heights" and Rembrandt Peale's Port-Hole head of the same subject were shown, and he must have seen Chantrey's statue of Washington, unveiled in the State House that fall.

Perhaps inspired by these works, Greenough modeled during the summer or fall a bust of Washington.[1] Possibly as studies for it he made sketches of Stuart's portrait and Raimon Trentanove's bust in the Athenaeum.[2] He also modeled portraits of some of his contemporaries, made casts, and evidently proposed to take subscriptions for putting them into marble in Italy.

Apparently his price was about $100 each. His first commission of all was for an ideal bust called "Genius of Love," which came from a woman neighbor—the same for whom he had made the imitation of the Roman coin head—possibly at this time. Mayor Josiah Quincy sat for a portrait, ordered it in marble, and was apparently delighted with the finished work; it might have passed, his young son Edmund enthusiastically declared, for the head of an Apollo or a Jupiter.[3] It was, indeed, though one of Greenough's first, one of the best of his portraits.

When modeling dates are considered, the Quincy bust is, in fact, the earliest by a few months of all of Greenough's sculpture which seems to have been preserved and is thus of unique interest and importance. The shoulders and chest are draped, the hair treated naturalistically, the features heavily modeled. Quincy may have been responsible for the drapery, for Greenough preferred none. Otherwise, the work typifies his chief style in male portraiture: forthright, aiming at fidelity to life, yet achieving considerable monumentality by a certain baroque quality.

Possibly Greenough also modeled about this time a bust of Andrews Norton, professor of sacred literature at Harvard. That attributed to him is similar to his bust of Quincy, except in being undraped.

In the fall of 1827 Greenough also had occasion to exercise his talent for literary composition. He wrote a review of Richard Dana's *Poems,* published about November, for Robert Walsh's *American Quarterly Review* in Philadelphia. It appeared, unsigned, in the issue for March 1828, and for it he received twenty dollars. In general, he praised realistic characterization, condemned extravagant language (Dana, he said, was never "lantern-led by conceits"), and judged by impressions rather than theory. Between artists in all media he recognized a kinship. Most significant of all, he set forth at the beginning of his essay a theory of American culture. The most important fact about America, he declared, was its coming into existence at a point late in history.

> We have had no intellectual infancy. The discovery of our country was the result of science; its settlement was effected by the operation of religious principle. The eye of mature reason has been on every action. We remember our first hour. We have had no age of barbarism; no dark remote antiquity. We began with experience. We laid our foundation in results.

The ages of violence and superstition had produced the world's store of myths and legends, which it was the artistic prerogative of civilization to refine. There could be no return to the primitive. "Discovered America," he wrote,

> like the statue of Prometheus touched by an enlivening fire, awoke, as far as poetry is concerned, in adult vigor. She raised her voice, and lifted her arm for the first time in battle. She can neither have the associations of childhood, nor remember the romance of youth. She must begin, where others have ended. Her poetry must be one of refinement; it must be the result of a study of nature, and character, on educated minds and tastes formed.[4]

As the year 1827 drew to a close, Greenough formulated plans which bodied forth this conception of an American art mature from birth. He decided to go to Washington and model the bust of President John Quincy Adams. His larger aim was by thus advertising his ability to obtain more commissions and so hasten the date at which he might return to Italy. Apparently above all, however, he wished to learn at first hand what possibilities there were for a sculptor to be employed by the national government. Shortly after January 27, 1828, he set out from Boston, carrying letters of introduction from Quincy to Adams, Allston to Samuel Morse in New York, and Richard Dana to Gulian Verplanck, then Chairman of the Congressional Committee on Public Buildings. Allston also wrote Verplanck about him (his modesty, the painter remarked, followed him like one of the "quiet backgrounds of Vandyke").[5]

Early in February Greenough was in New York, where he met Morse, William Dunlap, and—either then or in April—the painter Thomas Cole and William Cullen Bryant, soon to become editor of the *Evening Post*. Morse was then at the height of his artistic career as a painter and president of the National Academy of Design, founded a few years earlier in opposition to the autocratic American Academy of the Fine Arts. At the annual meeting of the National Academy in May 1828 Greenough was elected an Honorary Member (the title signifying that he resided outside New York). From the following year until 1838 he held the title of Professor of Sculpture. He showed works at the annual May exhibitions each year from 1832 to 1835 and also in 1841 and 1848—more frequently than he exhibited anywhere out of Boston.[6]

After stopping briefly in Philadelphia, where he evidently met the painter Thomas Sully and where he viewed with disapproval specimens of the new Greek Revival architecture, Greenough reached Washington about the second week in February. Soon he was enjoying himself socially as well as professionally. He engaged a "noble studio" in the house of Charles B. King, the portrait painter, and became acquainted with another such artist, Chester Harding; he planned to model Harding's bust and Harding to paint his head, but the projects were probably not carried out. He attended a Presidential levee and a White House dinner; called by request on the aged architect William Thornton, who entertained him with recollections of Washington; was thrilled by the funeral cortege of General Jacob Brown, with its "glory of many horses"; and became interested in a delegation of Indians ("I should like much," he wrote Henry, "to model an Indian skulking").[7]

Meanwhile he obtained President Adams' permission to model Adams' bust and began work on it. The first sitting occurred on the 20th of February, for about an hour, at King's. Apparently four others followed, on the second of which Adams sat at the same time to Greenough and Harding for nearly two hours. The model was to be cast on March 10.[8] The character of his subject seeming to Greenough eminently serious, he decided to avoid the attempt, made by Sully and others, to make Adams look cheerful. He made his work severely plain, of the Hermes form (head and undraped chest terminating in a solid marble block), with an inexorableness of modeling which seemed to eliminate all superfluous material and which achieved considerable intensity of effect. He was apparently pleased with it, and a German count in the city was so delighted as to hug him. Adams was apparently less enthusiastic. He told Greenough he did not wish the head otherwise, but he pronounced the bust of him made a year later by the Italian sculptor Luigi Persico, "perfect."[9]

Nevertheless at the fourth sitting Adams commissioned Greenough to execute during the summer a bust of his father, John Adams, to be placed in the new edifice of the First Church of Quincy, in whose yard both his parents were buried. Within the next few weeks Greenough made a sketch from a dageurreotype and possibly the model as well. Being allowed freedom in the composition, he adopted the Hermes form again and modeled the head with the same simplicity as he had the younger Adams', though with less severity. The marble, executed in Italy, was put in its place, surmounting a plaque dedicated to the memory of John Adams and his wife, on October 1829.[10]

In almost every aspect, Greenough's busts of the Adamses represent an immediate departure from his "Quincy." Yet they too are typical examples of a style which persisted in his work and which became more generally apparent in it than any other. It was a simple, plain, sometimes austere, often delicate style, which can, especially in contrast to his heavier or "baroque" style, be called "classic." Yet the two do not represent a contradiction, being adapted to different ends. In adopting the second for the Adamses, he was suiting style to character, as he insisted that style should always be suited. He may also have been idealizing his subjects to some extent; this was the style in which he executed most of his ideal works. The head of John Adams especially provoked his thought. Twenty years afterward he expressed the wish that at the time he had modeled it his

age and acquirements could have opened to me a full communication with it. It is the only head that I have seen which has conciliated body and Soul, brought the wisdom of retirement into life and keenly lived in time without forgetting where time leads us.[11]

He was probably describing his conception of a type rather than an individual—the type of republican aristocrat, for which he had the greatest admiration and which, despite his hostility to Federalism, was best represented to him by the Adamses and Washington.

Greenough also modeled in Washington the bust of Chief Justice Marshall, who was, like Adams, being painted by Harding at this time. At the first sitting, February 28, Greenough produced a sketch which Judge Joseph Story praised, and two weeks later he completed the model. Marshall evidently ordered a plaster cast of it and after his return to Richmond in the spring considered buying more than one if the price were not "held higher than I think my head worth."[12] In any case, there seems to be no record that the work was ever put in marble.

Whatever hope Greenough had of receiving a public commission in Washington, he was disappointed. The chief architectural project in the city, the construction of the Capitol, was drawing to a close. The building had just been finished and most of the decoration either finished or arranged for. The little sculpture in it, notably the frieze for the House of Representatives and the four reliefs in the rotunda—had been executed chiefly by a few Italians. The best of them, Persico, was about to begin work on the pediment of the east portico. Though Latrobe's plan called for a good deal more statuary than this, nothing else was contemplated.

Other aspects of the artistic situation in Washington were calculated to discourage Greenough further. The work of the foreign artists in general was undistinguished—"a dozen dunderheads," he called most of them, "whose ignorance and presumption" had ruined the Capitol.[13] Congressmen had spoken even more eloquently on the subject. When Enrico Causici petitioned in 1828 (at the time of Greenough's visit) for the seventh successive year to secure an appropriation to finish his two relief groups, a senator prayed that they not be finished in another seven years and opined that "A Yankee sailor with a jack-knife and a shingle, would carve images that would be better imitators (?) of humanity."[14] Yet the work of a native painter of excellence was no more sympathetically viewed by such critics. Trumbull had painted four of the eight panels in the rotunda (the remaining four were not commissioned for another decade), for which he was paid $32,000. In the opinion of one senator, they were not worth thirty-two cents. A few weeks before Greenough's arrival in Washington Trumbull's "Declaration of Independence," with its display of a dozen pairs of legs, was dubbed by John Randolph "The Shin Piece." The national legislators were reluctant to employ artists and dilatory in seeing that they were paid. The "annual epidemick—economy,"[15] as critic John Neal put it, was, in fact, largely responsible for curtailing the whole art program at the Capitol.

It was perhaps with some feeling of envy that while there Horatio read the letter he received from John in London, with its glowing account of English painters and their generous patrons. "Really, I do wish Allston would go there," he wrote

Henry. "He always seems like an eagle tied to his roost. There is no atmosphere of art." He felt doubly justified, a few weeks later, in delaying his return to Boston in order to model a few more busts because of the importance of profiting "by every gleam from such a sky as that under which art must here grow."[16]

The land which he had likened to Prometheus' statue was indeed beginning to stir into artistic life, but not so quickly nor so fully developed as he hoped. Yet from another point of view, this life was perhaps premature. In the absence of a strong tradition of folk art, elements in American society which might have found themselves represented by such a tradition failed to understand and tended angrily or derisively to reject the work of those artists who sought to take their place in the artistic history of civilization.

Nevertheless a further means for Greenough to advance his career did present itself in Washington. There he met his first major patron, Robert Gilmor, Jr., wealthy Baltimore merchant, who owned one of the best art collections in the country. On a visit to Washington during the first week in March, Gilmor called on Greenough, was pleased by what he saw of the sculptor's work, and engaged him for the modeling of a bust of himself or his wife or possibly one of each for $100. He also asked for an estimate of a figure of Venus rising from the shell, which Greenough promised to give after making a sketch.

About the middle of March Greenough went to Baltimore and there modeled the bust of Mrs. Gilmor. His first female portrait, it is typical of his others in being less heavily modeled and less inclined to flatter the subject than some of his male portraits, and in being draped. (He is not known to have executed any portrait in contemporary dress.) Preferring as he did the male ideal, Greenough tended to understatement in his female portraiture. The bust of Mrs. Gilmor, nevertheless, like those he made of several other women, has an unassuming charm. He thought it—as he inclined always to think his most recent work—one of his best achievements thus far, and Gilmor was so well satisfied that he eventually decided to have it put in marble. More momentously, Gilmor at this time ordered from Greenough a group or statue, to be executed in Italy of a subject to be determined later.

Greenough remained for some two or three weeks in Baltimore, entering into the whole experience with his natural zest for new scenes and associations. He luxuriated in the "air of art" in Gilmor's Gothic library; enjoyed making the acquaintance of Causici, who was then executing a statue of Washington to be placed atop a marble column in the city; called on the aged Charles Carroll of Carrollton, last surviving signer of the Declaration of Independence. He also found time to read a few books, among them Montesquieu's *Grandeur des Romains* and Quatremère de Quincy's *Life of Raphael.*

Probably he left Baltimore on his return north about the middle of April. He may have stopped to model a bust in Philadelphia; Gilmor got him the order of one there, but nothing further about it seems to have been reported. He stopped in New York and made plans to return to the city to take a vessel for Le Havre.[17] Evidently he had by now acquired almost enough orders to enable him to return to Italy and contemplated going by way of Paris.

When he reached Boston, however, about the first week in May, he was offered passage to Gibraltar by Colonel T. H. Perkins, prominent Boston merchant, on one of Perkins' vessels and so changed his plans. His immediate financial needs were taken care of by a group of Boston merchants, who, at the instigation of Gilmor, lent him $1000.[18] Apparently he sailed on Perkins' brig *Bashaw,* bound for Gibraltar and Canton, which left Boston on Sunday, May 18.

3

Art Colonist : 1828 - 1836

Quarries of the Renaissance

Before Greenough left America for Italy the second time he had already considered taking up residence in Florence rather than Rome, influenced chiefly by the Tuscan city's more healthful climate and equally rich if not richer art collections. When he left Boston in May 1828 he expected to be in Florence in eight or ten weeks. But, as in the summer of 1825, a quarantine imposed because of a smallpox epidemic delayed him at Marseilles over a month. (Again he sailed from Gibraltar there with John Apthorp, again on the *New York*.) Apparently he left this city about the middle of August for Genoa, where he spent several days, and there embarked for Leghorn.[1]

Meanwhile, he changed his immediate plans and decided to spend several months at nearby Carrara, the principal village near the chief Italian marble quarries, before settling in either Florence or Rome. He arrived probably early in September. Working conditions were so satisfactory and the scenery and climate so delightful that he could contentedly have spent the winter, he said, but for the attractions in Florence of galleries and possible commissions.[2] Evidently he stayed about three months.

The marble from the mountains around Carrara, in wide demand since Roman times, became most famous as used by the Italian sculptors of the Renaissance; Michelangelo often went to the quarries to select his blocks. It is of a finer grain than the Parian and Pantelic marbles of Greece and generally of a rich whiteness, though it tends to exhibit veins and spots in large blocks. In the early nineteenth century it was still extracted and transported by ancient, crude methods, which cost the lives of numbers of oxen and some men annually. Largely on this account it was expensive; at the time Greenough went to Italy a block for a bust cost apparently about eighty dollars in most places. At Carrara, however, the stone cost only a quarter as much and workmen about half as much as elsewhere.[3]

Greenough's chief motive in going to Carrara was to take advantage of these lower rates. Even so, his decision was an unusual and a significant one. Because of the prevailing sculptural technique, most sculptors of his day seldom if ever went to quarries. By this time, in fact, a sculptor might never even touch marble. He was now chiefly a worker in clay, who usually modeled first a small figure and then a full-sized one. The clay model was given to a molder to reproduce in plaster and the plaster model to a marble-cutter, customarily being sent to Carrara, so that if impurities were revealed in the block a new one might be more quickly begun. The figure was roughly cut or blocked out in the marble by a mechanical process known as "taking points," then gone over by workers with rasps and files, last by finishers and polishers who used fine sand or pumice stone. For details such as hair, plinth, and lettering there were other specialists. The wages of these workmen varied according to their skills. When Greenough first went to Italy a blocker-out, or boster, in most places got from twelve to fifteen dollars for a bust.[4]

This system of relying upon various workmen to put the work into its final substance and shape had far-reaching effects upon the practice of sculpture in Italy in the nineteenth century. It not only often long delayed the completion of a work but it could not be depended upon to reproduce the model exactly. Of this fact Greenough became keenly aware at Carrara. The best of Canova, he decided, was the "exquisite chiselling." In the model, which he saw at Carrara, he thought Thorvaldsen's "Christ" for the cathedral in Copenhagen "the finest wo[rk ou]r art has given the world since the golden time of Leo," but he predicted that some future spectator, seeing the marble (Thorvaldsen himself did not see it until years later, in Copenhagen), would doubt that this work ever brought tears of admiration into an artist's eye. "Yet in truth it has," he wrote Allston.

Let any man ask me where the beauty, the glory of the Venus and Apollo lie—I say in answer that . . . it lies within the thickness of dollar [*sic*] in every part of their bodies.[5]

He now determined to follow the example of the Greeks and Michelangelo and master the skill of working the marble himself. Throughout his career he entrusted principally the blocking-out to workmen, and long past the time when many sculptors would have released a work he habitually applied finishing touches. He did not even finish some of his clay models, which on this account he rarely exhibited.[6]

While in Carrara Greenough put two busts in marble and saw others begun.[7] Presumably the number included those of the Adamses and Quincy, which apparently were dispatched early in 1829. Of John Quincy Adams he made two marbles—one for his father and one which the Boston Athenaeum purchased from him, in October 1829, for $200.[8] On the latter and on the bust of John Adams he incised the letters ΓΡΗΝΩ ΕΠ, after the manner of ancient Greek sculptors; it was a simplified Greek version of his last name and an abbreviation of the verb *εποιει*, meaning in English "Greenough made." Though on the whole he was pleased with these works, they fell far short of his ambitions. "You will have seen before this some of my busts," he wrote Allston in April 1829.

I sigh while I write it. . . . Believe me I am sensible of many of their defects and though I can *do* no better now yet I can I think see my way clear to much better things.[9]

The "Quincy" and the Athenaeum's "John Quincy Adams" were shown in the annual Athenaeum exhibition the next year. From then until his death Greenough was represented there every year.

Meanwhile he had begun to receive requests from friends at home to carry out artistic errands for them. Allston wanted casts from life of a human ear and some ultramarine, painter Alvan Fisher also wanted ultramarine, and Boston dilettante G. W. Brimmer asked for statues for one of the city's theatres. Chiefly to look for these statues Greenough went the second week in October to Florence, a day's journey away, and spent about a week.

By this time he had decided to spend the winter in Florence. He highly enjoyed, he wrote Allston on the eve of his departure, even the anticipation of being again in "that city so dear to my imagination" and sitting in the "noble square" of the Piazza della SS. Annunziata, "with the capi d'opera of the cinque cento around and before me." "I will not try to tell you my feelings," he added a few days after his arrival, "at finding myself again in this city which seems and always seemed to me the most inspiring place in the world."[10]

He timed his visit so as to be able to attend the annual exhibition at the Academy of Fine Arts, and there he went soon after he arrived in the city. What he saw did not alter his opinion of most contemporary Italian art. He still thought that it had declined through having lost the "right path"—the study of nature. But he was again thrilled by the permanent collections of the Academy and of the Uffizi and Pitti Galleries—"two great instructors," he called them. The early works of Leonardo,

Raphael, and Michelangelo in particular, he felt, "point out as directly the road to excellence as one could wish."

In Florence he found one contemporary Italian who commanded his admiration: Bartolini. This sculptor he now saw with "an eye altogether different" from that of three years before. In Carrara he had been struck by Bartolini's little figure of a boy treading grapes, called "L'Ammostatore," which he pronounced "full of nature" and which he drew in the sketchbook he began in Rome. With an appreciation born of his recent development, he heard Bartolini tell him, "Where there is a beautiful model . . . there is Rome"[11] and recommend the maxim by which Bartolini had taught himself: "Che' la Natura e bellezza e benedetto e quello che le va un' po' vicino" ("That nature is beauty and blessed is he who goes a little near her"). Bartolini lacked Thorvaldsen's "fertile mind and . . . poetic imagination," he thought, yet was "perhaps before any of them" in "carrying out his conceptions" and working the "marble like a Greek." In Bartolini's account of his life, too, there was much to fire the enthusiasm of a young republican: his humble origin, patronage from Napoleon, persecution for liberal opinions. Altogether Greenough was so attracted that he asked Bartolini to be his instructor in drawing and modeling when he came to Florence for the winter. Bartolini agreed and even offered him an apartment in which to live.

In thus recognizing at last the genius of the Tuscan sculptor Greenough was exhibiting an independent critical sense and largely repudiating the academicism in the current sculptural tradition. "L'Ammostatore" came to be regarded as marking the end of the classical revival in European art and the beginning of a broadly naturalistic movement. At the time Greenough first knew him, Bartolini was fifty-five years old, at the height of his powers. Yet it was another decade before he received general acclaim.

About the first of December 1828 Greenough left Carrara and took up his abode at Bartolini's studio in Florence—a large, new establishment in Borgo San Frediano.[12] Probably he stayed through the winter, though no longer than the next summer. He also had the free use of Bartolini's models (several years later the cost of two was about $10 to $12 a month),[13] instruments, and workmen. Without this aid he would soon, as he said, have spent his last dollar.

Most important of all, Bartolini gave his new pupil characteristic advice. "Have you found your model?" he inquired when he learned of Greenough's intention to execute a statue, and on receiving a negative reply admonished,

> Look for one. Don't think at your age of beau idealizing and squeezing 4 ugly men into one handsome one. I see by your busts that you are capable of what you intend if you find a model you will do yourself honour in your statue.[14]

A few years later, complaining about young artists who took their models from the antique instead of from nature, Bartolini told Frances Appleton, the Boston belle, that "Greenough was doing himself much harm by this till I talked it out of him."[15]

Greenough was, indeed, more deeply influenced by Bartolini than by Thorvaldsen. Bartolini's opinions were, Greenough wrote Allston a year after settling in Florence,

> the very ones calculated to make him the best of instructors. Nature is his idol and to imitate her exactly his whole desire.

Yet he specified that he did not "go all" Bartolini's "lengths" in these opinions.[16] (A few years later Bartolini set his pupils to draw a hunchback as a lesson that all nature was beautiful.) Greenough too insisted that the artist should imitate nature, and without doubt he became established in this conviction under Bartolini's tutelage. But he never conceded that all nature was beautiful or even that it was all the province of art. In another letter to Allston in the fall of 1829 he expressed himself more fully on the subject than he ever did elsewhere :

Sublimity—Majesty—beauty truth—seem to me the only true elements of my art either in conception—composition or form—perhaps I might have said truth supposing it to contain beauty—but truth is not always beauty—therefore I have mentioned both yet I still contend that beauty is always truth nor can I admit as genuine in form a single plain or curve not belonging to the organization. . . . though I can bring myself to allow it's sometimes necessary to make a work merely true—I consider such a work the lowest in order of works of sculpture. Still I prefer it to the half way attempt to reconcile and mix a grand whole with mean detail. . . . I love reality dearly and when I want to enjoy it I go to the market place—the church the wharf and I get a glimpse [of] more of it than is to be found in all the works of Chantrey. Nor can I help thinking as I see the peasant standing or moving how feeble my art is in imitation and how improper an object reality is for a medium so abstract so refined so poetical as sculpture—I think therefore that instead of attempting to convey trivial detail we should seek to ennoble our works by putting into them all that we can conceive to move the mind—all that's dear in beauty all that's moving in passion all that's grand in thought. I would not go so far as M Ang whose drapery is often unlike any kind of cloth in its plains and foldings. For the eye is disgusted at the impossible. Such is my notion of my art. I am sensible how necessary repeated efforts are [to] enable me to embody them."[17]

Bartolini, moreover, was notoriously difficult to get along with, chiefly because of his jealous disposition. By the late 1830's all relations between him and Greenough had apparently been severed.

During the winter of 1828–29 Greenough probably met most of the other artists in Florence, notably painters Benvenuti, Bezzuoli, and the English Wallis, and sculptors Ricci and Pampaloni. Even before he settled there he wrote Allston that he had many acquaintances among the "first conversaziones of artists & dilettanti" and urged the painter to send him a picture that he might show them "how nobly *we American apples swim.*"[18]

For some of its artists and *dilettanti* and especially for its writers and intellectuals Florence was famed at this period. Such men as Bartolini, Marquis Gino Capponi (later historian and statesman), the Swiss litterateur Gian Pietro Vieusseux (founder of the review *L'Antologia*), the dramatist G. B. Niccolini, the poet Giuseppe Giusti, and others here and in nearby cities were effecting a general cultural and intellectual awakening throughout northern Italy. Insofar as they agreed esthetically, they advocated a severe classicism (as distinct from neo-classicism), containing large elements of the simple and natural and represented as the indigenous Tuscan style; and they anathematized romanticism, as signifying disorder, a violation of natural law, and foreign barbarian influence. Politically, they looked to the eventual independence of Italy, then under Austrian rule, thus aligning themselves with the national Risorgimento. Though Greenough did not associate himself with this Tuscan movement until the Revolution of 1848—and then only briefly, he knew personally many of its most prominent leaders in Florence. The particular intellectual milieu generated by it, moreover, was especially congenial to him. In many respects it was like that which he had known in America.

One of the most favorable circumstances affecting the beginning of the Tuscan Renaissance and one which probably encouraged Greenough to remain in Florence, the capital of the region, was the liberal government by the Austrian Grand Duke Leopold II. During the early part of his reign Tuscany became an asylum for political exiles from all over Europe and an attraction to travelers from as far away as America.

In consequence, Florence took on at that time a distinctly cosmopolitan character. The most celebrated foreign residents were the Bonapartes, brothers and sisters of Napoleon I and their families. The largest foreign colony was the English. At least one American was living there when Greenough arrived—the nonagenarian painter James Smith, who spent most of his life in Italy. Greenough was in effect, however, the founder of the American colony in the city.

Though Florence did indeed seem to many of these residents the "Earthly Paradise," it was Capponi's sad but wise opinion that it contained neither the Tree of Knowledge nor the Tree of Life. The benevolence of the foreign ruler discouraged the desire for independence which began to sweep Italy in the 1820's. As the spirit of the national Risorgimento penetrated Tuscany, moreover, Leopold became less tolerant of it; *L'Antologia* was suppressed in 1833, and the radicals left Florence. The Revolution of 1848 was abortive here as elsewhere in the country.

Greenough too was early disillusioned about modern Italy—"this beautiful but unhappy country," he called it in 1831.[19] Soon after his arrival in Florence, he wrote later, he stood before "those gigantic structures born of the wealth of Europe and of the Florentine genius and will" and asked himself why

> three centuries of "regular government" have ended in a dwindled population, political nullity and social corruption. The churches were filled on holidays—yet there was not much of what we call religion. Hospitals of all kinds seemed to forbid the poorest man to suffer unaided—labor in request, yet provisions cheap, and yet much misery, much sullen dying alone in dark corners, much distrust of man, much disbelief in God himself.[20]

He decided that for all its bloodshed the republic was better than anything Florence had had since, "for though it may be horrid to kill people, it is still worse to prevent them being born."

Nevertheless some of the enormous vitality of those republican days could still be felt in the city, especially in its architecture and its art collections. It was, more than any other in Europe, still a city of the early Renaissance, that rebirth to a great extent of Tuscan genius. More than any other it had resisted both neo-classical and baroque influences.

Upon Greenough the spirit of the early Renaissance, to which he was exposed at Florence, proved at least as influential as that of the classical ages of antiquity. The breadth of his interests, the masculinity of his work, and the buoyance of his thought were evidence of his response to it. Above all, his national consciousness responded. As the young republic in the west seemed to have a kinship with the republics of Greece and Rome, its spirit was equally kin to that which at the end of the Middle Ages awakened Europe by its large promises respecting nature and man.

"Glorious Fenimore"

Greenough's removal from Carrara to Florence in the fall of 1828 was hastened by the arrival in the Tuscan city of James Fenimore Cooper, the American novelist, with his family. At the suggestion of the American consul in Florence (the Italian James Ombrosi), Greenough was to model the bust of Cooper.[1] The two met possibly before Greenough concluded his visit in October, certainly by December, when he seems to have been settled in Florence.

It was a momentous meeting for him, for in Cooper he found a man whose place in his affections and whose influence on his career were second only to Allston's. Cooper, too, was older than Greenough—by sixteen years. An ardent democrat, a consciously American writer with an interest in the progress of all the arts in America, a man of independent and buoyant spirit—Cooper naturally attracted Greenough. "[Y]our father," he wrote Susan Cooper after Cooper's death,

was my instructor—he finished my education and he was my ideal of an American gentleman. . . . You know not how I have grieved that I was forced to live so separated from him.

"I shall write to glorious Fenimore in a few days," he once wrote Morse, capturing in a phrase what was to him the essence of Cooper's character.[2]

Cooper's bust was modeled for the most part during the first three weeks in January 1829, and by February the marble had been begun. At this point, satisfied of the sculptor's ability, Cooper gave him an order for a group in marble. Work on the bust was discontinued, and, because Cooper soon afterward gained a good deal of weight, Greenough later made another model.

With his order, Cooper aimed, he said, to serve three ends: enable Greenough to execute the sort of work he preferred, increase his chances of being commissioned by the American government, and encourage the art of sculpture in America. At the same time, he began to recommend Greenough widely for employment. "Without a rival," he confidently wrote the sculptor the next year, "almost without a competitor, you are certain of the patronage of every man who thinks for himself."[3]

Cooper's commission was a historic one, for no American had yet modeled a group. Greenough had put only a few busts into marble, and he accepted the order only on the condition that unless both he and Cooper were pleased the work should be regarded as simply one of his studies. As events turned out, it was the first work in marble of proportions larger than a bust to be executed by one American at the order of another.

The subject was proposed by Cooper: the two *putti* singing from a scroll in the foreground of Raphael's painting the "Madonna del Baldacchino," in the Pitti Gallery. This choice was partly influenced by the fact that Cooper could not afford a larger work. The price agreed on was $200, $150 of which was to be paid immediately and the rest when the work left

Greenough's studio.[4] But Cooper was also convinced that Greenough, then "bent altogether on the Michael Angelo or the heroic school," would be more successful if he catered to the popular taste for "the more graceful forms of children and females."[5]

Greenough, too, found the forms of children and of cherubs appealing, as some of the drawings in his Roman sketchbook and some of his later works testify. Raphael's pair, he thought, formed a "sweet composition," in which "angel beauty and infantile form" were "charmingly combined."[6] In one respect, however, he found Cooper's proposal objectionable: he was to copy another work of art. Though he evidently never expressed any such objection to Cooper, he made it clear to Gilmor a few years later when Gilmor made a similar proposal to him.

It was, on the whole, with the greatest excitement and a profound sense of gratification that the young sculptor launched upon his new commission. "Fenimore Cooper," he declared a few years later,

> saved me from despair, after my second return to Italy. He employed me as I wished to be employed; and has, up to this moment, been a father to me in kindness

"That group," he wrote Cooper,

> will always be most pleasingly associated in my mind. It was ordered at a moment which was a crisis in my life—when wearied with bust making I began to think that there was no hope for one of my turn of thought in America. It was commenced in ill health and melancholy. It was chiselled amid some difficulties. I found both health and spirits in the task and am likely to be much assisted by its being seen.[7]

He probably began work early in February 1829. He had finished drawings of the heads and a hasty sketch of the rest from which to work, but he took his figures from nature.[8] With pride he reported that he had not only modeled every part of the clay but chiseled every part of the marble from living models.

He had difficulty obtaining models because the Italian practice of swaddling infants affected the limbs of many. One—a son of one of her dependents—was sent him by the Marchioness Strozzi-Riccardi, who came to his studio by chance and was delighted by what she saw. The face of the cherub on the right was thought to resemble that of Cooper's young son Paul. While the work was being modeled Rembrandt Peale, then in Florence, was amused to see Greenough, to keep his clay moist overnight, "take a mouthful of water, and eject it by a peculiar practice, in a fine shower or spray over his work."[9] By the middle of May a cast had been made and sent to Carrara to be blocked out in marble. The rough-hewn work was returned to Florence in the summer with an eighth of an inch of marble left—evidently at Greenough's stipulation—for him to trim off. It was an unusually large amount, and Peale remembered seeing him

> at this pitiable labor, reducing the stone, which should have been done by more experienced workmen, and slowly copying, from his little naked and shivering subject, details of form which he had rendered sufficiently perfect in his clay model.

Meanwhile, at the end of July, Cooper and his family left Florence. In his absence Greenough's interest in the group apparently languished, and other concerns (including his negotiations as Cooper's agent with a Florentine printer and in a lawsuit involving the wages of one of the Coopers' Florentine servants) diverted him. Late in 1830 he designed for the figures two alabaster fig leaves attachable by ribbons, to be used if necessary, but evidently he did not execute them.[10] At last he incised on the back of the plinth "Sculptured in Florence for James Fenimore Cooper, 1830" and on the front "Gloria in excelsis Deo." The group left Leghorn in February 1831. By this time the title of "The Chanting Cherubs" had been bestowed upon it. Throughout the period it was executing it attracted much attention in Florence and was widely praised.[11]

At this point in his career, though Greenough had meanwhile received other commissions, his financial situation was no better than it had been when he and Cooper met. By September 1829 he knew, though he said Cooper did not, that the price of $200 would do little more than cover the expenses for executing the "Cherubs."[12] He agreed to deliver the group to America, but he apparently had to borrow five hundred francesconi (about $525) from Cooper to pay for its boxing and shipping. So far was he from being able to repay this sum by the end of 1831 that he had to borrow another five hundred. "What will you think of my eagerness to pay you the 500 fr you before lent me?" he wrote. "You will be amused at my expense. . . . What shall I say? I will speak of something else."[13] In the end Cooper assumed the cost of the work's transportation.

From December 1831 to September 1832 Cooper was Greenough's chief financial support. During this period he lent the sculptor a total of sixteen hundred francesconi, offered more on several occasions, and scolded when these offers were not accepted. "You are," he complained, "unnecessarily punctilious about our little money transactions."[14] Greenough always borrowed with apologies, repeatedly and effusively expressed gratitude, and returned the loans as soon as he was able.

It was thus doubly important to Greenough that the exhibition of his "Cherubs" in America prove successful. Both he and Cooper were sure that it would. Supposing that the work would be shown in Boston, New York, Philadelphia, Washington, Charleston, New Orleans, and Cincinnati, Cooper thought the receipts would total at least $1000, possibly $2000. At first he proposed that the initial exhibition be in the library of the Capitol in Washington, later favored New York, and when, because of the previous kindness of critics in Boston, Greenough dispatched the work there, protested violently:

You will be covered with twaddling criticism in Boston, which is no better, with all due reverence to your nativity . . . than a gossiping country town, though it has so many clever people.[15]

Neither his nor Greenough's anticipations, however, were quite borne out.

The group reached Boston's Long Wharf on April 8, 1831, and was exhibited to the public, beginning on April 18, at No. 4 Summer Street, daily except Sunday, between the hours of 10–2, 3–6, and 8–10. Single tickets were 25c, season tickets 50c. A dark crimson curtain was to hang behind it, and a boy was stationed to turn it around by means of a handle. On the first day over a hundred visitors came. Receipts of the first week were $140, of the second and third $160. The figures were especially popular with women (most of whom were gratified to discover a resemblance to their own offspring).[16]

At least six newspapers and two magazines carried notices of the exhibition, generally praising Greenough's work for its ideal subject and its realistic figures. Most extensive was the six-page "Letter on the Chanting Cherubs" which appeared in the *New-England Magazine* for July, written probably by George Hillard. After representing sculpture as the most difficult, abstract, and ideal of all the arts and the practitioner of it as a man who "dwells apart like a star," the author of this article considered Greenough and his group as typical examples. He described the cherubs as

good spirits sent down from heaven, wandering, hand in hand, through this vale of tears, and singing praises as they go.

At the same time he called attention to "the *creases* in the back part of the infant's leg (I am a plain-spoken man)." Two poems were also inspired by the group, one by Richard Dana.[17]

Most gratifying of all to Greenough was probably the praise of Allston, who walked in from Cambridge on the first day of the exhibition. He pronounced the "Cherubs" one of the most beautiful pieces in modern art and predicted the speedy elevation of its creator to a place among the very first sculptors of the day. Greenough was, he wrote the Charleston sculptor John Cogdell, a "brilliant, versatile genius." Incidentally he pointed out certain anatomical details in the knees of the figures which testified to "the intelligent use of the living model."[18]

On the other hand, two reactions to Greenough's work by less sympathetic visitors troubled its Boston sojourn. Some literalists, beguiled by its title and supposing the handle by which it was turned belonged to a concealed organ, were disappointed because the cherubs did not sing. "Well what are they good for then?" inquired one. Others objected so strongly to the nudity of the figures that about the third week of the exhibition dimity aprons were tied around them. Repercussions were immediate. "C." in the *Courier* denounced this "deforming" of the work "by a vile covering" and declared that any lady who feared she was courting the attraction of men by liking them had "corruption eating at her." A correspondent of the New York *Evening Post* suggested that the aprons be left behind when the group was brought to New York, to furnish Bostonians with night caps. Within a week or so the figures were restored to their pristine state. "We are happy to hear," announced one of the city's editors, "that the *gentlemen nurses* who have the care of Mr. Greenough's Chanting Cherubs intend to 'change *the diaper*' of the group in a few days."[19]

Greenough was surprised and chagrined when the news of this episode reached him in the fall of 1831. "I had thought the country beyond that," he wrote Allston. "There is a nudity which is not impure—there is an impurity which pierces the most cumbrous costume."[20] He proposed that his group be contrasted with hundreds of prints in English, French, and American annuals for his point to be proved. In a more lighthearted mood, probably in connection with this affair, he sketched a sober-faced cherub holding an enormous square cloth decorously in front of him.

There was, however—devastatingly enough—more public indifference than objection to Greenough's little piece. On June 1—months before the anticipated date—its exhibition in Boston closed.

In the fall it was shown in New York, at the arrangement of Alfred Greenough, with even less success. A room in the new Barclay Street quarters of the American Academy of the Fine Arts was secured (Morse, still president of the rival National Academy, was outraged when he heard the news) and the exhibition opened on November 6. Again the verdict of artists, intellectuals, and the press was flattering.[21] The National Academy passed a resolution thanking Cooper for his service to the country.[22] Young Thomas Crawford, then studying with Frazee, later called the figures "exquisite." Frazee, perhaps succumbing to professional jealousy, objected that they were not "really fine statuary" because the legs of one obscured those of the other.[23] Robert Weir, who saw the group in New York, subsequently represented it atop the organ in his painting "The Taking of the Veil," for which he had made a sketch in Rome. Yet some New Yorkers, too, were disappointed by the cherubs' failure to sing. In relaying this information to Cooper, J. E. DeKay called his townsmen "a race of cheating, lying, money getting blockheads."[24] Attendance at the exhibition was hardly three hundred the first fortnight, from which the proceeds were insufficient to cover the expenses.[25] Not long after the middle of December it closed. Cooper, who by this time had begun to feel alienated from his countrymen, was convinced that his ownership of the group was responsible. More ponderable was the advice of Trumbull, president of the American Academy, that Greenough should remain in Europe if he wished to further his career.[26]

It had evidently been planned that the "Cherubs" would be sent to Washington at the conclusion of the exhibition in New York. Apparently, however, because of the financial risk which loomed thereafter it went to no other city. Altogether Greenough realized only $400 from its showing, most of that amount probably in Boston.[27]

At the annual exhibition of the National Academy the next year—the first time Greenough was represented there—the "Cherubs," a bust of Washington by him, and a portrait presumably of him by Rembrandt Peale were shown. On this occasion a critic calling himself *Modistus* "effervesced through the press for some time," as one of the National Academy members put it, but no aprons were forthcoming. Subsequently the group appeared in other exhibitions in the city. Evidently Cooper never found a place for it in his home, and it remained stored in New York for many years. Still regarding it as chiefly of historical significance, he tried, unsuccessfully, to interest the House of Representatives in purchasing it. Shortly before his death he apparently sold it into private hands.[28] Unfortunately its present whereabouts, if it has survived, is not known.

Cooper's anticipation of a great vogue for sculpture in America was indeed realized within the next two decades, and his analysis of public taste was on the whole correct, though the public proved less fond of Cupids than of Venuses. The chief element in that taste which both he and Greenough failed to recognize was its Puritan and common-sensical attitude to nudity. That the Cherubs rippled the surface of both the American sense of propriety and the American sense of humor suggested that the nude, if presented to the mass of Americans, required special treatment. Such treatment Powers gave it with phenomenal financial success a decade or so later in his "Eve" and "Greek Slave," at which time Greenough's half-draped figure of Washington elicited precisely the same two responses that his "Cherubs" had. Yet if those early responses had any effect on Greenough, it was to strengthen him in the conviction that the only valid subject for great sculpture was the unadorned human form and to incline him to believe that between the great and the merely popular there could be no compromise. He elected to attempt greatness.

A House of Brothers

1

The latter half of 1829 was one of Greenough's most dispirited times. For several months after Cooper left he hardly had a word of English with anyone, and even after his acquaintances became more numerous he lived, he wrote Cooper a few years later,

> in a complete desert for the heart. The time you spent here spoiled me for living abroad. I never had expected to find that sort of intercourse out of my own country and to fall so suddenly from it to the regular artist's life here where one is met at every turn by interested or ill willed actions was chilling.

His letters to his family were evidently in the same vein. "I observe," wrote Alfred to Henry about this time,

> that when Horatio is travelling he writes the most amusing letters; but when he settles down to work he loses his gayety and looks back with a longing eye to home, recollecting all its joys and none of its fretting troubles and petty vexations.[1]

He began to have professional difficulties. The cast of Mrs. Gilmor's bust had arrived at Leghorn in January 1829 and been sent by Greenough directly to Carrara, accompanied by instructions to his boster there to await his arrival. He was dissatisfied with the drapery and intended to remodel it. The boster, however, began on the marble at once and refused to relinquish it or the cast when Greenough offered him only half the regular price. Consul Ombrosi had to intervene to secure them. Greenough proposed to finish the bust without drapery to be given by Gilmor to some friend and to execute a second with the drapery remodeled; yet in the end he evidently finished the work (which was done by November and shipped in February 1830) according to the original model. For it he apparently received $150—$100 at the time it was modeled and $50 when the marble was dispatched. On its receipt, Gilmor offered him another $100, which he refused. As a pedestal he recommended a truncated Tuscan column, with an ornamented torus.[2]

Greenough was probably also occupied in 1829 with a bust of Petrarch's Laura. Evidently he presented one this year to banker Rogers in Marseilles,[3] perhaps in gratitude for assistance at the time of his illness two years before.

As for commissions, however, he soon found that most of his countrymen abroad were less inclined to be patrons of art than was Cooper. "[T]ravelling Jonathan," he observed, "is very philosophical." Theologian Henry Ware, for example, who visited Florence in the spring of 1830, declared Greenough was working "beautifully" and expressing "such fine and high notions that I am sure he will be a great artist," but did not favor him with an order.[4]

With little or no income, he saw his funds rapidly diminish. In September 1829 his total capital was $200, of which his board and lodging for the coming year were to consume $108. He feared that unless his fortune changed, "the Demon Want" would within a year have dragged him on shipboard. Yet he consoled himself that

> a short voyage will bring me again into the light of eyes—within sound of voices and touch of hands of which I often dream and for which in my *fits* my heart yearns as if it would break.[5]

By the fall of 1830 he had "sunk" $1000 in addition to the prices of all his works,[6] and during the next two years he realized nothing from his commissions. He underestimated the cost of his work, feared to appear high-priced, and favored his friends. On one or two of his first busts he spent more than he received, as a result, he said, of his resolution "that nothing shall go from my study with which I have not done my utmost to please the employer." He lived with "the greatest economy" and denied himself "every indulgence." "If I cannot make some sacrifices to fame while I am young and have hope, when shall I do it?" he rhetorically inquired of one correspondent.[7] (Always a great smoker, he formed at this period a habit of twisting cigars in half because he could not afford whole ones.)[8] His career would probably have been cut short had it not been for his friends. In addition to Cooper's loans, he was aided about this time by an anonymous gift of $1200 from America; the donor he later learned was George Ticknor.[9]

Even more than by his finances young Greenough was depressed during his first years in Florence by the frustration of his ambition to execute a full-sized work. "I have great courage," he wrote Allston shortly after his arrival, "and great hunger after glory. I would fain be one of the small band of American 'Old Masters.' " By the fall of 1829 his hopes were flagging. "I'm pressing on from the boy to the man," he noted sadly. "Not one solid blow struck for a name—at an age when M. Angelo had nearly finished his colossall David." The commissions for busts and even small statues which he gradually began to receive (which fell "daily" into his hands, he reported with fine hyperbole) did not satisfy him; "though they feed my body," he chafed, they "starve my soul by keeping me constantly busy on trifles." As early as the summer of 1829 he began to consider methods of publicly financing a statue of Washington and by the fall had made preparations for modeling the work. "Any thing rather than floundering in lazy hopes!" he announced to Allston. He proposed to raise $1500 in Boston, which he thought would cover the cost of putting the work in marble.

and he hoped by exhibiting it to secure money to pay off all his debts. Reports about business conditions in Boston, however, discouraged him.[10]

One other fact contributed to Greenough's periodic depression during his first years abroad : he was not robust. His health, he wrote Gilmor in May 1829, "though even is delicate and requires much attention." Throughout the next few years it improved steadily and his strength increased, as a result he said of "prudent diet," regular habits, and "the exercise of the chisel."[11] Yet during most of his residence in Florence he was subject to colds in the winter and, upon exposure or sitting in a cold study after exercise, to attacks of fever. He also seems to have been for several years afflicted, as he was in Rome, with insomnia. A sketch of his of one of the sea-goddesses of Ammanati's fountain in the Piazza della Signoria bears the notation : "June 29 1830—4 oclock AM after a sleepless night." Two years later he confessed that he still passed some nights "a little poetically."[12]

In addition to modeling, visiting galleries, and reading the lives of artists, he taxed himself, especially during 1829, with particular studies in the technical aspect of his art. His "grand aim," he wrote Allston, was "the formation of a *method* both in drawing and modelling." Both arts he thought demanded a "scrupulous outline" and a proper shading of surfaces "in proportion to their obliquity to the source of light."[13] From the first he learned both these lessons, which he then applied in the second. He must have been encouraged in these studies by Bartolini, who regarded the management of light as an especially important part of the sculptor's technique.

Increasingly Greenough became aware not only of the "dignity" and the "glory" of his art but of its "immense difficulty." Soberly he concluded that his own "expectations" should be "very modest." Yet he was spurred by his ambition and by his sense of his historical importance. "I am the pioneer of a band which I doubt not will hereafter enrich and beautify the cities of the Republic," he proudly declared. "I am warmed with the thought that if I seize on the right path they will do me the honour of having begun well."[14]

It was to Allston that Greenough most fully reported his studies and general observations on art during his first years abroad. "As I pass," he began one of his letters to the painter,

> from time to time, one of those hills which lie so frequent across the road I am travelling, my first wish after my curiosity has been slaked, is always to communicate to you what I have seen and what I think, confident that your wishes for my advancement will prompt you to correct my errors to which my experience and the nature of the company in which I travel, make me liable.

Allston, however, was a notoriously poor correspondent and his replies were infrequent. By 1835 Greenough's letters were also, not because of "any change in my tastes or character," he avowed to Allston,

> but simply from the discouragement of your silence. I called a spirit from the vasty deep. He would not come when I did call to him.[15]

2

Lonely though Greenough felt in Florence after Cooper left, he was not long alone. More American artists soon appeared, some influenced by his example. Rembrandt Peale and his young son Angelo came in the summer of 1829 and stayed nearly a year; George Cooke apparently passed through from Rome in the fall; and Bostonian John Gore began at that time a residence of several years. Peale painted a Byronic-looking portrait of Greenough, which he showed, together with his portrait of Washington, at the Academy exhibition in September.[1]

In February 1830—most welcome of all—Henry Greenough arrived in Florence, having been advised to take a voyage for his health and intending to remain as long as Horatio did, studying painting and architecture. The two were always closer to each other than to any other member of their family, and Horatio always depended on Henry for advice in artistic and business matters. To the disappointment of both, Henry's health continued poor, and after three and a half years he returned home. Twenty years later he drew on his memories of these years when he described life among the art students of the city in his novel *Ernest Carroll*.[2] In 1830 John Greenough was also in Florence, already having the financial difficulties and exhibiting the temperamental instability which troubled his entire life.[3]

In the spring of 1831 the number of American artists in Florence reached a peak which apparently was not surpassed for another decade. In addition to the Greenoughs and Gore, there were Bostonian Amasa Hewins (in whose notebook Horatio drew Hewins' profile),[4] John G. Chapman of Virginia, John Cranch (whom Horatio had met in Washington), Cole, and Morse. Chapman painted a portrait of Horatio, depicting a handsome young man with an urbane yet frank expression; on his return home he presented it to the Boston Athenaeum, "as an ardent admirer of Greenough as an artist and a man."[5] During the spring and summer of 1831 Cranch, Cole, Morse and the Greenoughs lodged in the same house, Number 4488 Via Valfonda; rooms were about six dollars a month.[6]

They all visited galleries. They consorted at cafes (the most popular was Doney's). They coped with models (Horatio described one of Gore's as "a red-headed, long-bearded, fiery-faced, green-eyed fellow, that has killed his man and cuts all his bread with a pointed knife two inches longer than the law directs").[7] They attended the Pergola Theatre, where the sensational young Giulia Grisi had just made her debut, to hear opera for the price of a paul (about ten cents). They made excursions to nearby villages like Vallombrosa and Volterra to

HORATIO GREENOUGH by John Gadsby Chapman, 1831.
(Courtesy of the Boston Athenaeum.)

sketch. (Among Horatio's sketches are some of Etruscan sarcophagi at Volterra.) Some of them formed a class in drawing at the Academy. Horatio was one of those in a school of the nude.[8] Above all, they talked endlessly about each other's works and plans and about the characteristics of a national art.

Of these artists Horatio was particularly fond of Cole and Morse. At his suggestion Cole took up the study of the human figure. The painter's more permanent interest in architecture was also stimulated by the sculptor, as the two exchanged views on some of the great edifices of Italy. In his sketch book Cole drew, probably in 1832, a profile of Greenough, showing him with thin cheeks, drooping mustache and hairline beginning to recede; it seemed to be that of a man years older than the one in Chapman's portrait.[9]

In these years Morse and Greenough were drawn together by a common devotion to the classical tradition and the cause of a national art. "Alphabet Morse," Greenough teasingly called him, "wicked Morse . . . sousin' up niggers & writin' anti catholic pamphlets," "our Numa Pompilius." As the painter prepared to return to America in 1832 the sculptor implored him:

Pardon, I pray you, any thing of levity which you may have been offended at in me. Believe me, it arose from my so rarely finding one to whom I could be natural, and give loose, without fear of good faith and good-nature ever failing. Wherever I am, your approbation will be dearer to me than the hurrah of a world.

Temperamentally and philosophically, however, the two were poles apart. He did not, Greenough wrote Cooper, "believe infants are born charged and primed with sin as friend Morse does," and when Morse counseled him to accept adversity piously, he bluntly replied, "my stubborn head . . . refuses to comprehend the creation as you comprehend it."[10]

From the end of 1829 to the summer of 1831, when he made a trip to Paris, Greenough had in progress at least eight works in addition to "The Chanting Cherubs." In November 1829 he modeled a bust of Cornelius Bradford, a friend of Cooper's then in Florence, for which he was to receive $100;[11] since Bradford died a few months later, it was probably not put in marble. About the same time he began a bust of ex-president Kirkland of Harvard, which several New England travelers had him put in marble for presentation to the Boston Athenaeum. (Sprightly Mrs. Kirkland thought her husband did not have a face for a bust and feared the work would resemble the antique bust of Socrates.) It is ponderously draped, as if in compensation for the bland features. When he dispatched it late in the summer of 1831 Greenough stipulated that it receive "a descending & if possible a northern light, "since

Unless a bust be placed in nearly the same light in which it was wrought, its modulations of surface, its character, its flesh, evaporate. It becomes sheer stone.[12]

From merchant Joseph Grinnell of New Bedford (one of the purchasers of the Kirkland bust) came another order : for a three-foot statue of his five-year-old niece Cornelia. The price was one hundred Spanish dollars (approximately the same amount in American currency), half of which was paid the last of April 1830, the rest to be forthcoming when the statue was packed for shipping.[13] The model was promptly made and the finished work reached New Bedford in July 1832.[14] It represents the child clad in a tunic which hangs from one shoulder, looking down, holding a small bird in one hand and a dish in the other, making altogether an appealing little figure. This work was the first of five portrait statues and three portrait busts of children executed by Greenough, which compose an unpretentious but noteworthy group. Those which are available are among the most successful of all his works.

In the spring of 1830 Greenough also modeled the bust of Grisi, whom he thought "the loveliest woman" he ever saw (a year or so later Gore and Morse evidently thought him in love with her); apparently retouched the bust of Washington done in Boston in 1828 and got one or more orders for it; and made preparations to model a Newfoundland dog. The next spring traveling New Yorker James I. Roosevelt ordered one of his "Washingtons" and Morse and Cole sat for their busts. The latter two were made, he apologized, "at odd moments of leisure when fatigued and dispirited." Yet they are two of his most sensitive. Possibly the subjects obtained them by paying for the marble. Morse's (incised "1831") was made from the block out of which the first bust of Cooper was begun.[15]

Meantime, while Greenough was acting as Cooper's legal agent, a feud developed between him and Consul Ombrosi, who—as one of the city's worst rascals—was conniving with Cooper's former servant. But for this fact, Greenough might in these years have received a few more commissions. New Yorker Peter Schermerhorn, who arrived in Florence in March 1830 with the intention of commissioning a small group, did not do so evidently because of Ombrosi's interference. During the next two years the consul answered requests of travelers that the sculptor's studio be visited by saying, as Greenough reported, "that Mr. Green-gh was a strange sort of a man! rather odd! and that he had rather be excused."[16]

Late in 1830 Greenough again took up the project of a monument. By December he had decided to propose that one commemorating the Revolution be erected in front of the Capitol in Washington and asked Cooper to write congressmen to this effect.[17] By March 1831 he had completed the design and modeled the central figure. The ground plan was square, formed by four pieces of statuary on low blocks: Columbus seated, pondering on a globe; a mother clasping her infants, with a menacing Indian behind her; King Philip seated amid the bones of his fallen brethren; a seated female figure representing Civilization, holding implements of industry, with a boy reading beside her. Surmounting the central block was to be a statue of Washington, standing, fully draped, extending his sword in the act of resigning his command, a fasces beside him.[18] Morse, who saw the model of this figure, declared it the "grandest conception of the person and port of that illustrious man" that he had ever seen.[19] The sides of the central block were to be decorated with four scenes in bas-relief from the American Revolution, signifying Oppression, Remonstrance, Resistance, and Independence. In arrangement, union of historical and allegorical figures, and use of drapery for the central historical figure, the design was comparable to that of the monument which Bartolini was executing in these years to Count Nicholas Demidoff. Yet it was also a development of Greenough's proposals for statuary around the Bunker Hill Monument. The essential designs of two of the proposed accessory pieces were eventually put into marble: the brooding Columbus as an ornament on the chair in Greenough's later statue of Washington and the group of the pioneer mother and infant and the Indian as the central figures in his group "The Rescue."

Yet even as Greenough announced this project to Cooper he had misgivings. He had designed the work, he said, not so much from any hope of "ever being so respectably employed" as "from a thirst to get vent in something large. I like to think about great works though my stars have forbidden their execution."[20] Apparently there was no response in Washington to his proposal.

Undaunted, he proposed a year later to erect a statue of Washington in New York, presumably executed from the model already completed.[21] The announcement was made in New York newspapers early in December 1831 in connection with the exhibition of "The Chanting Cherubs." Subscriptions were solicited to raise $5000 for the statue and $1000 for expenses, and arrangements were made for the future proceeds from the exhibition to be applied to this end. The council of the National Academy at an extra meeting resolved to help raise the sum, and the press supported the project. By the following February it had been abandoned, chiefly because it conflicted with an earlier project of similar nature. Neither, however, received the necessary financial support.

3

The chief commission which occupied Greenough between "The Chanting Cherubs" and his statue of Washington was the statue ordered by Gilmor. Because of delays and miscarriages in the correspondence of the two men the subject was not settled upon until the spring of 1831. In the interim they considered virtually all possibilities: classical, pastoral, Biblical, ideal, and copies from famous paintings.[1] By February 1830 Greenough had conceived the subject of the dead Medora from Byron's poem "The Corsair," but the letter to Gilmor in which he proposed it was lost. Meantime Gilmor had found in a painting of the Madonna a boy which he wished to have copied in marble so as to hold a lamp or vase. Unable to identify this figure, Greenough modeled late in 1830 or early in 1831 one to fit Gilmor's description. Not being altogether pleased with it, however, and feeling that such an order "cramped very much that latitude in composition so dear to the imagination," he abandoned it about April 1831 and began a figure of Medora. "Here," he wrote Gilmor,

> I can unite beauty to touching interest and a convenient form for your house to novelty. I . . . can do what has not been done in Italy for many years—attempt to interest and charm the eye and mind with a female form without appealing to the baser passions.

Gilmor apparently approved of the decision without reservation.

The subject had a contemporaneousness which gave it special appeal. Byron's Florentine residence was but a few years in the past; several years later Greenough became acquainted with Countess Guiccioli. Thorvaldsen and Bartolini had executed busts of Byron, and Greenough finished one by the fall of 1833.[3] With its romantic nature, the subject of Medora was also a novel one for a sculptor of the time. In relation to Greenough's own career it is further notable for its feminine character. He executed only one other full-length female statue.

The nature of the subject, however, excited Greenough less than the fact that the "Medora" was his first own "poetical" or original piece. To have been "the mere mouth piece of another inventor" at this time, he wrote Gilmor, would have been "morally impossible." Gilmor would have been the sufferer and he himself would have been attacked

as a man who soared on the wings of Italian masters, because Nature had only given him his own sorry legs to move withal.

As he modeled the work he began to feel for the first time master of his art, not having to "spur" himself to his task, but only "laisser aller." At the same time, he paid his usual attention to anatomical details. To one visitor he proudly explained:

There is an anatomical reason . . . why my Medora is dead; the position is one no sleeper would assume, or at least could continue beyond a moment; breathing is impossible.[4]

By August 1831 the model was completed. It was a life-size recumbent figure, the lower half draped, one hand lying over the heart and the other at one side clasping flowers according to Byron's detail. The features were thought to resemble Greenough's own.[5] The "soul," he said, was best described in the lines from Petrarch's "Trionfo della Morte" which compare Laura's death to the extinguishing of a light rather than a flame. Points were taken during the fall and the marble was begun early in 1832. He went at it with "a strength and a motive . . .

never felt before" and in June was applying finishing touches. Yet probably chiefly because of the serious illness of Henry in the fall it did not leave his studio until the last of April or first of May 1833. "I have never allowed myself to bestow on it my jaded or ineffective moments," he wrote Gilmor as he relinquished it. "It has been a great object with me to perfect it."[6] In a final word he asked that a single veiled light, falling at a twenty-five or thirty-degree angle, be directed upon it.

As Greenough's first representation in marble of a life-size figure the "Medora" was his most ambitious undertaking thus far. Above all, it reflects the variety of influences operating on him during these early years: the ideals of repose and feeling, the lessons from nature and from art. In outline, it resembles some of the recumbent figures in the drawings of Flaxman, whom at this period Greenough, probably influenced by Bartolini, especially admired. Yet these influences, in conflict with each other in other works of Greenough's, are here largely balanced. In some ways, this work is his most successful combination of the ideal and the real.

For the "Medora" he received $500 (or as he reckoned it 475 francesconi). The sum was apparently about twice what Gilmor originally intended to pay, yet it probably did no more than cover Greenough's expenses. Such were his straits that he drew on Gilmor for a total of 700 francesconi—over 400 by the end of 1830 and the rest by the end of 1832. It was all repaid evidently by the summer of 1833.[7]

The "Medora" was first exhibited, for Greenough's benefit, in Boston, again the city of his choice. At the arrangement of his brother Alfred,[8] it was shown from October 24 through December 31, 1833, in the rooms of Chester Harding in School Street, between 9 A.M. and 10 P.M., at the prices which had been charged for "The Chanting Cherubs." It rested on a low, green-covered platform. Printed extracts from Byron's poem were given out at the door. By the first of December some two thousand persons had attended.[9] At first the morning hours were exclusively for women. Even so, one female visitor confessed that she had "summoned courage" to go alone. She was "horrified at the size of what Moore calls woman's loveliness which actually took my eye so that I could not see the face," and would have been better pleased had the drapery been drawn a few inches higher.[10] After a male season-ticket-holder who was accustomed to visit the statue daily protested loudly because two ladies walked out in a huff when he appeared one morning the segregation was abandoned.[11]

Again the Boston papers (and several in New York) were kind. Dana contributed a poem to the *Independent Chronicle.* The *Transcript's* correspondent expressed the desire to have Greenough execute a group of Conrad and Gulnare from the same poem. The union of the arts of poetry and sculpture was applauded and the avoidance of impure suggestion approved. Again the *New-England Magazine* carried an article chiefly devoted to Greenough. The author, probably Hillard, perspicaciously noted that Homer was reported to be the sculptor's "constant companion" and observed that he had

> evidently benefited very much by his classical taste in literature. He is perfectly free from fantastic ornaments, and tasteless trickery; he shows a preference of the pure and the simple over the gaudy and ornate.[12]

The efforts of Alfred and Gilmor to have the statue exhibited elsewhere were on the whole unsuccessful. Finding no one in New York or Philadelphia willing to take it, Gilmor had it brought to Baltimore in June 1834. There it was shown, probably in the fall, by an exhibitor in Market Street, the receipts being equally divided between him and Greenough.[13]

Evidently it was not advertised or commented upon in the Baltimore papers.

When at last it reached its owner's mansion, an awkward discovery was made: there seemed to be no appropriate place for it. Eight months later the crate was still unopened. Greenough was "mortified and grieved" when he learned of the problem late in 1835. He offered, as he had promised to do if Gilmor were dissatisfied, to take it back or exchange it for another work—specifically for the small Cupid which he had just completed. But Gilmor preferred to keep his statue and finally took both pleasure and pride in it. A few years later Mrs. Gilmor attended a fancy dress party in Baltimore as Medora, in a white muslin dress, with her hair falling down to her feet.[14]

A third commission which Greenough superintended for Gilmor was the reproduction of Mrs. Gilmor's profile, taken from the bust, in a cameo. Gilmor seems to have ordered it in October 1830, thinking it might be made by G. A. Santarelli of Florence, who had done work for him before. But that artist was dead and the art virtually a lost one in Florence. The work was evidently done in Rome in the spring of 1832, finished by the help of Cole.[15]

During these years Greenough also procured for Gilmor's collection, by request, several older objects of art. In four shipments he sent six paintings (an original "Repose in Egypt" by Francesco Albani, copies of a landscape by Salvator Rosa and a portrait of Michelangelo, two landscapes on copper by Zuccherelli and a battle scene on stone), and a few miscellaneous items, including a salver and vase cast in scagliola from a piece of plate by Cellini. Altogether he expended two hundred and one francesconi.[16] He had carte blanche to buy anything he thought Gilmor would like, but the collector's preference for original "old masters" was hard to satisfy, prices were high, and the dealers notoriously tricky.

4

Late in 1830 Greenough hit on the notion of modeling the bust of Lafayette and wrote Cooper, then living in Paris, to obtain permission for him to do so; the work would, he thought, be "worth a fortune" to him in the public attention it would attract.[1] Though at first reluctant (chiefly because of his agreement that the bust of him by P. J. David should be the official one), Lafayette soon yielded to Cooper's importuning, stipulating that the novelist should be present at all the sittings, and Greenough made preparations to go to Paris the following February. Some crisis in his personal affairs, which necessitated his asking Cooper to advance the rest of the price of "The Chanting Cherubs," postponed his journey, however.[2] He went at last in August 1831, while the "Medora" was being roughhewn.

All along the way he had an ear for the different dialects and an eye for the architecture. In Genoa he admired "a feeling for the broad and massive almost Greek," though complaining that the Academy of Fine Arts was "showy" rather than "useful"; the baroque of Turin he found "paltry to an eye that comes from farther south." The Alps, which he crossed at Mt. Cenis, enthralled him. "The ocean's self," he declared, "never produced on my imagination any thing like the effect of those first born of creation." "You seem to stand on the battleground of Jupiter and the Titans, and trace the origin of the fable."[3]

On reaching Paris (on September 6, his twenty-sixth birthday), he put up at the Montmorency Hotel on the Boulevard Montmartre. About ten days later, Morse arrived in the city and the two took rooms together. They and Cooper were together almost daily, "now talking seriously and now letting ding any how," having "a grand discussion of the means of renovating art," looking forward to their return to America.[4] "In the year 1833," Greenough scribbled in a pocket French–English dictionary,

S. F. B. Morse and H. Greenough will be in the city of N. Y. decidedly the merriest and best fellows in the place—given Rue de Surenne, No. 25—1831—sitting in the dumps without any fire in Nouv—[5]

Such moods were short-lived, however, "As for describing Paris," Horatio wrote Henry, "I should as soon think of writing an encyclopaedia. It is splendid!" He went to the theatre, bought books for a friend in Florence, visited the Louvre (Paolo Veronese reminded him of Shakespeare in that "he must be felt"), visited Bartolini's friend Ingres and presumably Baron Gerard, but disdained French art in general (the "french-greek physiog" of J. L. David's ideal figures he pronounced "nauseous") and compared the French unfavorably to the Italians. His chief associations were with the republican community in Paris of which Lafayette was the head. He went to the wedding of Lafayette's granddaughter in company with

deputies, generals, Poles, Italians, Yankees (last, not least), all in harmony, all liberal, all grieved for Warsaw,

which had just fallen in the abortive Polish revolution. He attended some of the morning *conversazioni* of Princess Christina Belgiojoso-Trivulzio of Milan, exiled for her support of the Italian revolutionary movement. Among the Americans in the city was the social philosopher Albert Brisbane, then associated with the Saint-Simonians. He and other members of this group tried to convert Greenough to their doctrines, but without success. "Hateful word . . . metaphysics," he wrote Morse shortly after leaving Paris, referring to Brisbane. "Let's have reasoning till all's blue, but let's have *hold* of something."[6]

So many were the demands made on Lafayette at this period that Greenough had to wait over a month before seeing him and even then had difficulty obtaining sittings. Apparently they took place at Lafayette's home at Lagrange, just outside Paris. On October 13 Greenough got the first, at which time he made a sketch. He had asked for and been promised six of an hour each, yet for more than a fortnight he was allowed only a few minutes. Again Cooper came to his rescue, "pinned the old gentleman to his chair one morning for two whole hours with stories and *bons mots,*" he said,, and was "the saving of my bust."[7] The work represents Lafayette with a drapery over one shoulder and a strap over the other, suggestive of the costume of a Greek or Roman warrior. It is, however, realistic in details, especially in contrast to David's idealization. The sagging jowls are those of an old man, and the ears are peculiarly Lafayette's —set so close to the head that, as Greenough pointed out to Cooper and Morse, they could not be seen by one standing directly in front a few feet away. In Morse's opinion the bust was the strongest likeness Greenough had made. Eventually he had an engraving of it made, by Enrico Bandini and Davide Testi, inscribed to Cogswell.[8]

Meanwhile Greenough was busy with other work, which he began almost as soon as he reached Paris. He modeled Cooper's bust again; undraped, looking belligerently straight forward, it represents the novelist's vigor though little of his attractiveness. He also modeled the busts of Princess Belgiojoso (because her fortune was just then confiscated it may never have been put in marble), another Italian woman, Brisbane, and presumably two French women, who wanted theirs in plaster only.

While in Paris, Greenough put some of his ideas about art and artists in writing. In a letter to Rembrandt Peale he urged Peale to convince Americans that "one American Work is of more value to the U. S. than 3 foreign ones even of superiour merit," and that they should employ native artists "manfully and not tell us to learn to swim before we venture into the water." American scholars, he declared,

have looked so much abroad for salvation in letters arts and manners that they have not only overlooked home but unfitted all under their influence for judging impartially of any thing American. They have carted sand in upon fine soil and nothing but a flood of satire can remove it and bring to light the fertile bottom which they have encumbered.

The entire letter was printed in the *New-York Mirror* the following March. He wrote Allston, too, from Paris, chiefly criticizing American architecture and setting forth at length architectural principles of his own. This letter, in fact, contained the essence of his architectural theory, not made public until twelve years later. During his Paris visit he also did some work on a review, probably of Allan Cunningham's *Lives of the Most Eminent British Painters, Sculptors, and Architects,* in which he planned to incorporate objections to the style of art criticism in America and to the policies of the American Academy of the Fine Arts.[9] This essay, however, seems not to have been printed.

Altogether Greenough had such an enjoyable and stimulating visit in Paris that his departure, about November 30, pained him. For several months he yearned after the city, he confessed, "to an extent amounting to boyishness" and thought all who arrived from there seemed "to smell sweeter than ordinary artists."[10]

5

When he reached Florence on December 14, Horatio found Henry established in their new quarters in an edifice known as Casa dei Frati, located behind the church of SS. Annunziata and reached from Via San Sebastiano.[1] It was owned by the Frati dei Servi di Maria and for years partly rented to artists. The Greenoughs were on the ground floor. The room above them was briefly occupied by Cole (who painted the view from it into the adjoining garden) and later in 1832 by N. P. Willis, who was impressed by the building's "vast staircases and resounding arches and halls" and also by the fact that the Neapolitan ambassador lived on the same floor. The rent was three dollars a month. Meals in the city were correspondingly cheap: dinner might be had for twelve cents or with wine for twenty-five cents.[2]

As part of his and Henry's menage at this time Horatio had a man who worked for food and clothing and employed a woodman and a cook and chambermaid, formerly a servant of the Coopers', who persuaded him to hire her by misrepresenting herself as destitute. The woman gave him so much trouble, however—on one occasion stealing Medora's shroud—that he soon discharged her.[3]

A few new artists were added to the American colony in Florence in 1832, among them Bostonian Francis Alexander and South Carolinian Francis Kinloch. The number of American travelers, too, increased this year; in all Tuscany there were reported to be three hundred.

Greenough now began to go more into society. He had hitherto "read my Dante, etc.," he wrote Morse,

> and when thrown into contact with folk have gotten through as quick as possible, with the idea that every word spared was so much clear gain.

But he had found that "a man needs a circle of acquaintance" and determined to "scour away a certain ferocity which 3 years of independence and solitude" had produced. He escorted two spinsters from Albany, obliged the celebrated heiress Harriet Douglas (to whom his brother John had unsuccessfully proposed) by drawing in her sketchbook heads of Washington and Lafayette, went to the home of the retired Episcopal minister Samuel Jarvis and his wife for prayers on Sundays and tea on Wednesdays, made a few agreeable English acquaintances (in general he was a violent Anglophobe), and began to think of marriage. A "man without a true love," he aphorized, "is a ship without ballast, a one-tined fork, half a pair of scissors, an utter flash in the pan." Jokingly he asked Morse to advertise for him in America:

Wanted a young woman of knowledge without being aware of it —very humble at finding herself found—A blond and inclining to the petite—not slothful in business fervent in spirit serving the Lord.[4]

During the first eight months of 1832 he was kept moderately busy in his studio. Early in the year he began to put in marble, in addition to the "Medora," the bust of Lafayette (signed "HG") and probably one or two others modeled in Paris. (The "Lafayette" was purchased by Kinloch and presented to the Pennsylvania Academy of the Fine Arts in Philadelphia in 1834.) In the first months of 1832 Greenough also modeled the bust of Colonel Arthur P. Hayne of South Carolina (then U. S. Agent for Naval Affairs in the Mediterranean) and made a new model of his bust of Washington as a companion piece to his "Lafayette." The "Washington" was for Commodore James Biddle of Philadelphia, then with the American squadron in the Mediterranean. He may also have executed Kinloch's bust.[5]

In May 1832—a record month—Greenough received three orders, totaling $600 : one for a bust of Henry Miles, an American merchant living in Florence, and two for small statues for Henry S. Hoyt of New York. The bust was modeled in three sittings. The statues, for which he was to receive $500, were two and a half feet high, one representing the "Genius of America" (a sketch of it he made showed a nude male figure, with a drapery flying from one arm, holding out a "bud of promise" presumably to "posterity" with one hand and pointing upward with the other) and the other the "Genius of Italy." They were promised by November and the first was modeled by July, but they probably did not reach New York much before the spring of 1834, when they were shown at the National Academy.[6] Their subsequent fate is unknown.

At least two busts occupied him in the summer and fall of 1832. He began to put Cooper's in marble, and he modeled

N. P. Willis'. The latter was cut from the block which had already yielded Cornelia Grinnell's statue, and years later, when Willis had married Miss Grinnell, Greenough presented it to him. In the opinion of Willis' biographer Henry Beers it was "a fair likeness" though "somewhat heavy and unideal." Probably in the summer of 1832 Greenough also modeled the "arch looking" (as Tuckerman called it) bust of Alexander; it was finished by the fall of 1833. About this time he probably executed his bust of John Jacob Astor, who was then traveling in Europe, and perhaps his bust of Alexander Hamilton, adapted from Ceracchi's. From the wealthy and flamboyant Colonel Herman Thorn, then in Florence, he received several orders in 1832, but they may never have been executed—Thorn was "so occupied in *living,*" he said.[7]

Early in 1832 Greenough was also working, by request, on two drawings for Morse's sketchbook. One represented David singing to the mad Saul, attended by a son and daughter. A study for it resembles Flaxman's illustration of Ulysses weeping at the song of Demodocus. (Other sketches he made about this time of scenes from the *Iliad* resemble some of Flaxman's illustrations of that work.) On the back of this study he sketched the scene of Phaedon being restrained by Helios from mounting the sun-chariot—possibly the subject of the second sketch for Morse.

Throughout the early months of this year Greenough continued to consider means of financing a large statue. Nathaniel Niles, physician and politician, whom he had met in Paris, briefly negotiated with him about executing a colossal head of Washington, to be paid for by several persons; the price he set was $500, exclusive of packing and shipping charges. Shortly afterward Cooper, Kinloch, and others proposed to raise a subscription among some fifty persons for a statue by him and to petition Congress, on the strength of it, to give him a commission. His conditions were that for $1000 from them and $1000 from other friends in America he would execute a seven-foot figure to be disposed of by the subscribers after its exhibition for his benefit. "I would fain do something in the large before *habit* shall have cramped my hand to the little," he wrote Cooper at this time. "I wish to emulate others who have made statues for my country, while I'm young." He felt if he did not secure some such order soon he would have to make a drastic change in his affairs, and he considered giving up his establishment in Florence and going to Germany. "I must cut through the snarl into which four years have wound my relations," he wrote Morse, "and come smack on my feet. I'm afraid of a habit, and the habit of being assisted is one of the most ruinous."[9]

Meanwhile, early in 1832, Greenough was commissioned by Congress to execute a statue of Washington for the Capitol. Official notice of this fact did not reach him until the summer, however, and not until the summer of 1833 was he provided funds with which to begin work. It was on the whole a period of great exhilaration, yet of much uncertainty, and, above all, of many doubts about where he should fix his residence.

He felt increasingly pessimistic about his professional fate among his countrymen. Early in the year an uncle wrote advising him to take lessons in fire-eating and rope-dancing if he thought of returning home, fearing that "an ourang outang or a calf with seven legs will at any time throw all the chisel can do into the shade." His own experience and that of other artists whom he knew seemed to corroborate the report. At the same time he was unusually homesick. Morse and Cole returned to America in the fall of 1832, and Cooper planned to go then, though he did not until the next year. Gore and Cranch left Florence. He would soon be a "vox clamantis in deserto," Greenough lamented. "This world is all a fleeting shew," he kept lugubriously repeating. He felt he could not leave his studio even to go to Paris to bid Morse and Cooper goodbye. "Cruel invitation," he replied to Morse's letter urging him to come. "Lead us not into temptation."[10]

In September Henry fell ill and for three months Horatio did little more than care for him. At the end of that time they moved into new quarters, where Kinloch also lived. Probably these quarters were in Casa Ximenes, Number 6718 Borgo Pinti, adjoining the great Palazzo Ximenes Panciatichi. Horatio was living there five years later.[11]

Late in 1832 he began two works for Boston merchant Samuel Cabot, who with his family spent a month in Florence then. One was a bust of Cabot's eleven-year-old daughter Elizabeth; for it Greenough received a hundred Tuscan crowns (or francesconi).[12]

The second work was a group, whose design Cabot selected from Greenough's portfolio. Like "The Chanting Cherubs," it consisted of two nude infant male figures in the *putti* tradition, one supposedly just entering a spiritual from a mortal realm and the other a spiritual being acting as guide. In the beginning Greenough referred to it by the title of "Journey to Heaven"; afterward it was called "The Ascension of an Infant Spirit," "The Ascension of a Child Conducted by an Infant Angel," and simply "Angel and Child." "The points of expression," Greenough said, he intended to be "the contrast between the ideal forms and face of the cherub and the milky fatness and shew-baby, half doubting, half pleased look of the child." Cabot at first objected to his desire to "make em both stark naked," but as he reported, he

fought hard and carried the day—the little fellows are to be provided with alabaster fig leaves which shall fall at a tap! of the hammer when the discerning public shall have *digested* the fruit of the knowledge of good and evil.

The model was nearly finished by March 1833 and the marble

apparently about a year later. It was made a little over two and a half feet high, and on the front and back of the base respectively were incised "Quae nunc Abibis in Loca?" ("To what place will you now go?") and "H° Greenough F^{t} 1832" (the second abbreviation standing for *fecit* or *faciebat*). The price Greenough first asked was 700 Tuscan crowns, an increase over that of the "Cherubs" which he said was necessary to keep him from going in debt. But in the end he reduced it $200 because of his obligations to Cabot's father-in-law, Colonel Perkins.[13]

The "Angel and Child" was the third and last of Greenough's works to be specially exhibited in America. It was shown at Amory Hall in Boston from November 4, 1834 to February 24, 1835, between 10 A.M. and 10 P.M., at the usual prices. Receipts went to Father Edward Taylor's Charities for Seamen's Children, in which Cabot was interested. A green screen was erected behind the work, and a rose-colored silk curtain hung between it and the sun. Like the "Cherubs" and the "Medora" it was widely and flatteringly noticed by the press, and this time there were evidently no prudish or flippant reactions—thanks possibly to the alabaster leaves. One critic thought the subject was the best of the three (the "Cherubs" being too perfect, the "Medora" being associated with guilt), and Hillard (writing once more in the *New-England Magazine*) pronounced the work Greenough's best—an "Idea, embodied in a material form," having the power to deflect those who saw it "from the hot pursuit of wealth or vain distinction." At least three handbills were printed and four poems composed. One of the poems was by Dr. Charles Follen, professor of German at Harvard, and his wife. Another was by Allston, who paid tribute less to the artist's creation itself than to it as a symbol of his creative powers—"The living presence of another's mind." Ticknor was so impressed that when he saw the work of various sculptors in

Rome a few years later he thought that, Thorvaldsen's excepted, there was "more depth of meaning" in Greenough's group than in "all of them put together."[14] Actually, however, idea and form are not united in the "Angel and Child," as they were in "The Chanting Cherubs" by the nature of the subject, and the work suffers accordingly. It is also—a rarity among Greenough's works in this respect—sentimental.

Through Cabot Greenough also received an order from Colonel Perkins, of which he had heard a rumor a year earlier.[15] But whereas at that time he was in great need of work, he now felt that the commission added onerously to his obligations. Apparently it was not now undertaken. By the spring, when he dispatched the "Medora," he was for the most part caught up. Still waiting for money from the government with which to begin his work for it, he set up by mid-May a seven-foot Achilles (reportedly modeled from his own figure) "to divert my melancholy," he wrote Cooper, adding zestfully, "he's a whacker." Cooper continued to gibe at his Michelangelean leanings. "What do you intend to do, with the burly Ajax? . . . I beg your pardon—I believe it is the invulnerable: Achilles," he inquired. Evidently Greenough was not altogether pleased with this work and did not finish it. "I feel a great void under my waistcoat," he confessed to Cooper a few weeks later. "I suppose I always shall. Did you ever feel really satisfied?"[16]

For a year after he received the first payment for the statue of Washington for the Capitol, Greenough was largely occupied with beginning this work. During the latter part of 1833 and the first of 1834 he apparently undertook only four or five new private commissions, all busts. Probably in the fall of 1833 he modeled one of the celebrated belle Mrs. Joseph M. "Florida" White, who with her husband, the congressman from Florida, was in Florence at that time. It is one of his best female portraits, capturing much of the subject's sophistication. Early in 1835 it was in Washington, creating something of a stir: some gallant placed a rose on it, which was allowed to remain until faded; Hiram Powers, just beginning his career, was glad to model the wife of Senator Preston in competition with it. For this work, Greenough was reported to have gotten $300. Probably late in 1833 he also modeled the bust of Mary Frazier Curtis, the child of T. B. Curtis (later his brother-in-law), then in Florence with her and his first wife. It was finished by the spring of 1836. In the winter of 1834 he modeled from a print and mask a bust of Edmund D. Griffin, a recently deceased young clergyman, for the father, a wealthy New York lawyer; evidently a second marble was executed in 1835. By the end of 1834 he had completed the bust of naval Captain Alexander Claxton of Baltimore.[17]

In the summer of 1834 Greenough made a trip to Paris to secure certain authorities for his statue of Washington. He was there from late in August until September 6 (his twenty-ninth birthday), occupied for the most part with his errand. But he found time to visit galleries, call on Ingres with a proof of the "Lafayette" engraving, and buy books (including some in Spanish and Latin). Missing his companions of a few years before, he complained of there being a "melancholy about a superb capital," of Paris being "flat," and even more than before of the French artistic sense being inferior to the Italian. In his opinion "frippery taste" had produced a "Vanity fair aspect" in Parisian streets and affected all but "merely practical works," in which he conceded the French were great. "I shall return to Florence," he wrote Morse,

with an unwillingness to leave it again but for my own home. I prefer the Italians with all their faults to any other people. I thank God I've seen people that can beat them all hollow at cheating.

"Dear, compact, bird's-eye, cheap, quiet, mind-your-own-business, beautiful Florence," he exclaimed to Henry, "how does my heart yearn for you! There stands your bell-tower and your Palazzo Vecchio. What care I for those who inhabit you? There will I build my church!" Evidently he journeyed back to Florence in a calèche with Bostonian Jonathan Mason and Colonel and Mrs. White, by way of Milan and Venice.[18]

In the fall of 1834 he at last set up his "Washington," and from then until the first of 1836 he was chiefly engaged in modeling it. At the same time he executed a number of other works—fifteen busts in the winter of 1835 alone. Colonel White now probably sat for his; it was finished—bold and realistic in treatment—by May 1835. William Cullen Bryant was modeled on his visit to Florence in the fall of 1834; an enthusiastic viewer pronounced the likeness "redolent of poetry in every feature." Two marbles were executed of a Madame "Para," the second early in 1835, "with which all the world seems satisfied," Greenough reported.[19]

One family had the distinction of being entirely put into marble: that of David Sears, prominent Boston merchant. They were in Florence in the fall of 1834, at which time the commissions were apparently given. Of Sears and his wife Greenough made busts, producing in the first a handsome and much admired work but not succeeding very well in the second. Of the Sears children, Grace and Knyvet Winthrop, he made a small group, about two and a half feet high. His first drawing for this work represented the girl teaching the boy to read, but Sears thought this design too matter-of-fact.[20] In the design agreed upon, the girl was seated on a grassy plot, the boy bending over her, both playing with a squirrel, both draped. They were entitled "Forest Children." One of Greenough's most ambitious undertakings in the category of children's portraiture, the work is one of his most pleasing. By May 1835 all three works for Sears were to be seen in his studio, though the group, at least, was not in marble.[21] It was evidently completed in the fall of 1837, being delayed by his visit to America in 1836.

From Colonel James Thomson, a New Yorker of several years residence in Florence, Greenough received another order about this time for statuary of children. He executed the figures of the two Thomson boys playing battledore, designed to stand in opposite ends of a room. The one with the shuttlecock was being finished in the spring of 1836, the other sometime after 1838. They "please everybody highly," he reported, "for the novelty and the expressive action."[22] Unfortunately they seem not to have been preserved.

He also executed during this period a three-and-a-half-foot statue of Cupid, the hands clasped behind the back and one ankle chained to a stone, on which sat an owl. He called it "Love Captive" or "Love Prisoner to Wisdom." It embodied, he said, a conception of Petrarch in the "Trionfo della Castita." In the form he tried to represent "that twisting impatience which a boy manifests at restraint" and in the face mingled "treachery and mischief." It was rough hewn by early 1835, and at the end of the year he was applying finishing touches. It was, he thought, his best figure thus far. Visitors to his studio were taken by its expression, "original" and varying when looked at from different angles.[23] Superficially it is comparable to "The Chanting Cherubs" and the "Angel and Child" group, but the anatomical treatment is closer to that of archaic than of Renaissance tradition.

Several other patrons negotiated in 1834 and 1835 for statuary which for the most part Greenough executed much later. John Lowell, Jr., arriving in Florence in February 1834, ordered a statue, apparently of Venus Victrix, for the reported amount of $1000, to be presented to the Boston Athenaeum. In May 1834 Baltimore lawyer David Hoffman, bringing a letter of introduction from David Greenough, gave an order for a work not to exceed $300. In the fall of 1835 Greenough evidently designed for Miss Sarah Gibbs of Portsmouth, R. I., then in Florence with her sister and nephew W. H. Channing, a monument which she planned to erect to the memory of her parents. She was not satisfied with it, feeling that "personal private feeling was somewhat too much expressed," and the project languished for several years. (So impressed was young Channing with Greenough's ideas about art, that he urged the sculptor to introduce a gallery and deliver lectures on the subject in America.)[24]

Throughout these years of increasing artistic activity Greenough maintained his broad interest in letters. Morse carried for him one of Niccolini's tragedies to Edward Everett. In the summer of 1835 he sent Josiah Quincy, then president of Harvard, a catalogue of the celebrated library of Count Boutourlin, which was being offered for sale, in the hope that it might be acquired by the college. He pronounced Longfellow's translations from the Italian "inimitable," exulted over Drake's *Culprit Fay,* objected to the personal satire in William Snelling's poem *Truth* and to the national prejudice in Doblado's *Letters from Spain.* Late in 1834 Everett asked him to write an article for the *North American Review* on the current state of the arts, but he declined, presumably because he was too busy setting up his statue of Washington. He had considered, he wrote Cooper, the next year,

> giving my notions on Italy France England—America as respects those topics that lie within the range of my judgment, in the form of Travels in the East by a Boston Boy—Italy I mean to designate as the Empire of Già fù [formerly was] England as the island of Sellemall [uncomfortable saddle?] . . . France as the Kingdom of Ornsiorano [they ornament themselves]—America as the Republic of Peroravabbene [for the present it goes well].

Cooper had forestalled him, he said, in *The Monikins.*[25]

In these years, in fact, Greenough formed more close associations with writers than with artists. Most of the American artists who appeared went home after a short stay. "[I]t takes a great deal of resolution," he wrote Henry in 1835, "to work through the elements in a foreign land, with one's milk-teeth unshed and little money."[26] That year R. H. Wilde, the poet and ex-congressman, arrived in Florence to spend several years; and G. W. Greene, who had been there earlier, returned. Greenough knew both well. On one occasion probably during their early acquaintance Greenough and Wilde amused themselves by translating an unflattering Italian inscription on the tomb of a Cardinal in Florence.[27] Greene promptly gave some of his poems to Greenough for criticism and reported to Longfellow that Greenough was "a glorious fellow in every sense."[28]

On two other men of letters Greenough made in these years a lasting impression. Emerson, who spent a month in Florence in the spring of 1833, admired his "handsome" face and "well formed" person, expressed interest in his sculpture, but above all was struck by his artistic philosophy, which he expounded for Emerson late into one night. By this time he had come to think of art as a vast cooperative enterprise and of all artists as members of a great brotherhood. He was convinced, Emerson wrote in his description of their Florentine meeting in *English Traits,* that "art would never prosper until we left our shy jealous ways and worked in society" like the Greeks, who "had wrought in schools or fraternities, the genius of the master imparting his design to his friends and inflaming them with it." It was, Emerson wrote Greenough nearly twenty years later, "quite the most magnanimous theory of art and artists, I have ever chanced to hear from one of themselves." Greenough also introduced Emerson to W. S. Landor, who lived on the slope of the Fiesole hill, just outside Florence, and the two Americans breakfasted with the Englishman.[29]

A few months after Emerson young Henry T. Tuckerman of

Boston, who became Greenough's biographer, arrived in Florence for a visit of several months. He thought it was "a somewhat dreary *palazzo*" the sculptor lived in but was fascinated by the "huge fragments of marble" lining the court and stairway and delighted by one of the rooms fitted up "in the American style." Here beside a wood fire on winter evenings Greenough liked, Tuckerman said, to entertain a few friends

> around the tea-table, speculate on the news from home, criticise works of art, and tell stories. . . . He would often occupy himself with pen or crayon while thus enjoying a social hour; sometimes covering a sheet of paper with the remembered faces of the absent and the loved; and, at others, making elaborate and carefully wrought designs for a basso-relievo or statue.

Though in other studios he had seen "a more numerous and imposing array," in none Tuckerman declared, had he found "more of that individuality of design and execution which characterizes native intellectual results." When he left Florence, Greenough presented him with an original drawing of Orestes tormented by the Furies.[30]

Meantime, with Greenough's receipt of the "Washington" commission, the number of visitors to his studio increased and the circle of his friends in Florence widened. By December 1833 he sometimes had a "regular procession" in and out of his house, and he asked his father that all who were given letters of introduction be told to call after six P.M. in the summer and after four in the winter. Ombrosi resumed his introductions of travelers. Members of the American Mediterranean fleet called. Among the Bostonians were newlywed Charles and Martha Babcock Amory early in 1834 (disappointed, Mrs. Amory reported they saw "nothing very pretty" in Greenough's studio except a cast of "The Chanting Cherubs"), and in May 1835 Colonel Perkins, who was piloted about perhaps too zealously by his protegé. (Perkins confessed in his diary that his mind "was so struck with what I had seen that I was in a sort of maze. It is too much for my head.") Clergyman Orville Dewey of New Bedford was unimpressed by Florence, but thought Greenough "one of the most attractive and interesting, as well as kindest men I ever knew." The celebrated singer Mme. Catalani made an appearance in his studio, and Landor brought parties of English there. By 1835 Greenough was enjoying the quiet nightly receptions of Mme. Murat (sister of Napoleon). "I might have danced and frolicked to my heart's content if I had had a mind," he wrote Henry during the carnival season that year; at the Countess Orloff's masked ball he wore a costume of the time of the French Francis II. He also began to attend the soirées of banker Emanuele Fenzi, who handled his account during most of his years in Florence.[31]

After his receipt of the "Washington" commission Greenough also got an increasing amount of attention in the American press. The general response to the news was enthusiastic, though some jealousy and disapproval of his foreign residence was excited. An admirer of self-made Hezekiah Augur protested in the Boston *Transcript* in May 1832 that Augur was at least as good as Greenough, who was represented as "reaping laurels, acquiring fame, and accumulating wealth" and as having "acquired notoriety" by his residence in Italy and his "intimate acquaintance with the most popular American writers who have chosen to expatriate themselves."[32] During their Florentine sojourns Willis and the novelist Theodore Fay (who was in the city in the winter of 1833–34) referred flatteringly to Greenough in letters to the *New-York Mirror*. Tuckerman described a visit to Greenough's studio in the *American Monthly Magazine* for January 1836, and the same year his collegemate J. N. Bellows wrote an article on him for the *Knickerbocker*.

Dunlap's *History of the Rise and Progress of the Arts of Design in the United States,* which appeared in 1834, contained a relatively lengthy account of Greenough, including two letters written to Dunlap by Henry and Horatio. Horatio had requested that this account be brief, perhaps no more than thirty lines, since whaever importance he had might be only "local and temporary."[33] *"What is the use,"* he put it, *"of blowing up bladders, for posterity to jump upon, for the mere pleasure of hearing them crack?"* His letter was chiefly an acknowledgment of the aid he had received, particularly from Allston, Cogswell, Parkman, and Cooper; he would, he said, speak of others but that he feared to overlook some and shrank from calling attention tc what might prove "a fearful disproportion between the seed and the fruit." By now he was better able to assess his chances of achievement than he had been when he wrote Allston about them in 1829. He was no more confident than he had been then, for somewhat different reasons. "I fear," he wrote, "that the circumstances under which I began my career will ever prevent me realizing my idea of what sculpture should be." Presumably he was thinking of the meagerness of his early artistic environment and the extent to which he had been compelled to teach himself. Yet he continued to feel that his effort might be "useful to future artists, and yield some works of a relative and special value."[34]

With his studio work, his art purchasing, his reading and writing and his social activities, Greenough's life from 1833 to 1836 was a full and to all appearances a satisfying one. Yet there were tensions beneath the surface and periods of depression. He continued subject to colds and in the summer of 1833 had smallpox. At the end of that year—most of his close friends and Henry having gone home and commencement of his statue of Washington being delayed—he felt perhaps most alone. "I have much on my shoulders," he wrote his father in December, and depend entirely for comfort on what I hear from home, being here amid strangers who see too many foreigners and know too well that we are here for the moment only, to care anything about us.

To Allston he unburdened himself most fully:

I beg you will pity me as a sojourner in the land of strangers. I am a poor land-bird at sea. I am tired—but there is as yet no lighting place. I can't turn waterfowl. . . . a few years and I shall I trust sit by you and smoak and look out a window at the trees and sky of Cambridge. It will seem but a moment then—these months and years of absence.

Such moods as these he combated not only with work but physical exercise. Early in 1835 he took up horseback riding, which kept him, he said, in good health and "in spirits, and prevents melancholy from getting the mastery over me." In January of the same year he bought a greyhound, which he named Arno. "He puts his forepaws on my shoulders as I stand erect," he wrote Henry.

His nose is pink, and his ears look like rose-leaves. Everybody is enamoured of him. I gave five dollars for him, and have already received fifty-five dollars' worth of pleasure.[35]

Early in 1836 the figure of his "Washington" was cast. Several months being necessary for the plaster of so large a work to dry, he took this occasion to go to America, chiefly to secure materials unavailable in Europe to aid him in modeling the pedestal. By this time, too, he was evidently nurturing another large-scale project. He had plans "of great moment," he wrote Henry in March,[36] which partly depended on his getting to Washington while Congress was in session; he wanted Henry to meet him in New York and accompany him there. Perhaps he knew of the project just being launched by the government of ornamenting the blockings of the eastern front of the Capitol with two groups of statuary and hoped to apply for the commission for one or both of them. He made arrangements for the G. W. Greenes to occupy his apartment in his absence and early in April left Florence.[37] He stopped briefly in Paris and sailed from Le Havre on May 16, on the *François I.*

At Le Havre, the odor of kelp and seaweed which he met "after being ten years on the shores of that dead sea the Mediterranean" seemed to invigorate his mind and body by ten years. Yet as he looked back on the first decade of his career, he had a deep sense of fulfillment. "I ought to be thankful, certainly, for so much success and comfort," he wrote Henry from Paris. "If I were to be cut off to-morrow, I should not have lived in vain, either for happiness or for success."[38]

Death Masks

The *François I* reached New York on June 10. Probably on account of the illness of David Greenough, Henry did not meet Horatio there. On the 13th, apparently accompanied by his collegemate George Calvert and Hiram Powers, Horatio went on to Washington.[1]

His principal business there was an examination of the rotunda of the Capitol as the site of his statue of Washington, in consequence of which he decided not to have reliefs on the pedestal. Possibly while there he modeled the busts of Clay and Calhoun; both were in marble by the summer of 1839. Though Clay thought "Mr. Greenough utterly failed" in his, other critics pronounced it a "perfect" likeness.[2] The bust of Calhoun was evidently executed for a Charlestonian; after the owner's death in 1844 it was offered for sale for $1000.[3] Greenough may also have modeled the bust of politician Thomas Butler King of Georgia about this time.

As for the projected statuary for the east front of the Capitol, action had been taken a few weeks before Greenough's arrival in Washington to consider having it executed by Persico. Nevertheless, Greenough probably discussed the matter with government representatives while in the city. A year later both he and Persico received commissions for this statuary, each for a group.

About the middle of July Greenough traveled to Boston,

where his family was then living on Beacon Street. Three days after he arrived David Greenough, who had long been failing, took to his bed and on July 27 he died. He was cheerful to the end and his last words expressed his joy at seeing his children (all but John) around him. Horatio was much impressed by what seemed to him "a happy death, without any other security for the future than natural religion gives to an upright & benevolent mind." In great contrast to him was the "mannered jargon," the "helter skelter quotations from the Old & New Testaments to prove that we should rejoice in the event" of the minister who called on the family. "I cannot but think," he wrote Cooper,

> that Christianity is in the heart & in the heart only—any admixture of head-work spoils all—and in those of the trade all is spoiled.[4]

A few days before David Greenough's death, in consideration of his heavily mortgaged estate, Amos Lawrence offered to cancel the debt owed Lawrence on Horatio's account since 1825, but David would not agree, convinced that his heirs would soon be well provided for.[5]

Three weeks after the death of David Greenough another death shocked the whole city of Boston: that of Mrs. Emily Marshall Otis, the celebrated belle, at the age of twenty-nine. Portraits of her had been painted by Alexander and Harding, and after her death her husband asked Greenough to execute her bust. He and Henry took an impression of her face and from it he made a cast. He had never before thought her beautiful but declared he had never seen "more symmetry of features" than in those of her corpse. "Ah! Sir," he wrote Wilde, "it was a bitter experience that sight!" He may have been referring to that experience when he wrote Charles G. Loring a few years later that he had intended seeing more of Loring in the summer of 1836, but a calamity which befel me there, under circumstances that rendered me peculiarly vulnerable, took from me what I have of energy and of philosophy.

He modeled the bust in Florence, from the death mask and Alexander's portrait (which was sent him). By the fall of 1839 it was virtually finished, but he kept trying to satisfy himself better and to incorporate suggestions made by friends of Mrs. Otis. He feared it would be a failure and hoped Otis would not exhibit it. Apparently it was sent to America early in 1844. Others were disappointed in it, partly, however, because they remembered the subject as having had a peculiarly uncapturable charm.[6]

The death of still another Bostonian in the summer of 1836 affected Greenough—that of John Lowell, Jr., which occurred in Bombay. Probably Lowell's uncle, lawyer John Lowell, "The Little Rebel," took over the order for the statue placed with Greenough—perhaps at this time.

A few other orders besides Otis' were forthcoming. Throughout the summer, Greenough wrote Romeo Elton, then in Providence, he was kept busy modeling portraits.[7] One of them—that of merchant Samuel Appleton—was one of his most effective. Executed in his heavier style, it evokes the spirit of the whole mercantile class, upon which so much of his career and the careers of other American artists rested: self-confident and practical, yet dignified and willing to patronize whatever meant the growth of the nation. Possibly he also modeled at this time the bust of Jonathan Mason, which was put in marble early in 1838.[8]

While in Boston Greenough sat to Alexander for his portrait, was elected a member of the Harvard chapter of Phi Beta Kappa, and had the distinction of being mentioned among several examples of American "genius" (though all were called "tame") by Emerson at the first meeting of the Transcendental

Club. He himself was much of Emerson's mind. He complained to Wilde of the little doing in the arts:

Portraits are the only pictures, and bank notes the best engraving I have seen. The Architecture flounders on in obstinate Greekism and at enormous expence. . . . Rail Roads alone seem to be *understood.* Go ahead! is the order of the day. The whole continent presents a scene of *scrabbling* and roars with greedy hurry. They are chipping out a colossus and one must stand clear of the *flinders.*

At the same time, in a characteristic effort to encourage native talent, he took occasion in a letter to the editor of the *North American Review* to praise the portraits of A. B. Durand, the genre studies of W. S. Mount, and other American paintings he had seen in Boston. He hoped to submit for publication in that magazine some compositions of his on the subjects of architecture and the future of art in the country, but he was unable to finish them. On the whole, he found everything in America more to his mind than he had feared and even thought of settling down and dreaming "no more of foreign lands, or of any advantages not enjoyed here."[9]

By September, however, he was impatient to get back to "my mud and my hammer."[10] By that time, the health of his sister Louisa having become so delicate that the family feared another New England winter for her, it had been arranged that she should go with him to Florence and spend some time there. On their way they planned to see John in London. About the 27th or 28th of September Horatio, at least, went to New York. From there he hoped to make a quick trip to see Cooper in Cooperstown if Cooper did not come to him. No record of such a meeting seems to exist. On October 10 Horatio and Louisa sailed from New York on the *Quebec* for London.

The year 1836 may be called the midpoint in Greenough's life. The death of his father signified the end of his youth, and his marriage the next year, to a woman he met on his way back to Italy, ended his bachelorhood. He was midway in his career as a sculptor for the national government, having modeled one of his two works for it and being about to receive the commission for the other. His ideas about art and architecture, moreover, had so matured that he was now ready to set them forth publicly in printed form.

Part II

4

Spokesman for the Nation

GREENOUGH'S EXECUTION OF HIS two works of sculpture for the American government and his formulation of his architectural theory may be considered to constitute in themselves a chapter of his life. They are his major achievements. He was occupied with each over a period of a decade or more, and from 1837 to 1841 with all three simultaneously. All are, moreover, intimately related as manifestations of his thought and of his greatest desire as an artist: to be a spokesman for his nation. All assume art forms to be subservient to ends other than themselves, and all project the image of a mature and a humanistic civilization.

"The Birth of My Thought"

The commission awarded Greenough by action of the American Congress for a statue of Washington represented the consummation of a longstanding desire on the part of both parties involved. At the end of the Revolution the national legislative body voted to erect such a statue, subsequently proposed other memorials, yet took no final action about any. Meanwhile a host of artists addressed themselves to producing likenesses of the father of the country, and four statues (all by foreign sculptors) were erected under local auspices. Houdon's, in the Virginia State House, wore a Revolutionary uniform; Canova's, in the North Carolina State House, was clad like a Roman soldier, seated, composing the Farewell Address;

Chantrey's, in the Massachusetts State House, was in civil dress, enveloped in a cloak, holding a scroll; Causici's, in Baltimore, was in military dress, resigning as commander-in-chief.

About 1828 the Congressional project was revived. In 1832, as part of the centennial of Washington's birth, it was proposed to move his remains to a crypt beneath the rotunda of the Capitol and erect a statue over the site. Permission for the removal of the remains being refused, negotiations were made for the statue alone.

These negotiations were launched by Leonard Jarvis, chairman of the Committee on Public Buildings, who on Allston's recommendation named Greenough as the sculptor for the statue. It was Allston more than anyone else who was responsible for Greenough's being chosen. (Two years earlier Allston had recommended him for the statue then proposed.) Cooper assumed most of the credit, presuming that "The Chanting Cherubs" had influenced the choice, but evidently it did not. In March 1832 Cooper wrote President Jackson urging Greenough's employment, but this letter was too late to be effective.[1]

Greenough had long desired to execute not only a monumental work but a Washington, as the treatments of this subject which he had already produced evidenced. It was, indeed, a subject which preoccupied him throughout his career, longer and more fruitfully than any other. Altogether it inspired some half a dozen works or projected works of his: the bust he modeled in college, that he executed in the late 1820's and early 1830's, the statue he modeled in 1830, that he executed for the Capitol, the statuette in modern dress he designed in 1837, and the equestrian statue for which he made studies in the 1840's.

The original resolution providing for the statue for the Capitol was dated February 13, 1832, and was introduced in the House of Representatives the following day by Jarvis. It authorized the President to employ Greenough to execute, in marble, a full-length pedestrian statue of Washington, to be placed in the centre of the rotundo of the Capitol; the head to be a copy of Houdon's WASHINGTON, and the accessories to be left to the judgment of the artist.[2]

(Houdon's, modeled with the aid of his life mask of Washington, was of all likenesses most authentic.) On the 16th the resolution was adopted by a vote of 114 to 50, the negatives being cast by those who doubted that one legislative body could appropriate money.[3] On February 23, Secretary of State Edward Livingston communicated the news to Greenough, also suggesting that the base of the work be rectangular and ornamented with bas-reliefs of Revolutionary scenes and asking for an estimate of the cost and the time the work might consume.[4] With his letter went a copy of the resolution and a plan and section of the rotunda. The documents were transmitted through the American Minister in Paris, W. C. Rives, and thus took some three months longer to arrive than had they gone by ordinary mail.

A few weeks later Livingston recommended that an appropriation be made for the work of at least $20,000, to be paid in four yearly installments, and an installment of $5000 was provided for in the general appropriations bill. In April when the resolution, which had been accidentally passed as a House instead of a joint Congressional bill, came to the Senate, that body objected that the House had no right to act independently regarding a part of the Capitol over which both houses had jurisdiction and struck out the appropriation. A joint resolution was introduced on April 25, which was passed by the Senate on June 26 and the House on July 14. On the last date the $5000 was re-appropriated.[5]

News of these maneuvers reached Greenough first unofficially. About the middle of March 1832 Cooper wrote him of seeing a letter from an American referring to the first bill. He did not have "much faith in Congress," he commented to Morse, but confessed that he had lately told "the spectre Debt" that "Brother Jonathan talks of adopting me, and that he won't have her of his household." On April 22 Cooper informed him that the resolution had been passed by the House, thus making him reasonably sure of it. His first step thereafter was a significant one: he went to the hospital and for the first time dissected a cadaver, which he planned to make his "constant study" in the winter. He was determined to "strain every nerve lest this commission should prove the greatest misfortune that ever happened to me." "In a couple of hours," he explained to Cooper,

one sees more of the *why* of organization and form than in days of lecture reading and examining the living model. Its effect on one is most stirring. It seems as one follows the knife as if God himself were made visible and audible in the beauty strength and fitness of our frames.[6]

At the same time, Greenough thought of his commission as affecting not only himself but all American artists. "I have made up my mind on one score," he wrote Morse,

Viz. that this order shall not be fruitless to the greater men who are in our rear. They are sucking now and rocking in cradles but I can hear the Pung! Pung! Puffety! of their hammers and I am prophetic too! We'll see if Yankee land cant muster some ten or dozen of em in the course of as many years!

He urged Everett to see that Morse, who aspired to paint one or more of the panels in the rotunda, received a government order also and exclaimed to the painter, "We will have a knot of us here, which shall form an epoch, by the beard of Jupiter Flaminius!"[7]

On June 3 Greenough evidently received word from Morse that Livingston's packet had reached Paris. A "coldness" came over him, and his mind was "topsy turvy" as he replied:

here's work and care and all the material of life for several years with the hope of being enrolled among the American *Old Masters* if I do not sink under the burthen.

A week later came a transmitting letter from Rives and several days after that at last the official documents.[8]

On July 8 Greenough replied to Livingston, accepting the commission and the suggestions and describing his general conception of the work. He proposed to make the statue fifteen feet high, on about a ten-foot base. (He had decided on the dimensions after examining the grand altar in the Baptistery in Florence, a room approximately the size of the rotunda.)[9] He thought the figure "should not be a mere image of the man to gratify curiosity, nor a vain display of Academic art, but an embodying of his spirit"; that in contrast "Truth" should be represented in the reliefs on the pedestals; and that the accessories "should be stamped with the character of our institutions." He proposed to submit drawings from time to time to show his progress. The execution he thought would consume four years, and the price he set was $20,000. Of his profound gratification at receiving the commission and of the enormous importance attached to it in his mind he left no doubt. "The hope," he wrote,

> of being found worthy to execute a statue of Washington for one of the great cities of my country, has been my support through years of solitary study in a foreign land.
>
> . . . .
>
> Believe that in exertion I will be true to my country—and that I fully feel that if I prove worthy of this task I shall not have lived in vain.

As soon as Livingston's letter arrived, Cooper advised Greenough to go home for a visit, partly to examine the site proposed for the statue, and offered to advance the money for the trip. But Greenough felt he should first know of the Senate's approval of the bill and have Livingston's reply to his letter. He also had private commissions to be filled which committed him to his studio for several months. News of the Senate vote reached him in August and of the final vote and appropriation about September.[10] Throughout the fall Livingston's letter of announcement and Greenough's of acceptance were widely printed in American newspapers.

Livingston's reply to his letter, however, and funds for the commencement of the statue were delayed. Jackson had understood $5000 to be the total cost of the work and referred the approval of the sum named by Greenough to Congress at its next session. At the end of March 1833 Livingston wrote Greenough announcing the acceptance of his terms and enclosing a draft for $5000. Both documents reached Florence early in May—a year after Livingston's first letter. (Out of this sum Greenough paid what he owed Cooper and planned to pay the Bostonians who advanced him money in 1828.)[11]

Throughout this year Greenough debated, often agonizingly, where he should fix his residence while executing the statue. "I begin to doubt," he wrote Morse in the summer of 1832, "if ever I shall leave Italy; they write me that artists stand as ignorantly with the public as ever."

'Tis not the money we want, 'tis the consideration and weight. . . . I choose to reside in old Europe, and live secluded, and try to respect myself, rather than be waiting at the doors of the rich, at home, for the vain, or patronizing, or pitying proofs of their superabundance.

Yet exile was painful to him. "Like the ass between 2 bundles of hay," he wrote Cooper the following January,

I cast my eye from continent to continent and sigh that I cant plant one foot in the states and the other on the boot—chisel here with one hand and hold up to the christening font there with the other. Hitherto I have trodden on every sprouting inclination which threatened to shade or encumber my profession—shall I change tactics? . . . I think I have reached one of those cross roads of life where the choice of path has a great influence on subsequent happiness.[12]

In the end, the slowness of the government in concluding its arrangements with him virtually dictated his decision. By the time he received Livingston's second letter and the first installment of his fee, moving his base of operations would have involved an intolerable delay. He made immediate plans to execute his statue in Florence.

Even so, it was another year before he began work in earnest because of the difficulties of finding a large enough room and assembling authorities. He thought for a while he would have to go to Rome for such a room, but late in 1833 he rented a satisfactory edifice, which had once been used as a church, located about a mile outside Florence on the slope of the Fiesole hill in the neighborhood known as the Querce. Presumably it was the villa on Via Piazzola opposite the Collegio della Querce, in which part of the sixteenth-century Oratorio della Madonna della Querce had been incorporated. In its bare expanse he felt, he wrote Dunlap,

> like a spoilt boy, who, after insisting upon riding on horseback, bawls aloud with fright at finding himself in the saddle, so far from the ground!

Several alterations had to be made before he could use it.[13]

Shortly after receiving Livingston's first letter he tried, unsuccessfully, to get a cast of Houdon's bust of Washington from America or from Lafayette's copy and finally got in the summer of 1834 casts of the one at Fontainebleau. His other chief authority was Stuart's portrait of Washington in the Boston Athenaeum, which in 1833 he employed Alexander to copy. He also secured anatomical preparations, casts from the antique, prints, and books. He consulted, in fact, not only pictorial but historical authorities. No other artist, thought one acquaintance, "would have so diligently and enthusiastically studied his hero, in all the sources of history, biography, and correspondence."[14]

Meantime, in the fall of 1833 he made a clay model about half the size of life and the next April and May modeled a mannikin from life. In October 1834 he began the large model (by this time he had decided on a height of eleven feet) and sixteen months later he finished it. By March 1835 he was so engrossed that he wrote Allston, "I can as regards myself only talk to you of my statue which is my life," and by June he was essentially finished. Intending the surface to be "elaborate," however, he spent several more months on it, had the clay passed through a sieve and made "as soft as silk," one man being entirely devoted to its care.[15] He first hoped to cast the model in September 1835 and finally did in February 1836.

The design of Greenough's statue was an adaptation of that of the statue of Zeus made by Phidias for the temple of Elis in Olympia, regarded as that sculptor's masterpiece and one of the Seven Wonders of the ancient world. (It did not survive to modern times.) As described most thoroughly by Quatremère de Quincy, Zeus in that statue had been seven or eight times the size of life, had been half-draped with an elaborate mantle, held a winged Victory in his extended right hand and a sceptre in his uplifted left, and occupied a chryselephantine chair. More than any other monument in Greece it had embodied a national spirit. At the same time, it had constituted a fixation of existing iconographical types, which persisted in a multitude of variations throughout later artistic treatments of deities and human rulers. Roman emperors were commonly represented in the attitude of the god. Adaptations of the figure appeared in frescoes in Palazzo Pitti in Florence and in Flaxman's illustrations of Homer. Rembrandt Peale painted the head in the border of his portrait of Washington. Phidias' statue came promptly to the mind of Edward Everett, then a representative, when the statue for the Capitol was commissioned. He urged Greenough to study it, reminded him that the Capitol was comparable to the temple at Elis, and hoped that "Your Washington may be to the people of America . . . what that great national statue was to the Greeks."[16]

By September 1832, shortly after he received Everett's letter, Greenough was thinking of his figure in connection with that of Phidias. He was "full of plans and attitudes and conceptions," he wrote Cooper, but had "as yet fixed nothing—nor shall I till I have had a grand talk or 2 with you and one with an artist or so." Yet to Cooper's remonstrance that fifteen feet seemed "a devil of a pile of stone to put into the rotunda," he replied confidently that it would be "like a great summer cloud" and recalled that

the Jupiter of Phidias was so large that could he have risen from his throne he would have stove the roof of the temple.

His decision was not a hasty one, however. In May 1833 he had "questions to ask" and "plans to shew" Cooper, but he did not refer to them in his reply in July to Livingston's second letter. By the time he made his small model his mind was made up. On the first of November he sent a rough sketch to Morse and in January 1834 a finished drawing to Livingston.[17]

This drawing depicted Washington draped from the waist down and over part of the right arm by a mantle with a star-embroidered hem, holding a sheathed sword in his left hand and pointing upward with his right, resting his left foot on a stool, sitting in a chair ornamented with fruits, flowers, military and naval trophies, implements of economy, bas-reliefs of virtues personified, and eagles. Before it was sent Greenough decided to change the stool to a step, further extend the left arm, and make the hair natural. When he made the large model he lowered the position of the right arm, in order, it was reported, "to give greater gravity and repose to his figure, and to avoid every thing like over-strained attitude."[18] A few other changes were eventually incorporated (the sword's position reversed, the stars omitted from the mantle, the fold over the arm made fuller, the chair redesigned), but essentially this was the design which he put in marble.

Considering the historical significance of Phidias' "Zeus," both as a statue and as an iconographical type, Greenough's decision to adapt it in his own work was in one sense natural and even inevitable. In another sense, of course, especially in relation to other statues of Washington, it was a bold and original decision. His adaptation itself was thoughtful. In relation to the design of Phidias' work, Greenough's is less a deification of a man than a ruthless simplification and humanizing of a flamboyant god; in this respect it may be called distinctively American, democratic, and even Puritan. His work was, moreover, expressly designed for the edifice in which it was to stand, whose basically classical pattern had also been modified by native imagination.

With the drawing, Greenough sent Livingston a letter which briefly explained the pose of the figure and defended at some length the choice of dress. In preference to representing any one action, he had given Washington

> a movement which seems to me characteristic of his whole life. I wish while I impress the beholder with the idea of Washington, to remind him that Washington was an agent.

In the dress he had

> endeavoured to make the figure decent, dignified and simple. . . . It has not been without much reflection that I have set aside the dress of Washington's time. I am aware of the value of truth in the representation of the person of a great man. . . . but it seems to me that the fashion of his dress cannot be considered as such and where that fashion would interfere with the main object of the work, by calling attention to trifles, I think it should give way to considerations of what is natural and permanent.[19]

He also described and rejected a middle course between the literal and the ideal: the sculpturing of historical dress so that it would not be recognizable at a distance.

In these opinions about modern dress in sculpture Greenough was in agreement with both the neo-classical Canova, who had executed a nude Napoleon (Greenough's aim, according to one report, was "to convey a sentiment directly opposite" to that expressed in that figure, which held a globe in the right hand)[20] and the naturalistic Bartolini, whose figure of Demidoff was half-draped. In America in these years, however, the vogue of neo-classicism in art, at its height during the early national period, was rapidly giving place to that of realism. In approving the costume of Canova's "Washington," Jefferson had declared, "Our boots and regimentals have a very puny effect."[21] President Jackson expressed the new preference when he told Hiram Powers to model him as he was, even to his toothless mouth.

In these years of the second—Jacksonian—revolution in America, moreover, the image in the popular mind of a national hero was undergoing transformation, as the character of public leadership itself rapidly changed, from an aristocratic to a drastically democratized image. It was a fact of no small significance in the history of the statue for the Capitol that it was ordered by a Jacksonian administration and executed by a democrat of the old school.

Before Greenough's drawing reached Washington he knew his countrymen's general opinions of his design. By artists and intellectuals it was almost unanimously praised. Morse and others in his circle called the sketch sent him "sublime." To Chapman it was "glorious." Another artist, perhaps Cranch, declared that

as a grand ideal personification of the SPIRIT OF WASHINGTON—as a mighty work of *art*—simple, natural, grand,

the figure would give

a far truer idea of the *real Washington* than if it had been represented in the regimentals of the American General.[22]

By most Americans, however, it was condemned or ridiculed. The first public expression of this opposition came from Senator John P. King, who read an excerpt about Greenough's small model from his letter to Morse printed in the New York *Journal of Commerce* in March 1834.[23] The following month King wrote a letter to the New York *American,* objecting to the prominence of the sword, declaring that Washington's hand should be laid on "THE BOOK OF THE CONSTITUTION," and suggesting that the artist be given a suit of Washington's clothes from which to model the costume. Morse sent King's letter to Greenough, adding his approval of substituting a scroll for the sword.

Greenough replied at length to Morse in May 1834. Though he professed himself desirous of hearing criticism, he vigorously defended his design. Since "books are very like each other on the outside," to put a book or scroll in the figure's hand, he thought, would make the meaning "uncertain," and "doubt in a statue is feebleness." The sword, he felt,

> cleared the ground where our political fabric was raised. . . . I look on the military career of Washington as being, though not perhaps *his* highest glory—*our* greatest obligation to him. I can conceive of his having died at the close of that struggle without any very bad consequences to our institutions.

He repeated his earlier argument against modern dress and declared,

> If people would consider the abstract nature of sculpture . . . they would cease to look to it for information on points which are better explained by other arts in other ways. They would as soon expect to hear Washington's dress described in a 4th of July oration as to see it sculptured in an *epic* statue.

He accorded first place among statues of Washington to

Houdon's but indicated that he had deliberately eschewed the example of all these statues:

I choose to make another experiment. If it fails, the next sculptor who attempts the subject will have another beacon in this difficult navigation: the rocks will not increase: the sooner light-houses are on them the safer. Only don't send us landsmen for pilots.

His letter was printed in the *American* in August 1834.

His drawing, which reached Washington in May, was generally disapproved on account of the nudity and the upraised arm of the figure. Jackson suggested changes and asked Allston to come to the city for consultation about them, but he declined to go. (Greenough had described the design to Allston and proposed that the drawing be sent by way of Boston for him to see, but it was not.) Jarvis also solicited Allston's comment. Greenough had "undertaken to *idealise* Washington and to make an emblematical statue," Jarvis complained. "It is not *our* Washington that he has represented." Replying to Jarvis and judging from his description, Allston wrote that he and the Danas were also struck with "the inappropriateness of the *raised arm*" and questioned at length the idealizing of the subject. Yet he declined to dictate to another artist, ascribed to Greenough as much "genius . . . as any sculptor living," and reaffirmed his belief that Greenough was capable of producing "a statue that will do honour to the country."[24]

Greenough evidently received no official comment on his design. Not long after his drawing arrived Congress adjourned. When the winter session opened, Everett, who had expressed approval of the general conception, wrote him reporting the two principal objections and urging him to "make a popular, as well as a good, statue of Washington." Insofar as this report influenced Greenough, however, it did so adversely. Observing that in any case Everett's letter arrived when his large model was well under way, he drew from the politician's "various and inconsistent advice," he wrote Allston, "the strongest arguments in favour of an artists thinking for himself and acting resolutely from his own convictions." Other reports which reached him in 1834 and 1835 left him in no doubt about the objection of most of his countrymen to his design. "Volumes," declared an American in Florence early in 1836, were written him from America on the subject. "He has carefully, deliberately, and sagaciously weighed all difficulties," this visitor continued; "but, having once decided, he has adhered to his own convictions with commendable firmness." The advice Greenough received from William Cullen Bryant about this time expressed his own decision exactly:

As you are to execute the statue, do it according to your own notions of what is true and beautiful. . . . give us a Greenough; the statue deserving it, the popularity will come sooner or later.[25]

Determined as he was to obey his own creative instincts, Greenough was nevertheless of two minds regarding the opinion of others. He was convinced on the one hand that the greatest achievements were appreciated by few, yet on the other hand that the opinion of the many was in the last analysis just. "I have made up mind," he wrote Allston in March 1835,

to look for the approbation of a few. I rest my hopes of comfort during my life upon ground which has little relation with the success of my work with the world. Was it not always so? Yes and it will always be so.

Yet he was sufficiently impressed by the varying opinions of his design to propose in February 1835 that a cast of the model be sent to Washington, set up in the rotunda, and there remain to be criticized for six months or a year, the government having the right to reject it. This experiment he estimated would cost some $1500, but he argued that if the model were rejected it would save $10,000. It was not agreed to by Secretary of State John Forsyth because he had no authority to incur additional expense. "The responsibility falls entirely on me," Greenough announced to Gilmor in November 1835, "and I am ready to take it."[26]

By this time, almost ready to cast the model, Greenough had apparently begun to realize that he had not produced a work commensurate with his aspiration. He declined to say more about it to Gilmor than that

I have done my utmost. . . . I have acted conscientiously. At all events it will probably sooner or later give way to a more successful effort of some more [page torn] red artist.

About this time, the American engraver James Stout, visiting Greenough's studio with the Chevalier Saint-Georges and the Duke of Lucca, expressed the opinion, in which he said the two concurred, that it was weak in conception, "*sitting,* raw from its nudity," he later wrote, "theatrical in its upraised arm, and pointed finger." Greenough replied, he recalled, "you may be right, but it is too late to alter it." Without enthusiasm Greenough wrote Cooper in December 1835 that he had

the satisfaction of feeling that I have not sacrificed my art to any hopes of gain or favour or temporary reputation. The work is conscientious Sir & is a thousand miles ahead of any thing I have yet done.

Yet hopefully he added on this occasion, "I believe the old Hero is there and he looks like Old Hundred *you may depend.*"[27]

Early in 1835 he designed a new chair, which he thought had "none of that French air which sinned" in his first drawing. He postponed work on the pedestal, however, intending to secure authorities for the reliefs in America.[28]

When he examined the site for the statue in Washington in 1836 he found that the size of the rotunda called for more ornamentation of the chair than he had intended and therefore decided to redesign it and to leave the pedestal plain. He also found that the work could not be properly seen in the center of the room, since there it would be directly under the light from the dome, and decided the best position was between the center and the door leading into the library.[29] At this time also he tried to collect the fourth installment of his fee, then a year overdue, but it was not made available to him (because of official mismanagement) until 1838.[30]

On his return to Florence, early in 1837, he found that the weight of the uplifted arm and drapery had bent the figure of the cast out of line. The correction of this fault took about six months. The next process, the blocking-out of the marble, done in Carrara, was begun in November 1837. (The first block quarried, apparently in the fall of 1835, was cracked and another had to be obtained.) Bad weather, cholera, and "the dilatory habits of the Carrarese" delayed the operation, but by May 1838 it was in "full progress." It consumed seventeen months, nearly twice as long as he had estimated. During this time he made several trips to Carrara to supervise it.[31]

The marble, ready for his work on it, was promised in December 1838 and delivered in March 1839. During the following summer he employed as many as seven workers at once (the best he evidently paid about a dollar a day) and used up rasps and files by the dozen. He was "pretty regularly done up" every day, as he told Greene; ". . . this running up and down ladders to see one's effect is severe exertion." "I would recommend it to your dyspeptic gentlemen of Boston," he wrote Charles G. Loring, "that they should keep a lump of granite in their wood houses and pass their leisure in making Washingtons." By July the figure was so advanced he said that "the uninitiated would suppose it finished." Yet the time he spent in this last process also doubled his expectations. He promised the work finished by the summer of 1840 and had it ready to be shipped on the first of October. When no arrangement was made to get it then, he continued to work on it apparently for the equivalent of another month. About this time it was engraved by Jacopo Bernardi.[32]

Meanwhile he redesigned the chair, providing for reliefs on the sides and two small figures at the back. For both sets of accessories he considered a variety of subjects (including a Negro for one of the figures) and modeled several (notably, in the winter of 1837, six allegorical figures in relief, representing Agriculture, Trade, Facture, Legislation, the Army and the Navy).[33] He settled at last, by the fall of 1839, on the figures of Columbus and an Indian and reliefs of two mythological scenes which he gave modern historical signification: Apollo driving the chariot of the sun (meant to suggest the rising sun on the first national arms) and the infants Hercules, struggling with the serpents, and Iphicus, shrinking in dread (representing North and South America and their respective attitudes to "the obstacles and dangers of an incipient political existence"). For these reliefs he considered two mottoes from Virgil's eclogue on the return of the Golden Age—"Magnus ab integro saeclorum nascitur ordo" ("The great sequence of ages is born anew") and "Incipe parve puer cui non risere parentes" ("Begin small boy on whom parents have not smiled")—but adopted none. The body of the chair was left plain, the upper portion ornamented with acanthus and garlands, and the back pierced so as to make the figure visible. By the contrast between the plain and the ornamented portions he meant "to hint at high cultivation as the proper *finish* for sound government and to say that man when well planted and well tilled must flower as well as grow."[34] For the back of the plinth he composed an inscription in Latin, the final version of which was: "Simulacrum istud ad magnum libertatis exemplum nec sine ipsa duraturum Horatius Greenough faciebat." Literally it read, "This statue as a great example of liberty nor without the same about to endure Horatio Greenough was making."

Throughout the years the "Washington" was executing in

Florence it was seen and commented upon by scores of Europeans and Americans, most of whom praised it. Among the Europeans were Capponi, who embraced Greenough upon hearing that Columbus was to be represented on the chair and who ordered a miniature copy of the work for one of his daughters; Luigi Sabatelli, director of the Academy of Fine Arts in Milan; Lady Rosina Bulwer; and Landor, who thought that Greenough had given Washington "back to the veneration of the world." Among the Americans were Perkins, Bryant, Ticknor, Cogswell, Charles Sumner, Fay, Catherine Sedgwick, Everett, Isaac Appleton Jewett ("Every part of it is emphatic. . . . How completely is the marble purged of every thing but Washington!" he exclaimed), and George Calvert (who quipped that "Washington, to be best seen, ought to be beheld, not as he came from the hand of the tailor, but as he came from the hand of God"). The last five and Lady Bulwer commented on the work in books or magazine articles. Tuckerman and Wilde wrote poems about it, and Wilde probably also wrote a lengthy prose account. Generally speaking, the class of Americans who most violently objected to it did not travel abroad, but many of those who did anticipated that criticism awaited it at home. It would be amusing, Frances Appleton thought, to see

how many "down easters" will kinder think it a burnin shame to have the General rigged out like an old Heathen instead of the "buff & blue."[35]

As early as February 1840 Greenough began to show the statue publicly. About the fall of that year he opened a studio in the city, apparently for exhibition purposes only, in part of the suppressed monastery of the Cavalieri, adjoining the church of San Giovannino dei Cavalieri in Via San Gallo. Here on an evening early in January 1841 he showed the "Washington" and a few other pieces to a company by torchlight, with such success that he offered to repeat the performance for Capponi and some of Capponi's friends. The next month he announced through the newspapers that the statue might be seen from the 18th through the 21st, from 10 A.M. to 3 P.M. At that time it was flatteringly commented upon in the papers, notably in the *Giornale del Commercio*.[36]

By January 1841 he had composed an explanation and defense of the work to be printed when it reached the United States. This composition did not appear, probably because of the disturbed state of his relations with the government throughout this year, but probably the substance of it is represented in the letter he wrote Lady Bulwer about April. By this time, his thought about it had culminated in a conception more general, more abstract, and above all more religious than he had at first expressed. By the gestures of the figure, he told Lady Bulwer, he wished

to convey the idea of an entire abnegation of Self and to make my hero as it were a *conductor* between God and Man.

The preceding fall he had more fully expressed this conception in a letter probably addressed to Dr. John W. Francis, of New York, then president of the Apollo Association. His statue, he wrote,

contains two of the most improving and sublime ideas that I know of, and the most necessary to be *felt,* viz. the duty of all men toward God—the duty of great men toward the human race. However I may have failed for want of art to make these ideas clear, speaking eloquent, I shall never fail to feel a warmth at my bosom that I chose them for my theme;—my Washington is the *apotheosis of abnegation*—he is a conductor standing between God and man, the channel of blessings from heaven, and of prayer and praise from earth. I have struck a bold blow,—I have thrown to the winds the fear of ridicule, carping and one-sided criticism; and I have made all the enthusiasm, that a real American feels about his country, my guide. . . . I have left the hackneyed commonplaces of art alone—what will come of it I know not.[37]

As Greenough's thought developed along these lofty lines, he was all the more sensitive to petty criticism and ready to regard himself as martyred by it. Late in 1839 he wrote Sumner:

I cannot say to you how my blood is stirred by finding that you and he [Capponi] and 2 or 3 more have felt and been moved by my statue. Has it not been born amid the sneers of ignorance and pretension? . . . Nothing so wi[th]ering so exhausting as the Vox clamantis in deserto—Nothing so bitter as ignorant scorn for attempted services—proffered light—Was it not always so?[38]

The next year he had even more reason to feel unappreciated.

In February 1840 he wrote Secretary of State Forsyth, announcing the near-completion of the statue and broaching the subject of the pedestal.[39] For this part of the monument he preferred a solid block of granite from the Quincy quarries, near Boston, but he felt unable to pay the price, which he thought would be $10,000. If he furnished the pedestal, he said, he would have to use a core of blocks covered with marble, a construction of which he disapproved.

He also reported at this time his progress on his second work for the government and requested payment for the second installment of his fee for it, then a year overdue. The negotiations for this installment now became involved with his final arrangements about the "Washington." In consequence, his relations with the government respecting the statue were unduly embittered and he was unfortunately prevented from going home to superintend its erection.

His second work for the government, one of the groups for the east front of the Capitol, had been commissioned in 1837. For both groups all payments after the first were contingent upon the receipt of a certificate signed by the American consul at Leghorn or Rome to the effect that the works were progressing satisfactorily. Throughout 1839 Greenough asked G. W. Greene, then consul in Rome, to come to Florence to inspect his work, preliminary to the second installment for it being paid, and when Greene refused to do so without a government order, Greenough requested, though to no avail, that one be given.[40] (He evidently did not apply to the American consul at Leghorn, Thomas Appleton.) Two weeks after writing Forsyth in February 1840, he drew on the Treasury for $1000.

Greenough's letter to Forsyth was answered by the acting secretary, Aaron Vail, who rudely took Greenough to task for not having finished the "Washington," accused him of trying to evade his obligation to furnish a pedestal for the work, and asseverated that payment for the group would not be made until a consular certificate had been received. Greenough's draft was refused and his brother Alfred covered it.[41]

Angered and humiliated as he was by Vail's letter, which reached him in June 1840, Greenough in reply accounted, as he had done in previous letters, for all the time that had elapsed since he had received the "Washington" commission (only four months more than the four years he had originally estimated were actually spent on the statue, but he had failed to allow for the inevitable interruptions of the enterprise) and suggested that the issue of the pedestal be postponed until the statue was set up. He requested, however, that he be allowed to give up his contract for the group. "Whatever may be my ambition to serve the government in the capacity of Sculptor," he explained, "I cannot purchase it at the price of such a misconstruction of my motives and misunderstanding of my conduct as that contained in the letter now before me."[42]

Two days later he wrote James K. Paulding, then Secretary of the Navy, a heated account of Vail's letter and his own in reply. Characteristically asserting his role as an artist, he declared,

You my Dear Sir and you alone can sympathize with me. You can imagine what would be your feelings if called on to write a work of high poetry and deep feeling with the stings and the racket of illnature and of ignorance bursting in upon your retirement and overwhelming your aspirations.[43]

He was still smarting when he wrote Charles Sumner a similar account a few weeks later. By that time he imagined an attempt might be in the making to "poison the public mind against my work," and asked Sumner, then a senator, in this event to make known the facts about both government pieces. As for the group, he thought he might interest some state government in purchasing it. By October, when he wrote again, he was glad Sumner had not spoken publicly. "Whatever may be its claims as a work of Art," he said of his statue,

a moments sight of it will at once defend me from all charges reflecting on my industry. I have never seen 2 such works for size as the Washington and the Groupe modelled for the capitol produced in less time unless they were merely decorative and gotten up without ambition and without scruple.[44]

Shortly afterward he received Forsyth's reply to his letter addressed to Vail, in which Forsyth said that the Department of State had no authority to suspend his contract for the group and referred him to the acting consul at Leghorn (Appleton having meanwhile died) for the certificate. In December Greenough had that work inspected by Appleton's successor, J. A. Binda. At the same time, with characteristic professional sensitivity, he secured the approval and signature of Benvenuti, then president of the Academy of Fine Arts in Florence.[45]

Arrangements for the transportation of the "Washington" to the United States now began to occupy him.[46] They were initiated by Congress in May 1840, at which time the Secretary of the Navy was authorized to ship and erect the work, but not until the following December did Paulding act. He then ordered Commodore Hull, Commander-in-Chief of the United States Naval Forces in the Mediterranean, to pick it up at Leghorn. Late in April Hull contracted with Fitch Brothers, navy agents, of Marseilles, for the merchant ship *Sea* to do so. The price was an exorbitant $5000, which Hull got reduced to $3500 by agreeing that the vessel's Captain Delano might touch at other ports to take on and to discharge other cargo before landing the statue. The immediate supervision of the loading was delegated to Commander Ralph Voorhees of the sloop of war *Preble*. The *Sea* arrived at Leghorn from Marseilles on May 8 and the *Preble* from Toulon the following day.

Apparently Greenough had not been informed of the date. The statue was still in Florence, and most of the month of May was consumed in moving it to Leghorn. By the 15th it was packed, but the Florentine engineer Misuri, whom alone Greenough would trust with the operation, was not available for another ten days. By the 27th it was mounted on a car and probably the next day taken out of the city.[47]

Meantime Greenough learned to his dismay the terms of Hull's contract. He immediately arranged to pay Delano the $1500 taken off the original price in order to insure a direct transportation of the statue without other cargo. Informing Secretary of State Daniel Webster of his action, he claimed still, though he had been paid for his statue,

an interest in it—The interest of a father in his child. It is the birth of my thought. I have sacrificed to it the flower of my days and the freshness of my strength. Its every lineament has been moistened with the sweat of my toil and the tears of my exile. I would not barter away its association with my name for the proudest fortune that avarice ever dreamed. In giving it up to the nation that has done me the honor to order it at my hands, I respectfully claim for it that protection which it is the boast of Civilization to afford to Art and which a generous enemy has more than once been seen to extend, even to the monuments of his own defeat.[48]

About this time—early in May—he learned that his second

draft drawn on the overdue installment of his fee for the group for the Capitol had been refused. (This time the reason given was that the certificate needed to be approved by another sculptor and that the only one available was the German Ferdinand Pettrich, who was then out of the city; yet after Pettrich's return the draft was again protested.) The fact was doubly upsetting to Greenough. He had intended all along to return to America at the time the "Washington" was transported, assuming that the government would invite him, and even when it did not—to his grief—he planned to go. It was, he said, the government's failure to pay him the installment on the group which deterred him. His sense of persecution reached a climax. "I have driven through my work," he wrote Henry a few days after the arrival of the American vessels at Leghorn,

amid the sneers of envy and the tittle-tattle of detraction. I must be backed by my country, or I shall be forced to give way before so much *interest* against me.[49]

To see the "Washington" safely shipped, Greenough went to Leghorn and from here he wrote Webster final instructions about the erection.[50] Again he designated the spot where it should be placed, and though he thought its height above the floor would have to be determined by experiment, he stipulated that

at the distance of 30 feet from the Pedestal in front the *fold* of *skin above the navel* may be *visible* and *not hidden by the knees*. If that fold *be hidden at that distance* my work is *sacrificed*.

He enclosed a sketch to indicate the positions for the figures of the Indian and Columbus and a drawing of his proposed design for the pedestal, for which he again urged a single piece of granite from Quincy. The *Sea* left Leghorn with the statue apparently on the 8th of June, having stayed about twice the fifteen days allowed in the contract for detention both there and at Washington, at a demurrage of $100 a day.

About this time Greenough also sent Webster a final account

of his expenditures in connection with his commission,[51] which, exclusive of the $1500 paid Delano (which was refunded him), totaled $8935. The largest single item was the marble and its blocking—nearly $2600. The salaries of the workmen came to about $2740, and the work on the chair another $500. Supplies (including 24,700 pounds of clay) were about $850, the studio $700, transportation of the statue from Carrara to Florence (eleven yoke of oxen and fifteen men were required) and from Florence to Leghorn $680 (trees along the route were damaged), his own journeys about $250. The remaining amount was taken up by the cost of his authorities, his models, drawings of the statue in case it was lost, and postage.

For the government, too, the expenses connected with the "Washington" ultimately far exceeded expectations. The $20,000 paid Greenough represented slightly less than half the total, which was $42,170.74. The freight and detention on the ship came to $7700; the removal from the navy yard and erection in the rotunda, $5000; the construction of a foundation, nearly $2000; the shifting of the statue's position in the rotunda, $860; its removal to the outside and the construction and removal of an enclosure, $6000.[52] Greenough spoke for both artist and patron when he observed that in works of a colossal dimension "the expenditure increases in a geometrical ratio with the increase of weight."[53]

On July 31, 1841, the *Sea* reached the Washington navy yard, but not until August 13 was the statue discharged. In the interim, while demurrage again mounted, repairs were made which restored the vessel to her original state, as provided in the charter. Early in September appropriations were made to cover the cost of the statue's transportation and erection, including $2500 for a pedestal according to the advice of the sculptor.[54] (Evidently Greenough's estimate had been too high.) To furnish the pedestal, Secretary of the Navy A. P. Upshur engaged

Pettrich, who prepared to ornament it with allegorical or historical reliefs.[55]

A foundation pillar for statue and pedestal had been constructed in the crypt a year before,[56] under the direction of Robert Mills, then Architect of Public Buildings, who had it placed beneath the center of the rotunda. Though he knew of Greenough's objection to this spot, he thought it the best symmetrically and he was convinced that the light from the dome alone was insufficient for the statue to be properly seen anywhere in the room. He proposed to get more light by opening the floor and constructing a double row of stairs between the crypt and the rotunda and, if necessary, by piercing the dome. Neither of his plans, however, was adopted.

On October 21 the "Washington," still boxed, was removed from the navy yard to the Capitol. (The fear expressed by the city's *Madisonian,* and repeated by papers in New York and Boston, that the doorway would have to be enlarged to admit it proved groundless.) Several weeks later a temporary wooden pedestal thirteen feet high was placed in the center of the rotunda, and on December 1, in the presence of President Tyler and a small group, the statue was placed on it, the frame removed, and the accessories put in place. Its position was thus doubly unfavorable. The pedestal was so high that one foot was entirely hidden. (The figure looked to one reporter like a man in a tree.) The light upon it from above threw all the features in shadow, making it, Senator William Preston said, "the most horrid phantasmagoria I have ever beheld," and hardly allowed the ornamentation of the chair to be seen.[57]

As soon as the winter session of Congress opened, friends of Greenough acted to improve matters. Late in December, at the instigation of Preston, a joint committee was formed and a bill passed to move the work to the spot designated by the sculptor. Early in February the move was made and the pedestal lowered to eight and a half feet. Even there, as Mills had foreseen, the light was poor. Preston also had Pettrich's work suspended, after some difficulty. (Most of the Congressmen whom Wilde talked with about this time did not, he thought, "seem capable of even feeling what an affront" to Greenough was Pettrich's employment.) Pending Greenough's further instructions, the temporary pedestal was boarded up and painted the color of granite. Altogether Greenough felt, he wrote Preston a year later, "I owed it to you that my statue of Washington had not been sacrificed in every way."[58]

Meanwhile the division of American opinion about the work widely manifested itself. Throughout the summer and fall of 1841 the press, which was generally sympathetic, heralded its arrival and printed excerpts from the laudatory comments of Everett, Lady Bulwer, and others. Accounts of the erection were carried by nearly every paper in Washington, Philadelphia, New York, and Boston, in most of which accounts it was pronounced a great work of art.[59] Giles Yates wrote an explication for the *Northern Light* in the spring, and S. D. Dakin wrote a poem, which was printed in the *Knickerbocker* the following fall. Two years later an article by Alexander Everett, repeating the standard defenses, appeared in the *United States Magazine and Democratic Review*.[60]

The opinion of most Americans, however, was overwhelmingly unfavorable. They marveled at the workmanship, admired the head extravagantly, and agreed that the location was not flattering. Here and there they expressed a preference for different details—a standing position, a smaller figure, a more definite action, an English inscription. But chiefly and generally they objected that Washington was not dressed in the clothes of his day. His garb seemed to them foreign, pagan, and indecent and aroused in them either indignation or hilarity.

One of the more serious deprecations was written by Amos

Kendall, then editor of the Washington *Union Democrat,* who feared that the statue, with its combination of mythical and historical elements, might introduce a "barbarian taste" into the United States and who affirmed that civilized societies *"recognise as beautiful only that which is true."* Typical of the abusive ridicule was the piece in the New York *Herald* by "Georgy Porgy," who described the figure as risen from a coffin "with his winding sheet about him," pronounced the conception "the selection of an idiot," and asserted that if the work had fallen in the process of being set up there would have been applause from the spectators. Even the inscription proved vulnerable. The imperfect tense *faciebat* had been widely used by ancient artists to avoid the appearance of arrogance, yet a correspondent for the New York *American* called it "execrable Latin" and one for the *Times* inquired why, if the tense signified incompleted action, the statue was sent home.[61]

Congressmen, too, were inspired to witticisms. On the temporary pedestal the figure reminded one representative of a Hindu suttee on a funeral pile. In May, when the appropriation for making the shift in the rotunda came before the House, Representative Henry Wise (who several years before called Greenough the finest sculptor in the world) took the occasion to give the subject a full-scale treatment. He asked whether the government wished an image such as this in the rotunda or a statue of George Washington. Washington, he was sure, was a man whose skin had never been looked on by any living creature. The left shin of the statue, he said, echoing the old joke about Trumbull's painting, was shocking. As for the inscription, it was bad Latin, written in Italy. A country man reading it would think the figure was one Simul Acrum and on asking who Simul Acrum was (at this point a laugh was heard in his audience), would be told by the next word (*istud*). ("Increased merriment" in the House was here reported.) Some, he avowed, had thought the seat was a garden chair, the throne of an unmentionable temple. He preferred Houdon's statue. He would keep the head of Greenough's figure and throw the body in the Potomac. Wise's remarks were reported in detail though indirectly by *Niles National Register,*[62] but other publications professed themselves too shocked to do so. Too "vile to be reported," declared the New York *American,* "the filthiest allusions ever heard in the House."[63]

Meanwhile, throughout the last half of 1841 and the first of 1842 Greenough waited in Florence, hoping to hear what decision had been made about the pedestal and when he might draw the installment due on the group. No official word of any kind was forthcoming—even to the effect that the statue had arrived. Through the influence of Everett, then American minister to England, Greenough got N. M. Rothschild & Sons (the United States bankers in London) to advance him £500 late in 1841, but the Treasury refused to reimburse them.[64] He concluded that the government must be trying to sever its connection with him and evidently gave up hope of returning to America for several years.[65] In the fall of 1842, however, he did return (presumably partly in consequence of his wife's having gone a short time before).

At his first sight of his statue in its place, late in November, he was, Allston reported, "absolutely startled." "Poor Greenough," wrote Stephen Perkins, who accompanied him, to their friend Francis Higginson,

> when we . . . climbed the steps of the splendid Capitol & entered its dark, mantled, lofty rotunda—there sat Washington *in the dark.* No, there was a *little light* such as you get in a well . . . and another *little light,* such as you get at the end of coal mine shafts, right in the face,

which gave it "a rigid, almost a vindictive expression." Standing close, Perkins could not see the bas-reliefs or the small figures.

Greenough said little at first but as they walked home he commented that

he felt as a man might who had left his child blooming & smiling in the Evening & found it the next day pinched & worn away with disease. That he only wondered why the public had shewn so much forbearance & had not turned both their sculpture & paintings out of the Hall long ago.

He thought the only thing to do was to have the work moved outside and a wooden shed built over it, which might be replaced with a better one if it were thought worthy. " 'If it looks there as it does here,' " Perkins reported, " 'he should be the first to condemn it.' It was on the whole a trial to him & he bore it well."[66]

His feelings were the more painful because of his assumption that a connection existed between the government's behavior in relation to the statue and its refusal to pay him for the group. Writing John Quincy Adams, then a senator, a few days later to ask how to have the statue moved, he asked also how to discover if there was a determination to discharge him from work on the group. At the same time he was torn between his faith in popular judgment and in his own work. "I have always been and am still of opinion," he declared,

that Art should address itself to the mass of men like eloquence and poetry. If my utmost endeavour to make a statue of Washington is considered a failure and it is therefore thought unsafe to trust me with the monument for the Eastern front . . . I shall bear it as I may best—cherishing the consciousness that I have wrought diligently—that my whole heart was with my work and that if I have failed it has been in a different manner from other and greater artists who have before me undertaken the same godlike subject.

A few weeks earlier he had written Higginson,

Perhaps . . . you think that I must be unhappy at so much indifference if not dislike for my work. I am not unhappy. I have done my utmost and I believe that there is more *Art* in my statue of Washington than in all else that I have done a *thousand fold.* He was not confident, he told Emerson in Washington this winter, that he had "translated the public sentiment of this country for Washington into marble, but he is very sure of his own diligence & that what has been in his mind must sooner or later appear."[67]

He soon discovered he was wrong in imputing any hostile design to the officials of his country, whatever else they might be guilty of. The warrant for the overdue installment for the group was issued late in December, apparently without protest or explanation for the delay. He also began to be more hopeful about the ultimate reception of his statue. Senator Thomas Benton said the head "had often enchained him for half an hour together," and Representative T. D. Arnold confessed that though he thought it *"outré"* the first time he saw it, the second time he was "not shocked at all" and after that he "began to like it." Morse, in the city seeking an appropriation from Congress for his telegraph, found it more than he expected even from Greenough; he could not "pass around it, or before it, without feeling an indescribable solemnity." Emerson described it as "simple & grand, nobly draped below & nobler nude above," and declared that it "greatly contents me I was afraid it would be feeble but it is not."[68]

Early in January, in the presence of a small company which included Emerson and John C. Calhoun, Greenough experimented with illuminating the figure by torchlight. The "whole spectacle," Emerson wrote his wife, was "a great satisfaction" to him. For about two hours he sat on the floor in the "grand area," watched the "colossal" shadows of the few persons moving about, and listened as

every word that was spoken reverberated Greenoughs direction to his lamp holder "Higher, higher," sounded up into the dome &

down again a better poem than Longfellow's "Excelsior." The "great height above," he wrote Margaret Fuller,

> & the moonlight looking in at the sky light and the resonance of every word & footstep and the electric air of this place, the political centre of the continent made it a very fanciful & exhilirating spot.

He disapproved of Greenough's plan to move it. "I had rather have it in this Rotunda," he told the sculptor, "in the worst light, than any where else in the best: The genius of the place is omnipotent here. . . ."[69] Greenough, however, was unconvinced.

By the first of the year he had written and read privately to Adams[70] a Memorial petitioning Congress to move the statue to the western Capitol grounds and erect a building over it, and on January 10 and 11 the document was introduced in the House and the Senate respectively. Less than half its approximately two thousand words were devoted to his petition itself, the rest to a defense of his work against the chief criticism of it and to general strictures on art and architecture. For the building he had first thought of a structure of wood, partly because in that material experiments might be made which would produce a better form than one arrived at by theory. He finally recommended, however, one of sandstone to match the Capitol, of a harmonizing form, the interior to be left unpainted and a natural color, if any, to be used on the outside. The practice of painting stone, he digressed, seemed "to reduce the noblest masonry to a level with ordinary laths and plaister . . . like covering pure gold with tin foil." Though pardonable in certain ephemeral structures, it was

> inconsistent with the gravity and dignity of important public buildings; and, most of all . . . in republics. To add, by color, a shade which should have been given by form, is to accuse . . . the art of building.

Indirectly he answered the suggestions for an ornamented

pedestal by repudiating historical bas-reliefs altogether as an "invasion of the domain of a sister art." His defense of his design he rested, too, on historical and political principles. In rejecting contemporary dress in favor of the "work of God—the human form" in his statue he but "conformed to the canons of his art, as practiced in its purity," but it was only in free states that art had flourished in this condition; in oligarchies, monarchies, and aristocracies it had been debased to the position of a "handmaiden of luxury." He therefore had reason to hope that

> this republic, standing upon a broader basis of human nature and more fairly representing the general human will, must . . . make that choice of style in sculpture . . . most in harmony with the highest and the truest, because the only lasting philosophy of art.

Having outlived objections to his first undraped busts, he trusted that prejudice would

> continue to decline before the efforts of high art, until his successors in sculpture shall be enabled to show that the inspired writer meant not merely the face, when he declared that God had made man after his own image.[71]

The document was referred to the Joint Committee on the Library. During the next few weeks Greenough conferred with this Committee, agreed to the eastern grounds as the site and to a temporary structure, asked for personal control of the move, and named $5000 as the sum needed. On February 22 a joint resolution was introduced embodying his wishes (and alluding to his statue as a "noble" monument of "moral beauty and true grandeur"),[72] and on March 3 it was passed.

A week later he began his services in the removal operation.[73] Under his and Mills' supervision foundations were laid for the statue and a wooden building was constructed on the grounds directly in front of the eastern entrance to the Capitol. Greenough inspected granite in Baltimore, but he still preferred that of

Quincy, and at the end of April he contracted with Boston architect Isaiah Rogers to furnish a pedestal and platform of it within sixty days and to move the statue. On three sides of the pedestal were incised the words of the Congressional resolution at the time of Washington's death—"First in war, first in peace, and first in the hearts of his countrymen"—and on the fourth the date of the work's execution. In June Greenough went to Quincy to inspect Rogers' work, which was delayed. At this point circumstances of a personal nature made it advisable for him to return to Europe immediately (presumably his wife was pregnant), and he terminated his services with the government on July 7, delegating his responsibility to his cousin J. J. Greenough of Washington. The blocks arrived from Quincy at the end of August, and the move was completed by the end of September.

The account between Greenough and the government in connection with the removal was carried on for several years, because $936 of his expenditures was until the end of this time suspended by the government (chiefly $424 for his own services, $435 for Rogers' expenses in coming to Washington, and $65 for J. J. Greenough's expenses). The final settlement was made in April 1851.

The removal of the "Washington" to the Capitol grounds did not enhance its effect. Rogers designed a permanent building for it, which Greenough recommended. It was evidently circular, forty feet in diameter and twenty-five feet high, having an octagonal roof and ceiling with a skylight, and two entrances, each with a small Greek portico of two columns.[74] But no action about such a building was taken, and the temporary one soon looked shabby. The greater exposure of the figure now heightened the effect of its nudity. Washington, asserted New Yorker Philip Hone, was

too prudent and careful of his health to expose himself thus in a climate so uncertain as ours, to say nothing of the indecency of such an exposure—a subject on which he was known to be exceedingly fastidious.

The figure looked, he thought, "like a great Herculean, warrior-like *Venus of the Bath.*" A visitor about this time, in an account of his trip called *Mysteries of Washington City,* declared that one mystery was contained in "a certain low ill-looking shanty," which contained "a statue of *Jupiter Tonans,* easing himself, without a shirt on his back, holding a thunderbolt in his right hand!" Others were moved to take liberties with the figure. When another visitor saw it, some one had inserted

a large "plantation" cigar between the lips of the *pater patriae,* while another had amused himself with writing some stanzas of poetry, in a style rather more popular than elegant, upon a prominent part of the body of the infant Hercules.[75]

New proposals for the location of the work were made, among them those to incorporate it in a National Gothic Monument and to substitute it for the Navy Monument on the western front of the Capitol. In May 1844, at the time of the latter proposal, a House resolution was passed to remove the wooden shelter and erect an iron railing with the proceeds. On this occasion one representative suggested that a locomotive be established to carry the "ponderous mass of immobility" constantly from place to place, and another, who was for uncovering the work so the elements could wear it out, opined that the optics of the Committeemen were sharp if they could discover a place in the habitable globe where it would excite admiration.[76]

Throughout these discussions the chief champion of Greenough's cause was Senator Robert Winthrop, whose efforts to prevent the first action made Greenough especially grateful. When he heard of the second proposal he wrote Winthrop, objecting to both the site (a *"subordinate"* one for a figure of Washington) and the uncovering of the statue, designed as it had been for an interior. Had it been intended for an open square, he said, he would have designed an equestrian figure in Revolutionary dress.[77]

In the fall of 1846, pursuant to the Congressional resolution of two years before, the shelter was removed and an iron railing and four lamps put up around the work. A few thought it looked better. To H. W. Longfellow, who saw it in the spring of 1850, it had "rather a grand effect under the blue sky." Representative Gouverneur Kemble about this time declared it one of the noblest works of modern times, second only to Michelangelo's "Moses." But another observer felt it "looked forsaken and cold as it must ever be from the bluish tinge of the marble"; Persico's group in contrast had softened to a rich yellowish hue.[78] It was now in the most unfavorable situation, both for its appreciation and its preservation, as Greenough had anticipated it would be. Yet he wrote Winthrop in 1847 that he was glad to hear it had at last been uncovered, having struggled against the move only a little in the belief that marble in the open air was destined for a short life. The heart of his letter represented in many ways his final judgment on his work and his critics:

A colossal statue of a man whose career makes an epoch in the world's history is an immense undertaking. To fail in it is only to prove that one is not as great in art as the hero himself was in life. Had my work shown a presumptuous opinion that I had an easy task before me—had it betrayed a yearning rather after the wages of art than the honest fame of it, I should have deserved the bitterest things that have been said of it and of me. But containing as it certainly *must* internal proof of being the *utmost effort* of my mind at the time it was wrought, its failure fell not on me but on those who called me to the task. . . . I sat down the less disconsolate at my failure because I felt and feel that Canova and Chantry had both never passed the fatal line of *mediocre* in their images of Washington. Allow me to exult a little that during the months I passed at Washington while my statue was the butt of wiseacres and witlings, I never in word or thought swerved from my principle that the general mind is alone a quorum to judge a great work. I began the study of sculpture at 20 years of age—at 30 the model of the Washington was compleated. It was too little preparation I own—nay had my attempt threatened to close the door for others I should not have dared it. As it is—where is the harm?—30000$ have been in one way or another wasted on that stone. But is not the example—the warning if you will worth the money? . . . Sir when in future time the true sculptors of America have filled the metropolis with beauty and grandeur will it not be worth 30000$ to be able to point to that figure and say, Here was the first struggle of our infant art?"[79]

At last, twenty years after his youthful declaration that his country had come to birth in maturity, he conceded to the history of its art a period of infancy and to that period consigned his own most ambitious work. When he wrote Bryant in the spring of 1851 about several of his works, he did not have much higher hopes for his ultimate reputation. But he now thought that such works should be preserved also for their own sakes, that philosophic criticism finds in each development of art qualities peculiar to itself and valuable as distinct articulations of the human soul. As the Savage shines with certain qualities that may well excite the emulation of polytechnic culture, so the ripe fruit of art has not attained its fullness without losing a somewhat of poetry and hope and promise that was fragrant in the blossom.[80] In the end, his sense of history and of his position in it—though it was a less elevated position than he had aspired to—saved him from despair at his failure to realize his loftiest aims and to some extent compensated him for the failure of his countrymen to understand the precise nature of those aims.

His realization, too, that the great body of Americans had no such knowledge of art or of history kept him from blaming them too harshly. He felt that the proposal to throw the "Washington" in the Potomac would never have been made had the statue been exhibited in England first. "Those men," he wrote S. A. Eliot in 1851,

had not, neither could they have, any adequate conception of the scope of my art, of its difficulties, or of the other productions of ancient sculptors, with whose works those of modern artists must stand or fall.[81]

Meantime he had made plans—begun immediately on his return to Europe in 1842—for an equestrian Washington, clad in the uniform of the Revolution, which he hoped to execute in bronze for erection in Boston or New York. In later years Everett recalled a letter from him written, probably during the early 1840's,

in the bitterness of his heart, saying that he intended to make an equestrian statue of Washington in small-clothes and Hussar boots, to show his loving countrymen that he was a tolerable tailor and bootmaker, which they seemed to think was the main thing in a sculptor.[82]

Yet his launching of such a project at that time was in good faith. He worked on it throughout the last decade of his life, though without bringing it to a conclusion. The fact was the greatest proof he could have given of his regard for the public taste and impressive evidence of his ability to respond affirmatively to his experience, however painful.

In this light he came to regard his group for the Capitol. By that work he hoped to show, he wrote Eliot and Bryant, that he had not lost heart nor his allegiance to the public in consequence of the criticism of his "Washington." At the same time, however, he claimed for all artists the "right . . . which I believe a sacred one and which may be interfered with by a strong disapproval on the part of the present generation"[83] to have their works preserved. And to the end he vigorously defended his statue against ignorant and presumptuous critics.

A few weeks after his return to the United States in 1851 he was incensed by a letter in the *Home Journal* which praised a certain profile of Washington and disparaged the "classic drapery" of Chantrey's "colossal" figure and Greenough's statue, "seated like the 'Jupiter Tonans' of Phidias." He replied immediately in a letter to the Washington *Daily National Intelligencer*. Chantrey's statue, he corrected, was not colossal nor its dress classical, the "Jupiter" of Phidias was not Tonans, and to remarks about his own work he countered:

Greenough's statue is seated as the Guiliano of Buonarotti is seated, as the Copernicus of Thorwaldsen, the Maximilian of Rauch, the Rousseau of Pradier, the Galileo of Demi are seated, as people must be seated who do not loll. . . . If the treatment of a high and noble subject in art, as in letters, contain proof that its author has made a careful and conscientious study of the analagous works of his predecessors, shall this be made a matter of reproach? If Bancroft remind us of the models of Greece in writing the history of our land, has he sinned? Was not Dante, the most original of modern poets, so imbued with classic lore as to let slip the title of Jove applied to the Saviour? Did Milton cull on British ground the flowers that perfume the stern theology of his epic?

The argument of critics who urged their fellow countrymen to "cut the string" in art and letters, moreover, was made ludicrous by the fact that

we build at this moment in all the styles elsewhere invented, and stick up our shirt-collars because that arrangement is becoming to some scrofulous prince of the blood royal.[84]

He now saw his statue for the first time out of doors, so disadvantageously situated that he was moved to protest. His objections were incorporated in his pamphlet *Æsthetics at Washington,* printed late in the year. The dwarf cypresses and the rose bushes planted around the statue were "impertinent and ridiculous," the grass out of keeping whether cut close or neglected, the lamps ill-placed, the railings ideally unnecessary and practically useless—his statue and the "Columbus" of Persico's group for the Capitol having

received more injury in the few years that they have been so guarded, than many figures wrought before the birth of Christ have suffered in coming to us through the so-called dark ages.[85]

Nothing, however, came of his criticisms.

The next year, when, after Greenough's death, his group for the Capitol at last reached Washington and was set up, his statue came in for a new round of comments. The proper location for it, declared one correspondent to the *Intelligencer,* would be "the corner of the rotundo if it could be found." The sculptor's "independent spirit," countered another, had impelled him to dress his figure as he did; he had not cared "a 'continental'—fig for the old shad-bellied uniform." In the opinion of a writer in the *Union Democrat,* it was a statue "not intended for our day . . . whilst other works sink into insignificance, this must rise in estimation."[86]

Yet even artists now began to draw from the statue a lesson chiefly regarding the power of public opinion. Mills, who called it a "splendid work" (and who had also admired Canova's "Washington") counseled native artists to take warning from the reception of both works and "make classic ground *here.*" Thomas Crawford cited his Washington equestrian statue for Virginia as proof of his desire "to illustrate American history without having recourse to sculpture as practiced in the age of Pericles." Submitting a design for the Senate pediment in 1856, H. K. Brown assured the authorities, "You will see by it that my country is no myth in my eyes."[87] Within a few decades the triumph of realism in commemorative statuary in America was complete. The particular artistic problem which Greenough had wrestled with—how to represent a historical figure ideally—remained a problem, but it ceased to present a challenge.

Throughout the rest of the century his "Washington" continued to inspire wags. In time, in fact, it drew to itself a considerable body of oral tradition of a distinctly American nature, or rather a union of two strains of native humor. It became not only a joke on cultivation, but a tall tale. The early rumor that it was too large to be taken through the door of the Capitol was repeated as fact; it was said to have been moved out because it shook the foundations and even to have sunk the first ship which attempted to load it.[88] In such stories as these, indeed, Greenough's countrymen themselves at last endowed his statue with a kind of legendary character. In effect they remodeled his figure, giving it the familiarity of aspect which they had all along insisted it should have.

Meanwhile, the eastern grounds of the Capitol were reduced in size and pavements were laid to the base of the statue. In 1908, pursuant to a joint resolution of Congress, it was moved to the Smithsonian Institution, where a National Gallery of Art was being formed. In the process a lower pedestal was substituted for the granite one. In view of Greenough's general objections to Gothic architecture and his mournful observations on this building in particular, this move represented the culminating insult to his work.

The fate of the "Washington" could easily be regarded as the tragedy of Greenough's life. Everett went so far as to declare that the widespread terms of "disparagement and ridicule" regarding the work "stung the generous and sensitive artist to madness."[89] He over-simplified one set of facts, however, and did not take others into consideration. Greenough was at least as much disturbed during the last decade of his life by the government's indifferent treatment of him professionally as by the popular criticism of his work, and most of all by the government's delinquency throughout this period in paying him for the group it had commissioned.

Bitter as the general fate of his "Washington" was to Greenough, it did not embitter his life. On the contrary, the whole history of the work represented a vast enrichment of his experience. His preparation for it led him deeper into the study of anatomy. The need for defending its costume induced him to speculate about the relation of fashion to art. The problem of properly locating the work sharpened his architectural perceptions. It was the most ambitious of all his works and one of the most ambitious ever undertaken by an American artist, bringing together as it did three sweeping themes: art, history, and religion.

When Greenough's "Washington" is considered in relation to his other works of sculpture, moreover, it appears midway in an uninterrupted series dealing with the same general subject. Not only did he subsequently project two more "Washingtons," but to all his "Washingtons" should be added his two "Davids," his "Achilles," his "Rescue" group, and his projected "Apollo the Avenger"—all of which depicted national or folk heroes. The image of the hero as a public servant dominated his mind. Particularly disappointing as the reception of some of these works thus was, the image itself had the power to sustain him.

The "Washington" is not, as Greenough knew, a great statue. Its weakest element is the action of the arms, whereby the particular—though not the general—meaning of the whole is delegated to parts. It is essentially not a plastic conception at all but an intellectual one, translated into plastic terms. When he referred to it as "the birth of my thought," the "utmost effort of my mind," he was as close to explaining its failure as its success.

It is, however, a statue which attempts greatness with admirable boldness and simplicity. The colossal size, the seated pose, the half-draped figure, the broad gestures express a massiveness like that inherent in the material, while the severity of outline, the fidelity to nature, the subservience to a moral idea evoke the presence of an equally elemental force. Its greatest tragedy was in being deprived of the site for which it was designed: the center of the rotunda. There, with proper lighting, its surroundings would have supported its weakness and clarified its meaning. It belongs in the American-classic Capitol, a building also both original and traditional and also almost great.

Rescue by History

The background of Greenough's second commission from the government was briefer than that of his first. It was the last of four commissions awarded for the ornamentation of the east front of the Capitol during about a decade. The first two were carried out between 1828 and 1833, when Persico executed the figures in the pediment and those for the portico. When a project was launched to complete this part of the building by having two marble groups erected on the blockings of the steps, Persico aspired to do these groups also, and by the spring of 1836 he had modeled a group which he proposed for one.[1] Representing the discovery of America, it consisted of the figures of Columbus, standing and holding aloft a globe, and an Indian maiden, half-crouching at his right. In April, a resolution was passed by the Senate to inquire about contracting with Persico for both groups. In the ensuing discussion, Preston and Calhoun objected to the government's considering only a foreign artist and recommended Greenough as the chief American deserving attention.

The next year an amendment was attached to the annual appropriation bill in the Senate setting aside $8000 to enable the President to contract for both groups. By that time it had been decided to divide the commission between Persico and Greenough. A few weeks after the passage of the bill on March 3, Secretary of State Forsyth transmitted to Persico articles of agreement (based on proposals Persico had made to the Committee on Public Buildings in February)[2] drawn between him and the President for one of the groups (his Columbus and Indian maiden, it was understood) and began negotiations with Greenough for the other.

In the initial letter to Greenough, dated April 4, 1837,[3] Forsyth asked him to submit a design for the second group, which was to be approved before the work was contracted for; allegedly enclosed a copy of the contract with Persico; and directed Greenough, if unable to complete the work in the time allotted Persico, to secure Thorvaldsen's terms for it. The contract with Persico was not enclosed, however, and no details about the proposed size, cost, and time allowed for the execution of either group were furnished.

Forsyth's letter reached Greenough in Florence on July 1. Obviously he had anticipated some such communication, for he replied to it on the same day, suggesting two designs and relaying opinions of them expressed by artists in Florence. The subject of the group already commissioned, he pointed out, was unique, and he would be obliged to adopt "one of less import; & to rely upon the resources of the Art, for filling the space allotted to me." He proposed a group, of which he hoped to send a design in August,

> which shall commemorate the dangers & difficulty of peopling our continent, and which shall also serve as a memorial of the Indian race, and an embodying of the indian character.

The artists with whom he had talked had objected that this subject was not "a distinct individual historical fact," advised that he balance Persico's group figure for figure, and suggested that he represent Washington raising from the ground a figure representing America. Though he felt that this allegory bordered on the "commonplace," he asked for advice in choosing between it and the other subject. He said he would be satisfied with the same fee as that paid Persico, but only if the President would allow him his own time could he accept the commission, having long since determined

> that no motive shall tempt me to promise that which I cannot be sure of performing—Viz. my utmost at a given day.

On October 16 he sent Forsyth a design for the group, together with a letter.[4] Both documents appear to have been destroyed. Probably this design represented Washington and America. Among his sketches is one which is apparently a version of it, showing both figures draped, Washington with a sword and America crowned, and on the base of the pedestal a scene depicting Perseus coming to the rescue of Andromeda and the Ethiopians.

A month later, on November 15, he sent a second design, accompanied by another letter, in which he said he had endeavored

> to convey the idea of the triumph of the whites over the savage tribes, at the same time that it illustrates the dangers of peopling the country.

This design, which was later returned to Greenough, also seems to have been lost. Apparently it was essentially that which he executed: a pioneer woman clasping a child to her bosom, crouching on the ground, and a pioneer man towering over from behind and restraining an Indian with a wound in his side, who had been interrupted in an attack on the woman and child. He now asked for particulars about the site and a general description of Persico's composition.

A year elapsed before Greenough received a reply to either of these letters. Yet he evidently proceeded on the assumption that he would be employed to execute the second design. In February 1838 he wrote Allston that he had finished the "preparatory studies for my large groupe." More than once during the year he sent requests to Washington for Indian skulls, dresses, and drawings to aid him in modeling his Indian figure.[5]

In the meantime Persico had returned to his home city of Naples to execute his group. By the beginning of December 1838 he had completed the model and gone to Florence to confer with Greenough about the marble to be used in both groups. They decided on that of the Ravaccioni quarries, chiefly because of its hardness. Since, however, according to the contracts they were to use the "best Italian marble," by which was meant that of the Carrara quarries, Persico wrote Forsyth to obtain official approval of the change in plans.[6]

About this time, late in December 1838, Greenough received a letter from Acting Secretary of State Vail, written in October, stating that his second design had been adopted and enclosing articles of agreement between him and President Van Buren for its execution.[7] The design was therewith returned to him to be altered in any way he saw fit, with the stipulation only that the wound in the side of the Indian be suppressed. The dimensions of the blocking and a copy of Persico's letter of proposals to the Committee on Public Buildings the preceding year were also enclosed.

The articles of agreement between both sculptors were the same, depending for their details about the time allotted and the payment of fees on Persico's proposals. Each contract provided for two statues nine feet high, with a six-foot base, to be completed within four years (by this time Greenough evidently felt less strongly about having no limit imposed on him), for which the fee was to be $21,000, payable in five installments provided the consular certificates attested the work warranted payment. Greenough signed one copy of his contract on January 2, 1839, and returned it; the other he retained.[8] Shortly after the first copy reached Washington he received the first installment of his fee.[9]

He began the model of the work immediately afterward. He

still had received no answer to his request for Indian relics, but by the end of the year he had casts and drawings of such objects furnished by Chapman. Early in February 1840 he was ready to cast the male figures, but the chief molder in Florence, whom he usually employed, fell ill and he may have had to secure one from Rome. In August he was apparently still working on the woman and child. By October both parts were cast.[10]

Of all Greenough's works, his group for the Capitol is perhaps least representative in design, being in one sense more realistic, in another more romantic, and altogether more complex. The figures are clad in the costume of their times, the Indian (without the wound) wearing a loincloth and having a blanket hanging from his uplifted left hand. In his right hand is a tomahawk, and on the ground is a rifle, presumably the white man's. As the figures now stand, the woman with the child is at one side of the men, but she may have been intended to be in front of them. Sumner, describing the group in the summer of 1839, said the woman was on the ground so as not to conceal the Indian.[11] At the time the parts were assembled at the Capitol, after Greenough's death, there was doubt about their proper arrangement, and a few years later members of Greenough's family asserted that the woman belonged in front. Certainly the position of the Indian's tomahawk calls for her to be there. Her position there would also clarify the pyramidical outline of the whole. Among Greenough's sketches for the work, however, one shows it arranged as it is now.

The design of his group for the Capitol reflects, nevertheless, some of Greenough's deepest artistic, moral, and political convictions. Its action is arrested, like that in some antique groups; its general arrangement resembles that of the group of the "Farnese Bull," in the Naples Museum. For all its historical aspect, it embodies an abstract concept, and this concept, despite the superficially romantic nature of the figures, is essentially anti-romantic. At the time, the standard picture of the American Indian by American artists and writers was that of a noble savage. Cooper evidently long urged Greenough to turn his "truant eyes" from "the models of antiquity, to contemplate this wronged and humbled people."[12] Greenough did so when he included the figure of King Philip in his design for a Washington monument in 1830. (One of his sketches from that time depicts Pocahontas rescuing John Smith.)

In the Indian of his group for the Capitol, however, as in the Indian on the chair of his "Washington," Greenough depicted a representative of a state of society which from his youth he had disparaged. In his conception there was not even a genuine conflict between the states of primitivism and civilization; they were rather stages in growth. His pioneer merely restrains his Indian, without wielding the rifle against the tomahawk, and the left hand of the Indian is rendered useless by the toils of the blanket. Most significantly, the pioneer is characterized by a composure intended to express not only self-confidence but compassion for his enemy. His superiority is principally moral, least of all technological. It is to some degree, however, a racial superiority. By 1848 at the latest Greenough had evidently decided to give the work the title "The Rescue."

In form and content, Greenough's group is in striking contrast to Persico's, apparently by intention. Greenough's too has a crouching female. But it has more figures, greater mass and a more complicated design. Its version of the relationship between the white settlers of America and the Indians is, moreover, at variance with Persico's. Having decided that any effect of balance between the two works was impossible to achieve, the American sculptor aimed instead at something of a tour de force. In part he must have been prompted by the desire to put in competition the art of the discovered land with that of the land of the discoverer.

The next stage in the execution of both groups had meanwhile been launched. Early in 1839 Forsyth wrote both sculptors that the President was willing for the "next best" marble to be used if the "best" could not be obtained in six months. Accordingly Greenough visited the newly opened Serravezza quarries near Carrara, which also yielded a pure, hard stone, and, deciding that it was superior to that of Ravaccioni and being assured that large blocks could be obtained by the middle of July, wrote Persico proposing it be used. Late in the summer, after Persico too visited Serravezza, he and Greenough agreed that the quarry of Polla there was the best, and Persico at least contracted for two blocks from it. Greenough's first block was not quarried until late in 1840 and early in 1841, however, and because of bad weather was delayed in being transported from the mountains.[13]

Even at this late date, in a letter to Forsyth in March 1841, Greenough urged, as he evidently had previously, that his work be executed in bronze rather than marble, giving examples from works in Florence of the different effects of exposure on both materials. Edward Everett, then in Florence, wrote John Quincy Adams, suggesting that he try to get Congress to agree to the proposal.[14] No official comment on the matter seems to have been preserved, but undoubtedly the higher cost of the bronze was sufficient to discourage approval of it.

About the time the marble for Greenough's group was ready, his disagreement with Vail over the payment of the second installment of his fee led him to ask for release from his contract, and late in 1841 or early in 1842, in his uncertainty about the government's intentions of paying him, he evidently suspended work on the whole operation. (Most of Persico's payments were two years in arrears, but none was so long delayed as Greenough's second, third, and last.) Soon after his return to Florence from America in the fall of 1843, the blocking-out of the figures of the pioneer and the Indian was apparently begun at Serravezza, and about a year later this operation was finished. Evidently he had hoped to have his own work on the marble under way before this time;[15] but circumstances of a personal nature now intervened to delay him another year. (On account of his wife's illness he took her out of Florence.)

When he again turned his attention to the work, in the fall of 1845, he made rapid progress. On a visit to Serravezza in December to obtain marble for the figures of the woman and child, however, he found to his dismay that all marble from these quarries had been engaged by the Czar of Russia for a church in St. Petersburg until its completion—an estimated period of two years.[16] It was actually four years before Greenough obtained his second block. In the interim, during 1846 and 1847, he completely remodeled the figures of the mother and child.[17] Probably he finished his marble work on the male figures during the same period.

Meantime he had difficulty collecting the third installment of his fee. About November 1844 he arranged for the certificate for the blocking-out to be sent, but Consul Binda delayed doing so, and this fact, coupled with Greenough's absence from Florence in 1844 and 1845, forced him, he said, to suspend the operations of his studio. When the certificate reached Washington about the summer of 1845, it got mislaid, so did a notarial copy forwarded (apparently by Alfred Greenough) soon afterward, and nothing came of inquiries made by T. B. Curtis (then the husband of Greenough's sister Laura) in the fall of 1845 and by Alfred in August 1846 as to why the payment had not been made. "You can have no idea," Henry's wife Frances wrote her sister-in-law Charlotte Greenough Parker early in 1847,

of the annoyance & anxiety this delay has caused Horatio, *unnecessary* vexation we have thought, as he was sure in time to get it, but that, with the strictures upon his Washington seem to me to have *(between ourselves)* diminished his love for and interest in his art. . . .

In January 1847 — a week after he petitioned George Bancroft, then minister to England, to ask the Rothschilds to advance him two or three thousand dollars — Greenough received his third and fourth installments, along with a letter from the Secretary of the Treasury explaining the delay.[18]

Marble for the figures of the mother and child was at last secured late in 1849, and during the next several months they were blocked out in Serravezza. By October 1850 Greenough had it ready for his own work. He now added to the composition a dog, which he thought was "a note wanting in the tune"; he sent Henry a sketch to show him the "excellent effect." Probably the dog was intended to stand, as it was erected, on the left of the men, but it was a largely unassimilated detail. Early summer of 1851 saw Greenough applying the finishing touches to the work, and in July he completed it.[19]

During the first and the last of the twelve years "The Rescue" was executing it received almost as much attention as the "Washington." In the spring of 1841 Greenough publicly exhibited the model of the group in his studio in the country and received at least one flattering reference to it in a Florentine newspaper. His friends Sumner, Everett, Bryant, Hillard, and Cogswell (who thought it "far, very far superior" to any American piece of sculpture he had seen) were again complimentary. As it neared completion it was almost unanimously praised by the Americans who saw it for its "national" and "American" character and widely contrasted approvingly with the statue because of this character. The group was assured, Bayard Taylor wrote in his *Views A-Foot,* "much more favorable reception than a false taste gave" the "Washington." Only a few noted with disappointment the unromantic treatment of the Indian. Margaret Fuller Ossoli, for example, wished

Greenough had immortalized "the real noble Indian in marble. This is only the man of the woods—no Metamora, no Uncas." Europeans, too, were enthusiastic. Early in 1851 a French draughtsman apparently requested permission to lithograph the work. No one, Greenough thought, expressed what he meant more happily than another Frenchman, who admired "la douce fermeté de cette nature superieure, qui, tout en conquerant, sent la compassion" ("the sweet firmness of the superior nature, which, in conquering all, feels compassion").[20] Apparently his own conception of the work deepened and became more intellectualized as he worked on it, as had his conception of the "Washington."

The most detailed analysis of "The Rescue"—and one of the most appreciative critiques of Greenough's sculpture ever written—appeared in a letter in the *Home Journal* in the summer of 1851, presumably by the American engraver J. A. Adams, who was in Florence that summer. The pioneer, he wrote, was

> He whose destiny is to convert forests into cities; who conquers only to liberate, enlighten and elevate; who presents himself . . . as the representative and legate of laws, and polity, and morals. . . . there is a sublime Washingtonianism of sentiment and character in the figure. . . . one conscious of an irresistible ascendant—too proud to feel triumph in prevailing over such a foe—too gentle not to contemplate with regret the necessary extirpation even of the treacherous and malignant. The hopeless, powerless inferiority into which the Indian has sunk . . . appears to be the result . . . of the action and movements of the victim.

In Adams' estimation, Greenough's style in the group was "essentially modern," uniting "complexity and action" with "grandeur and simplicity." He recognized three masters of this style—Bernini, Canova, and Greenough—but he thought Greenough alone had solved its peculiar problem by representing a moment of time "in which all effort and change are over, and continuousness of state has begun." He ranked Greenough, in fact, above all contemporary sculptors because of the "essentially intellectual" character of his work, it being of the

profound, complex and significant kind, which is interpreted by the mind as much as by the taste, and which rests for its full appreciation upon earnest reflection.

The power of speaking directly to the mind, Adams thought, distinguished the greatest artists, was the chief element wanting in modern art, and appeared in Greenough more than in anyone since Michelangelo. Yet far from being imitative, Greenough had a manner, he declared, which was

native, original, and genuine; copying no preceding school; strong, and marked and rich enough to establish a school for future times.[21]

Encouraged by the reception of his completed group in Florence, Greenough proposed to exhibit it elsewhere before it was set up in Washington, in the hope that it would arrive there provided with a better reputation than his statue had had. He asked the government for permission to show it in England and in New York and thought of having a cast made to show in other American cities. President Fillmore rejected his requests.[22]

About the fall of 1850 he began to make inquiries of the government as to when the group might be transported, but he got no replies. The next April Commodore Charles Morgan, Commander-in-Chief of the United States Naval Forces in the Mediterranean, offered to send the work in a store ship upon receipt of an order from the Secretary of the Navy. Greenough had Secretary W. A. Graham notified[23] and the work conveyed to Leghorn by the Florentine engineer O. Batelli. The figures were contained in four boxes; in another were eight pieces of marble for the base and marble dust with which to cement them.[24] In addition several cases containing Greenough's personal effects were to go. At first he planned to see the group dispatched himself, but he had by now decided to move to the United States and was eager to be on his way. He evidently felt sure that the shipment would be promptly ordered and that Morgan could be trusted to superintend it. More questionably, as it developed, he apparently left his agents, Chiappe Brothers in Leghorn, to furnish the statistics about the size and weight of the pieces to be shipped. In July 1851 he left Florence on his way home.

The transportation negotiations, however, were delayed and became confused. Two sets of orders were sent Morgan—in May and in October—instructing him to ship the work, according to the second order in the flagship *Independence*. Both orders reached him in December, at which time rough weather made loading the cases too risky. In the middle of April 1852, having ascertained from Binda their number and dimensions, he went to Leghorn prepared to take them aboard the *Independence*.

At this point it was discovered that Greenough's agents had underestimated the size and weight of the principal case. It weighed some thirty-two tons, twelve tons more than had been represented, and its dimensions were thirteen by eight by seven feet. Neither it nor the next-smaller case could be gotten below the spar deck. All the cases could have been put on the deck if a third of the guns had been struck below and the two larger cases lashed to the bulwarks. But since the ship would thus have been rendered inefficient for maneuvering and defense, Morgan decided not to attempt the transportation.[25]

Greenough had meanwhile arrived in the United States, in the fall of 1851, and had soon gone to Washington. There, for the first time, he saw Persico's group, which had been put in its place (on the upper of the two levels of the south blocking) in 1844 under Persico's direction. At that time the discovery had been made that from the level of the street an adequate front view of the work could not be had, and it had been elevated on a five-foot pedestal. It appeared awkward and interfered with a view of the front of the building. It was "anomalous and absurd," Greenough complained in his pamphlet *Æsthetics at Washington,* and did not treat the building properly "as a noble and important vase which it is called humbly to adorn and illustrate." To officials he "strenuously" advocated "a lower and more appropriate situation" for both groups. Presumably he advocated the situation of the lower level of the blocking. After his death, which occurred before his group reached America, there was a widespread rumor to this effect.[26]

After he arrived home Greenough was also concerned with collecting the final installment of his fee for "The Rescue." Apparently he had had Binda send a certificate to the effect that the work was completed, but no action had been taken on the matter. Early in June 1852 he wrote President Fillmore claiming not only the rest of the sum promised but recompense for the loss of his time incurred by the delay in transportation. The extra claim was denied on the grounds that the work had not been finished in the time stipulated, but acknowledgment was made that he was due $3500. In November, a month before his death, still unpaid, he asked Everett to intercede on his behalf. The final sum owing from the government was paid the following year to his estate.[27]

In August 1852 Congress appropriated the sum of $7000 for the transportation and erection of Greenough's group. The next month the Navy Department was given charge of the operation, and Commodore Stringham, then commander of the Mediterranean Squadron, was apparently instructed to make the necessary arrangements. These instructions did not reach Stringham until the following February. In December 1852, shortly after Greenough's death, the Secretary of State asked Binda to make the shipping arrangements, and early in February 1853 Binda did so. He chartered from Francis Malenchini and Company, merchants in Leghorn, for the sum of $3500, their brig *Atar Gull,* to transport Greenough's statuary and personal effects directly to Washington, allowing other cargo as well to be shipped if the weight allowed but not to be discharged first. The *Atar Gull* arrived at Leghorn about the middle of March and sailed the last of April or first of May with the Greenough cases. With the bill of lading went a letter written by engineer Batelli describing the way in which the parts of the group should be assembled.[28]

The *Atar Gull* reached the Washington navy yard about August 8. During the next two or three weeks the statuary was unloaded, transported to the Capitol, and set up.[29] The last two operations were under the general supervision of Commissioner of Public Buildings B. B. French; the placing of the work was done by the sculptor Clark Mills. As it was being brought from the navy yard to the city, French discovered that there was some question about where Greenough wished it placed. But he could not satisfy himself that Greenough had preferred the lower level and his measurements indicated that the group was two feet too wide at the base to be accommodated there. Accordingly, he had it placed above.

French was also unable to learn precisely what Greenough's intentions were about the arrangement of the parts of the group, though he "sought most industriously" to do so.[30] In the end he relied chiefly on Batelli's letter (now evidently lost) and his own judgment. He may have known Henry Greenough's opinion, but he could not have been much helped by it. Shortly after the arrival of the work Everett wrote Henry in Cambridge inquiring what the arrangement should be, and Henry, in a reply written on September 1,[31] drew a ground plan, based, he said, on what Horatio had told him in Florence when he was there in the 1840's. According to it, the two parts were joined to form a rectangular unit which would have been too broad to fit on the blocking. As for the position of the dog, added after he left Florence, Henry guessed optimistically that it must be "obvious." It would seem that he would have referred to the drawing Horatio sent him at the time the dog was added, but he said he knew of no pertinent drawing. In any case, by the time Henry's letter reached Washington, the assembling of the work was virtually completed.

A base about a foot high was constructed, two cases of the statuary were lifted to it on August 20th, and the other two in the course of the next few days. About October 12 the group was exposed to view (having been hidden by a palisade while it was being set up). An iron railing, similar to the one around Persico's group (to which Greenough had objected, as he had to that around the "Washington") was erected around it.[32]

For these operations and all others connected with the final disposition of "The Rescue" besides its transatlantic carriage, the expenditures were over $3100. Nearly $600 of this amount went to Batelli, the Chiappes, and other Italians for various services; the largest single sum was $1800, paid to Mills.[33] (The expenses for the transportation and erection of Persico's group were only about $1300, since it was transported by a United States Naval vessel and erected under his supervision.)

Almost all the advance reports of Greenough's group having been favorable, there was considerable expectation, especially among his well-wishers, that it would prove more successful than his "Washington" and firmly establish his fame. When it was erected it elicited indeed a good deal of comment in the city's press, though little elsewhere, and on the whole this comment was favorable. Again the sculptor's execution was praised, and this time his composition was approved as being distinctively American. But again the site of his work militated against it and again the essential ideality of his conception was misunderstood.

In general, the hopes which had been raised were disappointed.

Objections to the site were promptly expressed, chiefly because of the rumor that Greenough had preferred the lower level of the blocking and because of his criticism, in *Æsthetics at Washington,* of the position of Persico's group. To these objections French made two replies, printed in the Washington *Daily National Intelligencer,* explaining why he had placed the work on the top level and so constructed the base and suggesting that the most appropriate location for it would be the public grounds. "Would to God," he exclaimed, with feeling for both Greenough's fate and his own problem, "the lamented Greenough were here to superintend the placing of his own magnificent group!"[34]

The chief element in the composition which proved controversial was the repose of the figures. Over a period of a month, in November and December, two exchanges of articles appeared in the *Intelligencer,* written by two assailants and two defendants of the group. In the opinion of the first correspondent,

> there is a quietness which broods over the whole scene which is so far from a truthful representation that we would be induced to believe it were but a match at wrestling. . . .

He objected also to the dog ("Will some one more familiar than we profess to be," he inquired, "inform us what breed 'that dog' belongs to?") and to the open dress of the woman (which he thought immodest) and compared Greenough's work disparagingly to Causici's relief of Daniel Boone in the rotunda and to Mills' equestrian "Jackson." A respondent to this critic countered these objections severally. In explanation of the calm demeanor of the pioneer, he proposed a classical analogy: "He, like Apollo," he wrote of Greenough's figure, "knows his power; hence, like Apollo, you find no expression of fear or anxiety."[35]

The second exchange of letters about "The Rescue" was precipitated by an article in a series appearing under the title of

"From a Backwoods Traveller." Statuary, the author predicated, was a grand thing to an artistical eye, but he hastened to confess he had no such eye. Of the new addition to the Capitol he wrote:

The white man is too big for the Indian, and does not look half mad enough; the Indian seems to feel like the coon did when he heard Martin Scott's name mentioned. The woman looks too much like the one did when the bear and her husband had the fight. The baby seems wrapped in blissful ignorance; the toggery of the hunter is what the doctors call a disease when they do not understand it—suigeneris. That dog is some, but ought to be killed for not pitching into that *Ingun,* or else swapped off for a good rifle.

"Ill-starred Horatio Greenough!" exclaimed a champion in reply,

Was it not sufficient that while living the captious tribe indulged every opportunity to dispute your claim to an artistic reputation, but that now, since your clay reposes in the bosom of our common mother, your very last effort is scarcely awarded "faint praise?"

If the "Backwoods Traveller" had used whatever sort of eyes he did possess, this critic observed, he would have discovered the pioneer's rifle on the ground. "The 'Traveller,' however," he pointed out,

unintentionally bears testimony to the correctness of Mr. Greenough's idea. To show the triumph of civilization the white man should *not* look "mad," and the Indian *should* appear to surrender with a feeling similar to that of Captain Scott's "coon."

This letter produced from the now contrite "Traveller" an apology for having referred disrespectfully to the dead, but he claimed, "I did look for *that rifle,* and looked in vain; it certainly was out of place down among their feet."[36]

None of these critics questioned the arrangement of Greenough's group nor apparently did anyone else at this time. Six years later, in February 1859, formal objection to it was made by Greenough's family, through Edward Loring, brother-in-law of Frances B. Greenough, then Judge of the Court of Claims. Writing to James Pearce, Curator of Art at the Capitol, Loring asserted that

the mother and child are placed on the wrong side, & thus the artists conception is prevented expression—as he told the story—the mother and child were before the Indian and she in her maternal instinct was shielding her child from his grasp, to prevent which the husband seizes both arms of the Indian, and bears him down at the same time. . . .

Now all this is perverted, the mother and child are removed from the peril, which is the causa causans, of the action of the piece and she is looking unconcernedly away from it.[37]

He inquired whether the matter might be rectified and what evidence of the false position would need to be presented. His letter was referred by Pearce to M. C. Meigs, Captain of Engineers in charge of the extension of the Capitol, who replied to Pearce that any drawing of Greenough would be sufficient evidence, though he pointed out that a Congressional appropriation would have to be made for any move.[38] Probably because there seemed to be no drawing, no further action about the matter was taken.

Throughout the rest of the nineteenth century Greenough's group fared better than his "Washington" at the hands of critics, chiefly because of its realistic aspect. Eventually, however, it too aroused active opposition. In the twentieth century, groups of Indians more than once petitioned Congress to have it removed from the Capitol on the ground that it was a libel on their race.

Since Greenough's "Rescue" may never have been seen as he perhaps intended it to appear, it cannot be judged with entire justice. Nevertheless certain measures of it can be taken. In it, as in the "Washington," he aimed chiefly to express a moral concept through characterization, and on the whole he succeeded in doing so. In certain respects this idealization evinces greater artistic maturity. It is conceived of in terms of dramatic action and of naturalistic rather than stylized gestures. The group has, however, too many details treated with equal attention and thus forfeits the force of unity. The treatment of the Indian, modeled with an almost Hellenistic delicacy, tends to obscure the ideal meaning of the work, since the figure thus seems to represent an advanced state of development. (This was Greenough's only use of the nude as other than a symbol of moral perfection, a reversal of technique which he seems not to have recognized.) In contrast, the meaning of the "Washington" is single and unequivocal. Though the group, finally, was an original design, it tends to triteness. The bold and independent spirit in which the "Washington," for all its indebtedness to Phidias' "Zeus," was conceived was peculiarly in keeping with the subject of Greenough's later work, but no such spirit animates that work.

Nevertheless, despite its weaknesses, "The Rescue" is one of the greatest measures of Greenough's talent and of his total achievement. It is proof of his desire and his ability to explore new artistic traditions. It is evidence, too, though somewhat naïve in nature, of his determination to be a distinctively American sculptor. It is the closest he ever came to giving his countrymen the realism which he knew they wanted in a work of art, but it is instinct with his own belief in the superiority of ideal works. It is, finally, a testament of his faith that eventually his country would assume the role of civilized man—with all the power, magnanimity, and serenity he attached to that role—for which he believed it peculiarly destined.

Form as Function

Throughout Greenough's adult life he was concerned with a theory of architectural structure: from 1825, when he broached it in the letter he wrote the Bunker Hill Monument Association, to the last year of his life, when he attempted to draw public attention to it in his book, *The Travels, Observations, and Experience of a Yankee Stonecutter*. His most explicit statement of it is in his essay "American Architecture," which was published in the *United States Magazine and Democratic Review* of August 1843. It was substantially developed, however, by 1831, when he expressed its essentials in the letter he wrote Allston in October of that year from Paris.[1]

Greenough introduced the subject of architecture in that letter by way of continuing some of the conversations which he and Allston had had in 1828, in which Allston had agreed with him that "broader principles of art and a more intelligent imitation were necessary to the formation of a pure and masculine style of building." Probably he was prompted to state his opinions at this time, however, by some of the conversations which he, Cooper, Morse, and perhaps Brisbane were having. Certainly Cooper and Brisbane between them had ideas about architecture—notably that it should be simple, adapted to situations and uses, and expressive of national character—which were in general agreement with Greenough's.

Architecture, Greenough wrote Allston, had been "enthralled ever since a claim to *universal* and *indiscriminate* admiration" had been established for the Greek school. In deference to Allston's preference for the Gothic, he excepted this style for having validity by "recurring to nature." But he condemned the "bastard result" of ignorant adaptations of Greek and Gothic alike, citing as examples Italian churches and such American edifices as the Branch Bank of the United States in Philadelphia. This building, he wrote,

shoved in between the common buildings of a street—shorn of its lateral collonades and pierced every where for light reminds us of a noble captive stripped alike of arms and ornaments and set at work with the other drudges of his conqueror.

"These spirits in the vasty deep of past epochs *will not come when we do call for them,"* he declared. In the letter he wrote the Bunker Hill Monument Association in 1825, he recalled, he had endeavored to show that a monumental column was just such an "inconsequent and unmeaning" result.

Now, however, he was prepared, evidently for the first time, to offer a new authority for the principle of adaptation: the authority of nature. Nature, in fact, was

the only true school of art. Has she ever been the slave of any one idea of beauty or of grandeur? Her sublimity is manifest alike in the sailing eagle, the bounding lion and the rolling whale. Her beauty asks no sacrifice of the existence or even of the comfort of its wearer. . . . She always organizes the frame for its exposure and its work yet always leaves it beautiful.

He proposed that nature be imitated "in this important respect more compleatly" than before. "Nor do we mean," he added, making a significant distinction,

that the object for which a building is constructed shall be nowise sacrificed to an abstract idea of form—we would that the shell of each fabric be as it were, moulded on the wants and conveniences desired.

This, he observed, had been the method of naval architects, and he thought whoever had seen a ship at sea would "confess that in that work man has approached nearest his maker." As an example of a building to be designed in this manner he named a bank, in which light should be gotten "not by stealth as if we were ashamed of it, but as openly as tis given by the creator to our own brain"; ingress and egress should be "as convenient as possible to numbers"; and "every want that those employed in such buildings may have experienced" should be of first consideration.

Though such an architecture rested on the very "principles of creation," he pictured it at last as peculiarly American. "It is true," he wrote,

> that this style of art asks for much in feeling of which we have but the germ but why should we be discouraged? In our political institutions we have dared to be new. Can we not shew that art too has a reason as well as government?

Such an architecture was a peculiarly social creation. It required all the knowledge among us—all the light which can be thrown on the requisites of a building by those who are to occupy it all the science of our engineers and mathematicians . . . all the feeling and the imitation of our architects and painters. . . .

By 1836 Greenough had put some of his ideas on architecture and building into the form of "loose sketches"—among those he hoped at that time to have published, after he had revised them, in the *North American Review*.[2] His work on the "Washington," however, kept him from doing much else until the late 1830's. By 1839 he had written some essays on art and by 1841 a good deal on architecture. Edward Everett was particularly struck by an essay on architecture by Greenough which he read at that time, and he expressed a desire to see plans which would illustrate the ideas in it.[3] Greenough also had some hesitation about presenting himself to the public as an architectural theorist because he doubted his qualifications. He would insist on anonymity, he wrote the editor of the *North American Review* in 1836, relative to the publication of his views on architecture, fearing that he had done "a rash thing to speak of an art which I do not possess." It is perhaps significant in this connection that he issued his book, *The Travels, Observations, and Experience of a Yankee Stonecutter,* pseudonymously. When he first publicly announced his architectural theory, however, in "American Architecture" in 1843, he used his own name.

Greenough began this essay by citing the current opinion that the United States was "destined to form a new style of architecture" and offered explanations of its failure thus far to do so. Partly, he felt, the population had been too heterogeneous, but chiefly he blamed the late date of the nation's birth:

We forgot that reason had been the dry nurse of the giant offspring, and had fed her from the beginning with the stout bread and meat of fact; that every wry face the bantling ever made had been daguerreotyped, and all her words and deeds printed and labelled away in the pigeon-holes of official bureaux.

Reason can dissect, but cannot originate; she can adopt, but cannot create; she can modify, but cannot find.

The widespread appropriation in the United States of foreign styles without intelligent adaptation—in the past a sign of cultural decay—he attributed to the desire to display wealth, citing as examples both Gothic and Greek Revival buildings. It was "the purloining of the coat of carms of a defunct family." He urged, however, not more accurate imitation—which would be to "submit to an iron rule that begins by sacrificing reason, dignity and comfort"—but "experiment at the risk of license." He proposed, moreover, a new system for experimentation:

Let us consult nature, and in the assurance that she will disclose a mine, richer than was ever dreamed of by the Greeks, in art as well as in philosophy.

By consulting nature he meant examining the skeletons and skins of animals and recognizing the principle of construction embodied in them. It was not an "arbitrary law of proportion" or "unbending model of form" but an adaptation of the whole "animal organization" to the genus or species, its exposure, and its work. "The law of adaptation," he postulated, "is the fundamental law of nature in all structure." As examples of this law and this "organic beauty" he cited not only anatomical details in animals and birds, but instruments of destruction (for them he was willing to substitute the word *character* "as indicating the mere adaptation of forms to functions"), and ships.

He now turned to the application of this theory. "Instead," he wrote,

> of forcing the functions of every sort of building into one general form, adopting an outward shape for the sake of the eye or of association, without reference to the inner distribution, let us begin from the heart as the nucleus, and work outward.

The "most convenient size and arrangement" of the rooms, "the access of the light that may, of the air that must, be wanted" (the "skeleton" of the building), having been provided for, the outward appearance ("the dress") would follow. The "unflinching adaptation of a building to its position and use" would give "as a sure product of that adaptation, character and expression." A bank would then have the "physiognomy" of a bank, and a church would be recognizable. He allowed, however, for two classes of buildings with notably different kinds of functions: "organic, formed to meet the wants of their occupants," and "monumental, addressed to the sympathies, the faith or the taste of a people." Those in the first class might also be called "machines, each individual of which must be formed with reference to the abstract type of its species." He allowed also for another source of instruction besides nature—the "Greek masters . . . the true apostles of correct taste in building." He preferred adherence to the Greek "system of ornament" to the substitution of "novelty for propriety," but he urged, "let us learn principles, not copy shapes; let us imitate them like men, and not ape them like monkeys." And he was convinced that "the American builder, by a truly philosophic investigation of ancient art, will learn of the Greeks to be American." In conclusion he called on Americans to adapt architectural forms to climate and use and to develop ornaments in harmony with American institutions. He thought such a task could be accomplished only with the passage of time and the cooperation of many; yet he firmly believed that it would be accomplished, that "freedom and knowledge will bear the fruit of refinement and beauty."[4]

The only notable difference between Greenough's letter to Allston and his essay "American Architecture" was the stronger statement in the essay of his prejudice against the Gothic and in favor of the Greek. His theory was not, moreover, essentially altered in the nine years of his life after 1843. During his last year he wrote nine essays which more or less touched upon it. In five—"Æsthetics at Washington," "The Washington Monument," "The Smithsonian Institution," "The Cooper Monument," and "A Place for Everything"—and in a letter to Emerson written the same year he largely restated it. In "Æsthetics at Washington" and "The Cooper Monument" he seemed on the verge of relating it to some of the current developments in industrial building which proved to be important in the emergence of the new architecture and in which he became interested during this year, but he did not clearly do so. In four other of these essays—"The Stonecutter's Creed," "Relative and Independent Beauty," "Burke on the Beautiful," and "Criticism in Search of Beauty"—he was primarily concerned with the philosophic and religious implications of the functional principle. His application of this principle to architecture remained an achievement of his early manhood.

All his life Greenough regarded his theory of structure as distinctly his own. He was, of course, not entirely justified, since the central concept in it circulated in various contexts throughout Europe and the United States during this period. Yet he arrived at this concept largely independently, in response to various personal experiences. His essay "American Architecture" was, moreover, the first full and coherent public statement of the functional theory of architecture to be made by an American.

The first and apparently most important of the influences operating upon Greenough's architectural thought were those which led him to compose his letter to the Bunker Hill Monument Association. The argument which he therein advanced was in agreement with a body of ideas about building—to the effect that it should be simple, economical, and adapted to the environment—then current in America. The chief source of these ideas was the building craft. Architects of the Federal period—Asher Benjamin, for example, whose building manuals circulated widely—and those of the Greek Revival—like Robert Mills—alike inveighed against servile imitation of the antique and declared the use of buildings to be of primary importance. Indeed, the Greek Revival could be regarded as the first distinctively American style, in its simplicity, feeling for materials, and free planning. Though in 1825 there was only one truly Greek Revival building in Boston, these characteristics were to be seen in other edifices, including some of those built by David Greenough.

For these ideas about architecture and building there were also sources in the general currents of the Enlightenment, particularly in the neo-classical–common-sense esthetic. The most popular volume on esthetics throughout the period was Archibald Alison's *Essays on the Nature and Principles of Taste,* first published in 1790, in which fitness and utility were declared to be the chief sources of relative beauty; among the examples of fitness given were a surgeon's knife, disagreeable parts of the animal frame, and a ship (cited from Hogarth). The same principles were expressed by Dugald Stewart and Hugh Blair in books used as texts at Harvard when Greenough was there.

Yet farther in the past there were sources of the neo-classical esthetic itself, and with them, too, Greenough was familiar. In such Renaissance treatises as those by Leonardo da Vinci and

Alberti which he borrowed from the Harvard library, the principles of unity, proportion, and suitability were set forth, and in the writings of Horace and Vitruvius ostentation was scorned, fitness praised, and the laws of nature and reason invoked.

The new romantic esthetic, with its conception of form as organic—as the outward manifestation of inner life and growth—was already beginning to circulate in America. With this esthetic and very likely with this conception Greenough was made acquainted through Allston. Probably Allston called his attention to Coleridge (whom Allston knew personally and admired extravagantly), who had introduced the organic conception into English from the German. Insofar as it was a conception of unity in a work of art, it apparently made an impression on Greenough. Otherwise, however, he would seem never to have been deeply influenced by the romantic esthetic. In one of his last essays he referred to Goethe and Schiller, but there is little evidence that he ever read widely in romantic philosophy; his disparagement of "reason" as uncreative suggests that he was not familiar with the broader definition of this faculty formulated by the post-Kantians.

The most vital influence on Greenough's thought about structure seems to have been exerted by his study of anatomy. The new science of comparative anatomy in particular had revealed how pervasive was the phenomenon of adaptation to function in animal structure. Edward Tyson, father of this science, and Cuvier, its greatest codifier, were among the authors whose works Greenough borrowed from the Harvard library. John Bell, another of these authors, and his brother Charles were leading British physiologists. Charles Bell, who was also an artist, was the author of the popular *Anatomy and Philosophy of Expression as Connected with the Fine Arts,* first published in 1806, in which he set forth the thesis that the outward forms and expressions of men and animals were determined by the development and functioning of their organs. Greenough may have owned a copy of this book in later years.[5] He introduced more references to animal structure in later explications of his architectural theory, but even in his letter to the Bunker Hill Monument Association he employed the metaphor of the human body as an edifice. This metaphor, however, had been almost universal in architectural treatises since Vitruvius' use of it, and in the eighteenth and nineteenth centuries it was associated with the old rather than the new concepts.

Greenough's architectural thought was thus, in the beginning—as, indeed, it was always—expressive of predominantly classical and rationalistic values. It was not, however, the less revolutionary.

By the middle of the eighteenth century a revolutionary architectural theory and the beginnings of a new architecture had made their appearance in Europe, both the result of the strict application of reason to building. About that time the theory of functionalism in architecture was enunciated, for the first time, by the Venetian Carlo Lodoli, who declared that only that which had a definite function should show and that it should conform to the nature of the materials.[6] Neither Lodoli nor his followers, known as the *rigoristi,* developed new forms, however. Meanwhile a school of French architects, chief among them Boullée, Ledoux, and Lequeu, began to develop such forms, aiming in them to eliminate excessive ornament and to achieve both expressiveness and individualism.[7] Eventually the functional principle was broached by Ledoux, and by the beginning of the next century it was recognized by architects in France, England, and Germany.

The functional theory of architecture was also in line with romantic thought, particularly with the organic concept.

According to the organic view, the creative process was carried on by the imaginative and intuitive faculty, to a large extent by national and racial consciousness, and the organic edifice was typically one whose interior arrangement determined its external appearance. The romantic movement also fostered other ideas about architecture, chiefly the idea that it might express emotions and morals. Above all, it produced, in the decades from about 1830 to 1860, a widespread revival of the Gothic style, which was commonly regarded as being derived from nature and as supremely functional.

By the middle of the nineteenth century there was a general tendency to regard architecture simultaneously from two points of view : the functional and the expressive. New forms achieved by the use of new materials—especially iron and glass—were beginning to appear, but chiefly from engineers and industrial builders. Professional architects still dealt largely with historical forms.

Greenough presumably came into contact with most of these European architectural ideas during his first few years abroad. In Florence he was close to the sphere of Lodoli's influence. In the pages of *L'Antologia* the traditional Vitruvian and current utilitarian views of architecture were commonly expressed, but occasionally distinctively functional ones appeared. The leaders of the Tuscan Risorgimento saw all the arts, in typically romantic fashion, as expressions of national character; yet for this very reason they violently objected to the chief romantic architectural manifestation—the Gothic Revival. Throughout the period of Greenough's residence in Florence, moreover, a project pended which precipitated discussions of various architectural theories : the completion of the façade of the Duomo.[8] The chief argument revolved around two basic designs : the basilican, which would have preserved the lines of the structure; and the tricuspidate, which would have been a false front and hidden part of the dome. The basilican design, which better represented Tuscan taste and the functional principle, was the one at last, late in the century, settled upon.

Greenough was also acquainted with the French rationalistic tradition in architecture. The greatest French architect of his generation was Henri Labrouste, who was a pensioner at the French Academy in Rome during the years that Greenough was in the city. Possibly Greenough knew of his chief project from 1826 on, which was the restoration of the temples at Paestum. His drawings, which reflected his avowed objective to grasp "l'organisme de chaque construction" ("the organism of each construction") instead of depicting picturesque ruins, as was the vogue, aroused controversy at the Academy.[9] In 1830 he returned to Paris, was soon teaching pupils that "in architecture form must always be appropriate to the function for which it is intended," and was also soon experimenting with cast and wrought iron for public buildings.

Throughout this period Paris was the center of the chief revolutionary developments in both architecture and engineering. On Greenough's first visit he commented on the "beautiful and scientific" bridges of the city,[10] could have seen cast iron and glass used for the first time in a large structure (the just completed Galerie d'Orleans of the Palais Royale), and must have known of the Saint-Simonians' interest in the construction of docks, warehouses, ports, canals, and railroads. It was perhaps significant that he was in Paris when he wrote his letter to Allston in October 1831 and that there he spent the summer of 1842—the last period of relative leisure he had for possible composition or revision before "American Architecture" appeared in print.

The chief German architect exploring the new tradition was Karl Friedrich Schinkel, and of him only, among all these architects and architectural theorists, is there proof that Greenough knew. Evidently he learned of Schinkel's work first in the fall of 1839, probably from an intermediate source; he did not then know German. He wrote Sumner, then in Berlin, to send him an account of the impression made by Schinkel's buildings there, "as regards distribution & adaptation, *organization* in short," which he felt was "the germ of future architecture." It would, he thought be "an 'E Pluribus Unum' " style.[11] Had he known more of Schinkel, who sought to combine functionalism with feeling and historic association, Greenough might have found him most congenial of the new architects. By this time, however, his own architectural theory was essentially formed.

In any case, there was another influence upon the development of Greenough's architectural thought which was at least as vital as any of these European ideas and practices: the influence of his thought about his own art. During his first years abroad he simultaneously evolved definitions of the aims of sculpture and of architecture which matched each other in all essentials. As he rejected the strict neo-classical school of sculpture because it was intellectually shallow and false to the facts of anatomy, so he objected to the extreme aspects of revival architecture for the ignorance of history which they represented and for their impracticality. And as he defined a sculptural ideal which would project moral character through natural forms, he proposed an architectural style in which inner arrangement and outer appearance would agree. In both sculpture and architecture he rejected, in consequence, all extraneous details and ornamentation for its own sake.

At the same time, he struggled in his thinking about both arts, with his conviction that the highest artistic aim was the expression of thought or feeling or imagination. As he distinguished among sculptural works the beautiful and the "merely true," he divided edifices into two comparable classes. Yet even edifices of the more strictly functional class he conceived of as embodying national character and—especially as he thought of them in his last year—moral values and as being ornamented. And though he insisted upon the universality of the functional principle, he based his judgments of historical styles, as the Tuscans did, on political rather than esthetic principles. He was too deeply convinced of the vitality of tradition to be a genuine organicist and of the essentially ideal nature of art to be a complete functionalist.

In his own terms, Greenough distinguished chiefly, in sculpture and in architecture, between the imitation of forms and the application of principles—in favor of the latter course. Yet in practice he was less concerned with developing new forms than with revitalizing old ones, particularly classical forms. In varying degrees, he was responsible for the designs of at least three edifices: that by Rogers to house his "Washington" on the Capitol grounds (which he approved), the studio he had built for himself (presumably from his own design) in Florence in 1847–48, and a monument to Cooper which he projected in 1852. All were more or less classical in design. Yet in accordance with his theory, all were simple, plain, and adapted to their uses. For the last he proposed, as he had for the first, that a model be set up to be experimented with before the design was settled upon.

As an architectural theorist Greenough was far less committed to tradition than he was as a sculptor. In the former role he was brilliantly in advance of his time among his countrymen. From the 1840's on, the organic concept was commonly applied to architecture within the Transcendental circle, and experimentation with new materials in building—especially iron and steel—began, for the first time, to make new forms possible. Yet not until Louis Sullivan began to work in the 1880's was an organic and functional architectural theory comparable in scope to

Greenough's set forth by an American or was such a theory put into practice.

To this final achievement Greenough contributed. In the last year of his life he discussed his architectural ideas with Emerson, who was much taken by them.[12] In his own subsequent pronouncements Emerson emphasized the element of functionalism in esthetics more than he had previously. The central concept of Greenough's architectural thought was thus transmitted to the Transcendental tradition, which exerted an acknowledged influence on Sullivan and other architects of the new school. Emerson also called the attention of several of his friends to Greenough's ideas and alluded to them more than once in published essays and public lectures until at least as late as 1872. Among those who knew of Greenough through Emerson was possibly the new architect Frank Furness, whose father, W. H. Furness, was a lifelong friend of Emerson's and whose brother, the portrait painter W. H. Furness, Jr., was advised by Emerson to consult Greenough about the best place to study art in Europe.[13] In Frank Furness' firm in Philadelphia Sullivan was first employed.[14]

Part III

5

Florentine American : 1837-1851

Homage to the Goddess

ON THEIR WAY BACK to Florence from America in 1836 Greenough and his sister Louisa spent about two weeks (the last in November) in London, where they visited their brother John.[1] From the first of December until about mid-January they were in Paris. There they found a number of American friends: the David Searses, the Nathan Appletons and their two daughters (to the critical eye of Frances, Greenough was "too fresh from the hands of an American tailleur," but she liked the "intelligence of his face" and his "unaffectedness"),[2] Boston lawyer Francis Calley Gray, Cogswell, Joseph Russell and his stepdaughter Louisa Gore of Boston, and the newlywed E. P. Thomases of Baltimore. They were all often together—having dinners, hearing concerts (and taking ices at Tortoni's afterward), going on excursions out of the city, attending soirées.[3]

Of two members of this group—Mary Appleton and Mrs. Thomas—Greenough modeled busts in Paris. Mary Appleton's was for her aunt Mrs. Samuel Appleton. Quite a levee was held each morning during the sittings for it, as Gray, Cogswell, and others devoted themselves to keeping the subject smiling. Three of them composed a sonnet to it. (Frances drew a sketch in her journal to illustrate the episode.) Unfortunately the bust proved to be a failure. Greenough made two models; according to Gray, the first was too regular and the second (made a few months later in Florence) a "violent" likeness. The marble, which was evidently finished in 1838, disappointed Nathan Appleton and Greenough was "mortified" when he learned the fact. He proposed to try again, but apparently did not.[4] The bust of Mrs. Thomas, on the other hand, was highly successful. Cogswell thought the "pretty" lady herself not comparable.[5] It was put into marble during the next few months in Florence, signed "HG 37." Probably in Florence, when the Thomases were there in the spring, Greenough executed a bust of the husband. The two portraits made an elegant pair.

About the middle of January Horatio and Louisa left Paris for Florence. Promptly busying himself in his studio, Horatio added a shop where all carpentry work could be done and kept a man constantly busy.[6] In addition to his work on the "Washington," the Thomson and Sears commissions and the busts modeled in Paris, he modeled a few new busts. One was of Abélard's Héloïse, intended to embody the lines from Pope's poem, "Eloïsa to Abelard,"

> Dear fatal name! rest ever unreveal'd,
> Nor pass these lips, in holy silence seal'd:
> Hide it, my heart, within that close disguise,
> Where, mix'd with God's, his lov'd idea lies. . . .

The form was swathed in a veil—"a veiled magdalen," he called it, ". . . but a Magdalen who has to reproach herself with no grosser sin." One marble went to Philadelphian Charles Wetherill for approximately $370, and another, in the fall of 1838, to David Hoffman.[7] He also executed during the first half of 1837 a bust of the historian C. G. G. Botta, of which Capponi was to have one marble and Niccolini another.[8]

Early in the year he received from New York fur merchant John C. Halsey, then in Florence, an order for two two-foot statues of Aristides and of Washington in modern dress, together with two columns for pedestals. By December the "Aristides" was in marble, copied from the life-size antique statue of the figure in the Naples Museum then known by that name, later identified as Aeschines. (Again it was reported that Greenough gave his work his own features, but he did not noticeably alter those of the original.) He proposed to model the figure of Washington wrapped in a cloak, leaning on a sword. Halsey died in the summer, however, and his son was unable to assume the responsibility for the orders. He had Greenough make a medallion, possibly of the father, for fifty francesconi, but arrangements about the statues were temporarily suspended.[9]

By the summer of 1837 Greenough had also received orders from Gray for busts of Psyche and the young Augustus Caesar—probably copied from the antique. At that time the casts he made in America reached Florence[10] In July he received official notice of his commission to execute a second work for the government, and by the fall he had made sketches of his proposed designs for it.

Probably about this time he bought the proof-casts of five of Michelangelo's figures for the Medici tombs—all except the figure of Lorenzo, made by a molder sent to obtain copies for King Louis Philippe. He kept "Morning," "Evening," and "Guiliano" for his studio and sent "Day" and "Night" as gifts to Colonel Perkins, in appreciation of Perkins' giving him passage to Gibraltar in 1828. Perkins deposited the two in the Boston Athenaeum in 1838.[11]

Meantime the number of Greenough's social activities increased. Several of the Americans whom he and Louisa had known in Paris went on to Italy, stopping to and from the south in Florence, where they were escorted about by the Greenoughs. Among the number were Mr. Russell and his stepdaughter. Throughout the summer Louisa Greenough and Louisa Gore were evidently constant companions. Horatio had bought a horse, which he rode daily, and he now bought another and kept a carriage for "the ladies." He drove them himself on Sundays.[12]

By the summer of 1837 he had courted Louisa Gore, and by early August their wedding date had been set and a house for their occupancy secured.[13] The ceremony was performed on October 14th, at the home of the British Minister, Ralph Abercromby, by the Reverend Henry Hartopp Knapp, chaplain of the Anglican community in the city. Louisa had expressed a preference for an English clergyman; there was no American one. She used on this occasion the name of Eliza, by which she was often called in her early years. A settlement was prepared by Wilde and an Italian contract registered.[14]

Though their courtship was short, the bride and groom had been known to each other for several years. Louisa, who was seven years younger than Horatio, was the daughter of John Gore, wealthy Boston merchant and nephew of Governor Christopher Gore, who had been an occasional business associate of David Greenough. Her mother, Mary Green Babcock, belonged to a prominent family which patronized native artists through several generations. Her brother, John C. Gore, as an art student, had been a companion of Greenough's in Florence a few years before. She was a friend of the Greenough girls, and on one occasion she and her mother had sent Horatio greetings through Everett.[15]

According to her sister-in-law Frances B. Greenough, Louisa Gore was "brought up in the greatest possible self indulgence" and taught "to dawdle & fritter away her hours." Yet she had a number of accomplishments. She played the piano, knew French and Italian, often acted as Horatio's amanuensis, read a good deal, and during the early years of her marriage kept a commonplace book. Though generally more noted for sensibleness than warmth of affection, she had a good disposition, and though having, in Frances' words, a "stalwart" figure and "globular" forehead, she was attractive. Edward Everett, nearly as old as her father, was fascinated by her for years. Hiram Powers, who met her a few months after her marriage, was impressed by her appearance and manner, as well as by reports of her wealth. On coming of age, she inherited some $50,000, and at the death of her mother (in Paris, a few months before she and the Greenoughs met there) she got approximately that much again.[16]

Later generations of the family conjectured that Louisa's chief merits in Horatio's eyes were her fortune and her policy of not interfering with his work. Her money did indeed enable them to live well throughout their married life. Yet it was essentially a woman of broad cultivation and a particular station whom he married, not a mere heiress. Though no letters between them seem to have been preserved, other evidence indicates that the union was a happy one. "She is my only comfort in this exile, apart from my profession," Greenough wrote Gilmor of his wife in the spring of 1839. He was, Calvert declared, "blest as few are in his married life." G. W. Greene referred to his being "rich . . . in domestic felicity." No stranger in the realm dearest to her husband—art—Louisa showed visitors to his studio, offered advice about his work which he accepted, and sympathized with his most serious aims. As mistress of their house she was soon regarded as the social head of the American colony in Florence, a position for which one friend thought her "eminently fitted by her beauty, grace of manner and cultivation." She and Greenough, this writer continued, "kept entirely free from the envyings and jealousies which are apt to enter so largely into the society of artists. . . ."[17]

The newly married couple went first to live in Casa Brocchi, a thirteen-room house in Borgo Pinti, behind the Pergola Theatre. Louisa's step-father and Horatio's sister moved in at the same time and as long as they remained in Florence continued to live with their relatives. Within a few months Horatio was sending Henry reports of a settled and congenial menage. His work went on "in a still and noiseless manner . . . and with an efficiency and constancy" he had never known, while the "prospect of a pleasant evening circle" carried him through "the toils of the day." Though he did not always participate, he enjoyed watching the others play Boston and chess. In the spring of 1838 he was making a set of bronze and brass gilt chessmen and a billiard table for their use.[18]

At the same time, of course, his new mode of life entailed more responsibilities of various kinds. About that spring he employed Charles G. Loring as his business agent in Boston. He and Louisa soon began to look for another residence and hoped for a while to get the elegant Palazzo Giacomini in Piazza San Gaetano. Twice during the year Louisa had a miscarriage. In July Horatio was at Carrara with his sister, evidently emerging from a despondent mood; he walked some fifteen miles a day and began, he said, "to get my spirits again." By this time he was visited by almost every American who came to the city and importuned by Italians of all classes for favors. "A proud and savage concentration is sometimes necessary here," he wrote Henry. "*Porcupine* is the word here, you may depend!" "If I were to tell you," he wrote Greene in November,

> the titthe [*sic*] of what I have gone through in 8 months of excitement and botheration of one kind and another you would give me credit for a tough gizzard.

He had lived in a

> state of hurry anxiety & bustle . . . which with me entirely kills the conversible faculty and leaves me as soon as I retire from toil and battle only fit to mope and smoke or read merely to stop thought.

By this time he had moved with his family to Casa or Casino Leblanc, in Via di Bardi, across the river, on the hill above the

Ponte alle Grazie. At the top of the hill was a large garden, from where an extensive view of the city was obtained. Here he was two miles from his studio and got both exercise and quiet.[19]

Throughout their married life, however, the Greenoughs received much company and entertained a great deal. He was seldom without a guest in the evening, Horatio wrote Henry early in 1839, and later that year he reported that he regularly passed his evenings in a full room.[20] Among their visitors in the winter of 1838–39 were Benjamin D. Greene and his wife (one of Josiah Quincy's daughters, with whom Louisa had grown up). Horatio presented Greene with an original drawing and Greene witnessed his signing his contract for the group for the Capitol. Mrs. Greene was delighted by an evening spent at Casa Leblanc during the Christmas season in 1838. There were eight guests besides the four members of the household, and the meal, served at the American hour of half-past six, was, she recorded in her diary,

> entirely in the Italian style, & exactly to my taste. The dessert was on the table . . . presenting flowers, fruit & confectionary. After the soup had been dismissed, olives and butter were handed to each guest—then oyster patties, then fish, & a succession of dishes —pudding, pies, confectionary, wines of every kind, & black coffee —all left the table together.[21]

In the billiard room they had tea and cordials and heard music.

During this winter a young New York couple in Florence, the Frederick Bronsons, were also impressed by the Greenoughs' style of living. He had, Mrs. Bronson reported, "a very rich wife and . . . lives very handsomely." She thought, however, that his calling cards, inscribed simply "Greenough," suited "the rank of 'Bonaparte' rather than an American sculptor."[22]

By the spring of 1839 the Virginia painter William J. Hubard and his wife were in the city. Greenough told Hubard a Massachusetts legend about King Philip which he made the subject of a painting at this time, and sat to him for a portrait. A romantic treatment of a classical artist, it depicts Greenough, clad in a smock, seated in his studio, surrounded by a few artistic properties, presumably Arno and another dog, and a few of his works: the bust of Héloïse and possibly that of Venus and the statue of one of the Thomson boys. After his return to America Hubard often thought of the "charming hours" they all spent together and asked his wife to "play the music that Mrs. G. frequently delighted me with."[23]

This spring, apparently in company with the Hubards, Greenough's sister Louisa returned to America. About this time the news reached him of his brother Alfred's engagement. He felt "more & more as living in exile," he wrote Dr. John C. Warren. "I confess I often pine and languish for a sight of my friends at home," he wrote Henry; "and when I think how many years must pass before I can return, I feel as if I were living at a foolish sacrifice of comfort."[24]

He was not long, however, without relatives in Florence. This spring John Greenough and his wife arrived from London, John having fallen into debt again and abandoned that city permanently. In 1840 young Richard Greenough was also in Florence, just beginning his artistic career. In ill health, he returned to Boston in the spring of 1841, accompanied by John and his wife.[25]

According to John, Horatio was hoping at this time to be appointed chargé to several Italian states, planned to secure John as his secretary, and for this reason declined the consulship at Leghorn when it was offered him on the death of Appleton in April 1840.[26] No official record of such an offer, however, seems to exist.

Among the American visitors to Florence in these years were two or three whom Greenough knew particularly well. He and young Charles Sumner had some animated discussions of art,

HORATIO GREENOUGH
by William James Hubard, 1838–1839.
(Courtesy of the Valentine Museum, Richmond, Va.)

religion, and politics in the summer of 1839, and he drew a sketch of Sumner. In Sumner's estimation Greenough was

a wonderful fellow, an accomplished man, and master of his art . . . a thinker of great force, and a scholar who does not trust to translations, but goes to the great originals.

"As men—as specimens of the human race to be looked up to and imitated," he felt that Chantrey, David, and the English sculptors at Rome were "not to be mentioned in the same breath."[27]

In 1840–41 Edward Everett and his family were in Florence for a year, during which time the Greenoughs saw a good deal of him. He was impressed by their quarters and their "elegant" dinners. Soon after he arrived he was invited to one in company with Capponi, Sir George Back (the Arctic explorer), the Swedish Count Gräberg (a granducal chamberlain) and his daughter, the engraver Samuele Jesi, a printer and a jurist.[28] While in the city Everett wrote an article, printed in the *Boston Miscellany* in 1842, about all the American sculptors in Italy (by that time a sizable group). Of them all, he regarded Powers as the best.

About the time the Everetts left Florence, late in 1841, the George Calverts arrived, to stay until the following spring. In his book, *Scenes and Thoughts* in Europe, published shortly afterward, Calvert praised Greenough as a man and an artist.

The first three of these years after Greenough's return to Florence, full as they were of changes in his personal life, were his busiest professionally, and the first year of his marriage was his most productive of all. "No man since Canova has undertaken more," he wrote Henry early in 1839.[29] He thought of having an engraved edition of his works published by subscription, together with the poems that had been written about them. At the end of the year he had about $4000 worth of works ready to ship to America, but he decided to hold them until spring in the hope that the current high tax on such items might be reduced.[30] In the three years he put into marble or clay some thirty-three pieces and finished three others in addition to his work on the marble "Washington."

Probably he began late in 1837 to put in marble the casts he made on his recent visit to America. In December he modeled the bust of a Mrs. Cabot who was in the city with her husband (probably the Edward C. Cabots). Early the next year he was working on one of Colonel Thomson. That spring he finished an ideal head in American clay and executed for Henry's wife of a few months one of her brother Frank Boott, another Florence visitor; "no one," candidly reported Boott, "sees a likeness in it." In 1838 he also completed the busts for Gray, which were shipped by the end of the year, and two for Dr. Warren, who was in Florence that spring: one of Warren and one of his father Dr. John Warren. The latter was one of Greenough's most feeling portraits. In the spring of 1839 he was working on a medallion of the younger Mrs. Warren. He may have done one or two other busts in 1838. One of Machiavelli by him was exhibited by the owner, wealthy New Yorker Rufus Prime, at the Apollo Association in 1839, presumably soon after it reached America. Francis Alexander wanted a bust of his infant daughter Francesca and sent sketches which arrived in the spring of 1838. Greenough was disinclined, however to proceed with such uncertain data and nothing further of the project seems to be known. Early in 1839 he was finishing a colossal bust of Franklin, which he sent to America with the "Washington" and presented to the Boston Athenaeum in 1842 or 1843. He also executed, possibly at this time, a life-size bust of the same subject, for which his authority was evidently Houdon's bust. Late in 1839 he was working on a second marble of Clay for Clay's son-in-law James Erwin. By 1840 presumably he had modeled a bust of Wilde, which was eventually put in marble;

Wilde was to have had it for the cost of the material but never felt he could afford it.[31]

The other new works on which Greenough was engaged in these years were remarkably varied. Most ambitious was his group for the Capitol, which he modeled in 1839 and part of 1840. About 1838 he executed a recumbent statue of his greyhound Arno, for a Mr. Whitwell of Boston. It was finished by the spring of 1839, precise in anatomical details, yet handsomely stylized. Not long afterward it was acquired by Everett and for many years lay in his library.[32]

Three of these works were executed for John Lowell, "The Little Rebel": a life size statue of Venus Victrix, a bust of Venus (apparently a copy of the "Aphrodite" or "Venus Victrix" of Capua in the Naples Museum), and a bas-relief of the Judgment of Paris. Lowell was to have the privilege of exhibiting the first and third for his benefit in America. He died, however, in 1840 before they were shipped. In February 1842 they (and the following year the bust of Venus) were presented by the executors of his estate to the Boston Athenaeum.[33] Only the statue seems to have survived. The relief, at any rate, was ordered after it.

Of all Greenough's private works in marble to this point the statue of Venus was the most ambitious. It was nearly five feet high and the price must have been around $2000. Probably it had its inception three years before in Greenough's negotiations with John Lowell, Jr., but Cooper suggested another inspiration when he inquired if it were a "homage" to Greenough's bride or a "votive offering" to propitiate the goddess. The model was begun in the fall of 1837, about the time of his marriage. Being his first attempt to represent the complete female figure, it gave him, he wrote Allston, a "dreadful battle." He meticulously examined both nature and the antique, concluding that the "Venus dei Medici," though the best of all female statues, was unrealistic in details. So deeply interested did he become in his study that he thought of remodeling the figure, but he probably did not do so. The model was finished by February 1838, but work on it at Carrara was delayed nine months. It was far advanced by the fall of 1839 and probably finished by the next summer. By some admirers it was pronounced "exquisite," but it was not calculated for popularity.[34] It has character, however, in its freedom of conception and uncompromising fidelity to nature. Especially in contrast to the vogue established by Powers' nudes during the next few years it is praiseworthy for its avoidance of both the sentimental and the conventional.

Greenough's other patron of note at this period was Professor Edward E. Salisbury, oriental language scholar at Yale, then traveling in Europe. Befriending the bereaved Halsey family, Salisbury learned of the orders Halsey had placed with Greenough, and late in 1837 he took them over. The small "Washington" not having been begun, he proposed instead a work of "a more poetical character" and evidently suggested two subjects from the Bible: St. John forbidden by the angel to worship him (from Revelation) and Joshua bidding the sun stand still. Delighted by the prospect of a new ideal work, Greenough promptly sent a sketch for a bas-relief of the first subject, which he proposed to execute for three hundred crowns. The second he said he dared not attempt, doubting that the art of sculpture could treat it adequately. As alternatives he suggested the seraph Abdiel leaving the rebel host as described in Book Five of *Paradise Lost* (suggested to him years before by Allston) and Jesus driving the money-changers from the temple. Though he feared the last, too, was an impossible subject, he felt it would be "worth the disgrace of defeat" to have expressed it partially. He wished that if Salisbury ordered statues they would be life-size, for which he named a price of four thousand francesconi.

A three-foot size he priced at six hundred francesconi, including, as he now did in his prices, the amount for boxing though not shipping. In January 1838 Salisbury ordered a relief of St. John and the angel and a small statue of Abdiel.[35]

Greenough began the statue first. The subject was a loftier one than any offered by classical mythology, he wrote Allston, adding with characteristically mixed feelings:

Alas! I feel, believe me Sir, how far I am from being worthy to speak of these great works but I have always thought it best aim at what we dream of in our warmest aspirations rather than to measure our strength and mark out our course by the rules of logic.

In the design of the figure he was apparently influenced by Ammanati's bronze "Marte Gradivo" in the Uffizi Gallery. It was rough-hewn by April 1839 (with no more than one-twentieth of an inch left for him to remove) and apparently finished by the fall, signed "HG 1839." It and the "Aristides" were shipped to America the following summer. Despite its diminutiveness, the "Abdiel" has a heroic air. To Sumner it seemed a "winged, heaven-born Achilles."[36] Greenough proposed to make another statue of the same subject the size of the "Apollo Belvedere," but did not.

The relief for Salisbury, which went to the blocker when the "Abdiel" was returned, cost Greenough more time and money than the statue; he could, he said, have made two busts for eight hundred francesconi during the time he spent on it. It was his first experience with working marble in relief, a mode of sculpture which he had suggested partly from a desire to experiment with it and partly because he thought it well suited to the relatively small homes of Americans. Twice he modeled the work completely.[37] Some eighteen inches square, it represents a bearded man with outstretched hands, kneeling to a young, winged angel, who extends one hand in protest and with the other points upward. It is starkly simple and purged of emotion, like some of the early Greek reliefs Greenough admired. The effeminate details of the angel, however, are somewhat out of keeping with the design as a whole.

During these years Greenough was also occupied with the Gibbs monument, for which the design had at last been settled. According to a Gibbs family tradition, Allston designed it,[38] but he probably offered suggestions at the most. For the features of George and Mary Gibbs, Greenough depended on copies of Stuart's portraits of them, which were sent him by Miss Gibbs. By September 1839 he had finished the architectural part and modeled the sculpture, and before 1843 the complete monument was in America.[39] It was erected in St. Mary's Episcopal Church on the Gibbs estate at Portsmouth, Rhode Island, where the couple were buried. The overall dimensions are some nine and a half by five feet. It consists of a bas-relief and an inscription, flanked by two columns ornamented by fruit and foliage and topped by an entablature and pediment. The relief depicts two draped figures, representing Gibbs and his wife, between whom stands a winged angel, pointing upward with one hand and clasping with the other a hand of Gibbs, whom he is leading away. (Gibbs had died some twenty years before his wife.) There was nothing like it in America, Horatio proudly said when he urged Henry to go to see it. It was in notable contrast to the flamboyance of much contemporary grave sculpture in America and Europe, following rather traditions in antiquity and the Renaissance. The presence of the angel suggests that Greenough had modified his early admiration for the realism of the Greek steles and the tomb figures of Donatello,[40] but Miss Gibbs' objection to his first design may have had some such influence on the final one. Though the combination of mythology and portraiture is not particularly happy, that of austerity and sentiment is. It is perhaps the best of all his preserved reliefs, certainly evidence of the early mastery of his latest style.

The reliefs on which Greenough worked in these years—Salisbury's, Lowell's, Miss Gibbs', and those on the "Washington" chair—represent the emergence in his art of a new style or stylistic variant, the last which may be distinguished in his development. Generally classical in nature, it is less severe than that of some of his portraits and his "Washington." The male figures are softened, female and infant figures introduced, and details more often elaborated. He had, of course, been interested in the relief tradition of Greek sculpture from his Roman days. The date at which he began to work in this sculptural mode, however, was significant. It coincided with the date of his marriage. Perhaps his renewed interest in religious themes, which also dated from this period, was partly encouraged by his new status. Certainly he became more conscious, as the master of a home of his own, of the interior decoration of domestic edifices, for which many of his reliefs were designed. Cooper was essentially perspicacious in suggesting that in Greenough's art at this time an address to the female spirit was recognizable.

The goddess, however, proved not altogether kind. In 1839 Louisa had a third miscarriage, this time a boy of six months.[41] Not until 1845 did she give birth to a living child. The problem saddened and unsettled her and Horatio's life together during nearly a decade. Eventually it influenced them to leave Florence for several years. As a direct consequence the course of Greenough's career was deflected and indirectly the whole of his speculative thought was affected.

A New American School

A few weeks after Greenough's marriage another American sculptor and his wife took up residence in Florence: the Hiram Powerses. Born in Vermont, Powers had grown up in Ohio, had largely taught himself his art, and was just becoming known. His first years in Florence were difficult ones, but he soon became by far the most popular and financially successful of all American sculptors and more than any other established the character of the whole school.

In the beginning of their association especially Greenough endeavored to promote Powers' career. He lent Powers workmen and marble, introduced him to the chief artists of Florence (at a dinner he arranged beforehand for some of Powers' works to be placed conspicuously about the house and thus had the conversation devolve on him), purchased his bust of John Quincy Adams (for $1000), recommended him for government employment, and praised him more than once in print. He particularly admired Powers' busts of Webster and Adams. Powers' "Eve," begun in 1840, he found "somewhat cold and measured."[1]

One of the busts Powers modeled in 1838 was of Greenough. He began to put it in marble, but, one of the workmen having spoiled the block, it remained in plaster in his studio until after Greenough's death; at Louisa's request he then executed the marble. Greenough pronounced the model "admirable," and Powers thought it as good as any he had made.[2] It not only faithfully reproduced Greenough's handsome head but also suggested a great deal of his aristocratic air.

From the beginning the two sculptors cooperated in various professional respects, to their mutual advantage. Together they imported American clay for modeling; it was more tenacious than some Italian varieties and susceptible of a high degree of finish.[3] In the fall of 1838, together with three other artists in the city, they decided to form a club which would meet weekly The next summer they gave their support to efforts being made to reopen a new quarry near Carrara and to improve the methods of transporting the stone.[5] About the fall of 1843, apparently after preliminary consultation, they succeeded independently in developing a new modeling mixture, a plaster of Paris which, unlike clay, did not expand and therefore obviated the need of casting. They also devised instruments with which to stipple the surface of works modeled in this mixture to achieve a fine finish. Greenough was increasingly pleased with it and thereafter used it exclusively for figures; it was reportedly less desirable for busts. (After Greenough's death, Powers denied him any credit for the mixture or the tools.)[6]

There was also from the beginning a good deal of personal association between the Greenough and Powers families. During the fatal illness of little Jimmie Powers early in 1838 Greenough arranged for his friend Dr. Vincenzo Andrieni to be called in. That summer while he and his wife were briefly out of the city, his sister stayed with the Powerses and so endeared herself to them that their next child, born that September, was named for her. In 1838 Powers modeled her bust also. The wives of the two sculptors were friendly though not intimate. Mrs. Greenough "is a very fashionable woman," Mrs. Powers wrote to her mother a few years later,

> goes to balls, parties, operas, etc., and as I can do nothing of the kind, of course we are not such congenial spirits, but she calls on me two or three times each six months.

By that time the Greenoughs had moved to Palazzo Pucci, one of the great residences in Florence. They lived, Mrs. Powers thought,

> in splendid style. Being possessed of an ample fortune they live in a palace & she has her carriage, servants, etc. . . . of course has little time or inclination to visit me in a social manner. She is amiable & friendly and I have stated the above not as a complaint, but merely as a matter of fact.[7]

Much as they had in common, both Greenoughs and both Powerses were chiefly remarkable for their differences, and there could have been little genuine congeniality between the two couples. Powers, a Yankee mechanic type, had slight interest in books, the art of the past or Italy. His wife regretted that he had not allowed his interest in steam engines to determine his occupation, for then she thought they would never have come abroad. Partly because of his cultural deficiencies, in fact, he achieved his phenomenal popularity with his countrymen, and he cultivated the Yankee role as his fame grew. (It was reported that he preferred to model in American clay because of his intense patriotism.) His forte was portraiture, but his reputation was sensationally secured by his nude "Eve" and "Greek Slave" statues, which were widely exhibited in the middle 1840's, and he made his fortune chiefly by reproductions of a few ideal pieces (one hundred and twelve of his "Proserpine" alone). Less broadly artistic than Greenough, he seemed more nearly identified with his art. "In Powers," George Hillard thought,

> the whole man appeared to have passed out through the hand and chisel. Humor excepted, there was nothing in him which was not in his marble. Greenough was a man of large powers and various accomplishments, in whom the practice of his art was but one mode of intellectual expression.[8]

As he became more successful, Powers exhibited more conceit. Whereas shortly before he came to Italy he publicly disclaimed the assertion of a Washington critic that he was superior to Greenough, he told Hawthorne after Greenough's death that Greenough was unable to make a good bust. He so lorded it over his fellow sculptors in Florence that according to the painter Miner Kellogg most of them moved to Rome within a few years. Powers and Greenough had one minor rift—about the summer of 1847 (when Greenough, chosen by Powers to be the arbiter of a quarrel between certain other persons, gave an unsatisfactory decision), but otherwise they were on friendly and intimate terms throughout their acquaintance. The fact was, Charles Eliot Norton felt, "all to Greenough's credit."[9]

Yet it was to a great extent because of the tremendous sensation which Powers created that the whole profession of sculpture in America became during the 1840's and 1850's rapidly more famous, more lucrative, and more generally attractive to young artistic natures and that so many of the new sculptors went to Italy. Between the time Powers came and Greenough left (in 1851) some thirteen followed them: Clevenger, Brown, Ives, Mozier, Stephenson, Story, Galt, Randolph Rogers, Hart, Richard Greenough, Akers, Barbee, and Bartholomew. All but four —Bartholomew, Richard Greenough, Stephenson, and Story, who went to Rome—settled in Florence.

Of them all perhaps Crawford, who settled in Rome in 1835, was closest in spirit to Greenough. The two first knew each other through Greene in 1839 and first met when Crawford came to Florence in the summer of 1840. He was, Greenough thought, "a fine spirited young man" with "the proper spirit for an artist," whose ideas on art had received perhaps too little attention in Rome.[10] Crawford's interest in heroic and monumental sculpture and his republican sympathies agreed with Greenough's. There was little further personal association between the two, however, and little if any influence was exerted by the older on the younger man.

With most of the American sculptors in Florence Greenough's relationships were casual, partly because he was often out of the city in the 1840's, and on none was his influence noticeable. Mozier, one of the few interested primarily in ideal figures, wrote enthusiastically of Greenough's work in the late 1840's but after his death told Hawthorne that he had not the slightest inventive genius, though he was an excellent critic of art.[11] The forte of the whole group, like that of Powers, was portraiture, in which they, like him, aimed at a photographic realism of dress as well as feature. Their ideal works, in the general neo-classical tradition, tended, like his, to the feminine and the graceful rather than the heroic and severe. Even Richard Greenough, who might have been regarded as his brother's most likely follower, exhibited these characteristics.

Shortly after Powers, several new American painters also took up residence in Florence, among them Luther Terry, Kellogg, George Loring Brown, Abel Nichols, and James Cameron. A few Americans who were not artists also settled there in these years. Yet with none of these countrymen was Greenough's association so close as it had been with those in Florence in the preceding decade. The artists of the 1840's had, generally speaking, other backgrounds and other esthetic principles. About this time, moreover, Greenough's interests in areas other than his art deepened, bringing him into new associations. During the last decade or more of his residence in Florence his most intimate friends were neither Americans nor artists, but a small circle of European intellectuals.

In the Palace of a Bonaparte

A few months after his marriage—in the midst of his greatest productiveness—Greenough made a significant decision. Being at last financially able to do so, he determined to execute fewer works and to devote himself more to ideal subjects. "I find the imagination—" he wrote Allston early in 1838,

at least mine—will not bear fruit by plowing manuring & sowing. . . . I must let the sun shine and the rain fall only on the ground whence I would see a real flower of the heart & of the soul spring.

He particularly resented being urged by patrons to complete their orders. "Our good folk think," he complained a year later, "statues can be turned out like yards of sheeting." The tenor of a letter he wrote Gilmor this spring was typical of his mood. Gilmor had written to inquire his estimate of the cost of ornamenting a monumental column (possibly the Washington monument in Baltimore) with trophies. "I do not pretend to offer any great Bargains," he replied,

> because I employ the best workmen & pay them at a high rate. . . . I cannot say either that I can finish them at a given day—as I have suffered too much mortification and loss from the failure of my agents to fulfill their contracts ever to think of binding myself when I cannot bind them.

He strongly recommended bronze instead of marble, in spite of the greater expense. Evidently nothing came of the project.[1]

Between the end of 1839 and the summer of 1842, when he left Florence for America, he apparently executed only about eight new pieces. Late in 1839 he began a bust of Capponi, which by the next summer was finished and had brought him more credit, he said, than all he had done before in that line. In accordance with his wishes it was presented to the Academy of Fine Arts in Florence after his death.[2] By the fall of 1840 he had two "beautiful heads" far advanced for a Mr. Goddard.[3] That year he undertook a statue of two-year old Ada Reviczky, daughter of Count Adam Reviczky, Austrian minister to the Tuscan court, for the Countess. The model was completed by July and the marble by early 1841. The child, lightly draped, was seated, observing a butterfly on her hand, on a grassy bank, on which were a wreath of flowers and a lizard. A Florentine critic praised the work enthusiastically in one of the city's newspapers, noting especially the symbolic nature of the insect (the emblem of Psyche in classical mythology and in Dante of the evolution of the human spirit) and of the flowers (representing to him innocence). It was mounted on a pedestal of dark purple oriental marble, with raised gold lettering giving the name and age of the child, and placed in the center of the Reviczky salon. The next year Greenough was working on a bust of the young Countess, whom he thought very beautiful.[4]

Late in June or early in July 1841 he began a bust of Lucifer, inspired further by *Paradise Lost;* it was finished the next year. It was, he thought, his "highest effort in that line"—probably meaning in ideal busts. Calvert thought it effectively represented a countenance of beauty not yet blighted by deformity of mind. It was modeled appropriately in his heavy style, but its profusion of curls, dilated eyes and nostrils, and base of writhing serpents and two small devils' heads gives it a bizarre effect. In 1841 he also executed a bust of his nephew J. F. Curtis, two-year old child of T. B. Curtis' second marriage. Possibly this year he remodeled the head of his "Abdiel" for Elizabeth Howard Bartol (sister of his college mate John Howard and wife of C. A. Bartol), who had been promised a bust as early as 1837; the helmet is more elaborate than that of the statue and the features resemble those of the "Apollo Belvedere." Besides a miniature copy of the "Washington," Capponi evidently wanted a head of Washington, and the retired Russian diplomat Count Ivan Hippolyte Mouravieff-Apostol, living in Florence, was particularly eager for a bust of W. E. Channing.[5]

At the same time that Greenough's interest and creative energies contracted in some areas, however, they expanded in a variety of others. As he turned more to ideal subjects and gradually abandoned portraiture, he began to work in relief and adapted traditions besides the classical heroic to his purposes. He became interested in another plastic material—bronze. Repeatedly he recommended that his group for the Capitol be cast in this material and perhaps coveted the order for the projected bronze doors of that building. Everett recommended him as the artist for them early in 1841.[6]

He also became more interested in literary composition. In the summer of 1839 he read several essays which he had written to Sumner, who was much impressed. One was on the nude, prompted no doubt by criticisms of the "Washington." During the same summer Everett urged him to write a popular history of painting, architecture, and sculpture, perhaps to be published in a "Common School Library" series, but he was evidently not attracted by this prospect. In January 1841 he let Everett read seven of his essays on various subjects: the presepio of San Romano, in which he discussed the taste of the uneducated; the public monuments of London, to which he objected; decency in works of art (perhaps the same as his essay on the nude); academies (he accused Americans of being fond of getting up academic machinery but of not achieving genuine social cooperation); Gibraltar (apparently a descriptive sketch); the dress of Washington in sculpture, which piece he treated in the form of a vision; and architecture.[7]

During these years Greenough also devoted more time to reading. Here too he exercised a sharp critical faculty, often directed by his strong nationalistic bias. He thought Prescott had made a mistake "for his reputation with posterity" by choosing a European subject in his history of Ferdinand and Isabella "when so many of our local histories cry for a hand to record them." As an American author he would prefer to take his chances with a volume of "annals of Salem" than a history of the decline and fall of the Turkish empire. "This is what we want," he wrote Paulding thanking him for a presentation copy of *A Gift from Fairyland,* "not a starveling and puritanical abstinence from works of fancy & taste, [but] an *adaptation* of them to our institutions, and a harmonizing of them with our morals or what we mean shall be such." He enjoyed Paulding's *Letters from the South,* John L. Stephens' *Incidents of Travel in Egypt, Arabia, Petraea, and the Holy Land,* and Cooper's history of the American Navy; noted the appearance of Longfellow's *Hyperion* and Rufus Dawes' *Nix's Mate;* and objected to the strictures of F. J. Grund in *The Americans.*[8]

He began to buy more books of his own. His evenings were customarily spent in his library, he wrote Capponi about the end of 1839, though he felt obliged to add, "Lucus a *non* lucendo" ("A grove from not being light; an illogicality").[9] Compared to the libraries of some of his Florentine friends his was small, but eventually it evidently consisted of a thousand or so volumes. Six cases of books were shipped to America with his final effects,[10] and at the sales of what remained of them in 1890 and 1895 at least some five hundred works seem to have been offered. In the catalogue for the second of these sales other books were indiscriminately listed with his, but many of his may be almost certainly identified. Of the works presumably his listed in both catalogues the greatest number are literary, followed in order by art works, histories, descriptions and travel accounts, biographies, scientific works, philosophical and political works, and foreign language dictionaries. In literature most of the celebrated authors of Greece, Rome, England, Italy, and France and a few of Germany and Spain were represented. Among the American authors were his friends Cooper, Calvert, G. W. Curtis, Paulding, Prescott, Tuckerman, and Willis. The historians included Bancroft, Botta, Galluzzi, Guicciardini, Lanzi, and Pufendorf. The chief artists represented were Cellini, Leonardo da Vinci, Flaxman, Hogarth, Palladio, Raphael, Reynolds, and Vasari.[11] Altogether, it would seem to have been the library of a broadly cultivated gentleman rather than of a specialist.

He acquired, too, more paintings, engravings, and other objects of art. Among Louisa's possessions after his death were a "Herodias" by Van Dyck, a Bronzino, an "Adoration of the Magi" from the Veronese school, a portrait of Ugolino probably by Bezzuoli, the interior of Siena Cathedral by a Leblanc (probably Alexandre, whom Greenough knew) and landscapes by one of the Markós (probably Károly, who lived in Florence in the 1840's).[12] By 1840, the Greenoughs were, as Everett found, "charmingly situated amidst pictures of the Ancient Masters, books, & music,"[13]

Chiefly as a scholar and a gentleman Greenough became more intimately acquainted in various Florentine circles in these years. He now apparently saw more of Capponi. In the spring he was presented with portraits of Capponi and his daughters and about this time expedited some of Capponi's correspondence and exchange of books with Ticknor and Prescott.[14] He was also on familiar terms with Mouravieff-Apostol, over eighty years of age but still keen, who lived with his wife and daughter in the great Palazzo Pandolfini. A close early companion of Czar Alexander I, Mouravieff-Apostol had gone into exile because of his sons' revolutionary activity. He was a bibliophile—with an interest about this time in securing American historical works, a student of Greek literature, an essayist, and a moral philosopher—with an admiration for W. E. Channing. In 1841 Horatio had Henry send copies of Channing's works for him and for another such admirer, the Marquis Bocella of Lucca.[15] Yet another close friend of Greenough's by the late 1840's was Count Ruspoli, member of a distinguished Tuscan family noted for its liberal political sentiments. Two of the Count's sisters, he thought, were "just like our best Bostonians."[16]

Increasingly in these years Horatio and Louisa went into society. They had a box at the opera, in the second row. They went to court a few times a season (balls were weekly at the Pitti); to Fenzi's; to the Thomsons', whose parties in Palazzo Ximenes were voted the pleasantest in town; and to affairs of the British Minister (then Lord Holland). In consequence of visiting the "Washington," the Marchioness Lenzoni, last descendant of one branch of the Medici family, invited Greenough to her small, semi-weekly receptions, famed for being attended by a more intellectual company than any others in Florence. He began to know better and to like some of the English colony: Back, Lord Fitzwilliam's nephew Mr. Hume, Lady Davy, the sculptor E. B. Stephens, the painter Charles

Skottowe, probably the historian George Grote and his wife (who were furnished a letter of introduction to him from Sumner), and the poet John Kenyon. He invited Wilde, Powers, the Piedmontese refugee G. A. Bezzi, Capponi, and the actor Charles Kemble to dinner to meet Kenyon. In 1841 he and Louisa were particularly friendly with two English women in the city—Lady Bulwer and Mrs. Frances Trollope. Lady Bulwer wrote a complimentary article about him which appeared in the *Court Journal* in London in May. Mrs. Trollope was partial to the work of Powers, whom she had met in America. Wilde teased the two sculptors about their "rival belles" and in later years threatened to write an epigram about them.[17]

Among these Europeans Greenough habitually assumed the role of American spokesman. On one occasion, at tea at the home of a Russian woman, he was asked by an English official whether a certain American woman did not belong to "one of your great American families," to which his reply was, "We have no great families in America. We have colossal men." Another time, at Mouravieff-Apostol's, he "measured weapons" with the old Anglomane Count Golovkin, who "thought he could crush democracy with ease," proved that the Count's criticisms of America were based on errors of fact, and elicited an apology. A few years later at an English home, asked when America would pay her debts, he retorted, "As soon as she can get the better of some Oriental nation in an opium quarrel."[18]

During the years 1840 and 1841 Greenough's reputation reached its peak, in both Florence and America. In 1840, at its second annual sculpture exhibition, the Boston Athenaeum showed seven works by him—the greatest number shown at once in his lifetime: the busts of Kirkland, Cooper, Mary Curtis, and Psyche, the groups for Sears and Cabot, and the statue of Arno. That year in Florence he opened his studio in Via San Gallo, into which he moved his "Washington," statue of Ada

Reviczky, busts of Franklin and Capponi, and a cast or another marble of the "Psyche."[19] His exhibitions of these works there in January and February 1841 were highly successful.

Two Italian societies of artists bestowed memberships on him about this time. In September 1840 he was unanimously elected to the faculty of the Academy of Fine Arts in Florence with the honorary rank of Associate Professor of Sculpture. The only dissenting spirit was Bartolini, now claiming that Greenough trampled on him, who left the room. Greenough doubly esteemed the honor, coming as it did in the midst of his altercations with Acting Secretary of State Vail. Words of sympathy from the Academicians were, he wrote in his letter of acceptance to Secretary Niccolini, "di un valore inapprezzabile per chi non la vissuto lunghi anni di solitario esiglio" ("of a value not to be appreciated by one who has not spent long years of solitary exile"); they were "l'acqua nel deserto" ("water in the desert"). At the Academy's annual exhibition that fall he showed a bust, probably Capponi's, and in 1845 that work. In March 1841 he was made an honorary member of the Academy of Science, Letters and Arts of the Tiber Valley, recently organized in the nearby town of San Sepolcro.[20]

In April or May 1841 he and Louisa moved their residence again, across the river to the magnificent seventeenth-century Palazzo Pucci in Via Pucci. This edifice was then divided between two owners, one of them a Pucci and the other the Marquis Felice Baciocchi, a descendant of Napoleon's sister Eliza. The Greenoughs lived in quarters belonging to Baciocchi, which were entered from Via dei Servi. Greenough customarily referred to them as being in Casa Baciocchi. They were "splendid" quarters, Everett thought. The "carpets and wood fires" reminded Hillard, who visited there in the late 1840's, "of the comforts of home." Calvert remembered with pleasure "the easy, elegant hospitality of the *Palazzo Baciocchi.*" By this time the Greenoughs had a coachman, William, who remained in their employ for several years, and apparently two or three Italian servants: a cook, a maid, and probably a manservant. They customarily received on Saturdays.[21]

At precisely this stage in Greenough's career, however, a climax was also building up in the series of humiliations and frustrations which he suffered in connection with his government commissions. His difficulties in getting the group inspected, Vail's letter and his offer to resign the commission, the conditions of Hull's contract, the protest of his drafts on the Treasury, the government's failure to acknowledge the arrival of the "Washington"—all were deeply disturbing. His decision in the spring of 1842 not to return to America for many years represented the lowest ebb of his spirits if not the farthest tendency of his mind toward morbidity.

Meantime Louisa's health continued to be distressing. In July 1840 she had a fourth miscarriage. Probably on her account they made plans—soon abandoned—to go to America late that summer. In January 1842 she lost another child. The entries in her commonplace book during the following months were unusually melancholy, including several verses on death. On May 22 she entered a passage from Channing's second discourse on "Self-Denial" which included the sentence:

Think you it demands no power to calm the stormy elements of passion, to moderate the vehemence of desire [last six words crossed out], to throw off the load of dejection, to suppress every repining thought when the *dearest hopes are withered* [her italics] and to turn the wounded spirit from dangerous reveries and wasting grief, to the quiet discharge of ordinary duties?[22]

By this time her step-father had made plans to return to America, and she had decided to accompany him, spend the summer there, and come back to Florence in October. She dreaded going without Horatio, but she felt if she did not take this opportunity it would be "many long years" before she saw her friends again.[23] Apparently Horatio decided to spend the time of her absence in Paris. They closed their apartment, storing some of their household goods with the Powerses and the Clevengers, and left Florence about the middle of June. On the 16th of July Louisa and Russell sailed from Le Havre on the *St. Nicholas.*

Horatio passed some two months in Paris after they left, apparently occupying himself chiefly by reading and writing. Late in the summer he told Powers that he had been "studying," though he knew not "with what fruit." He renewed his acquaintance with General Cass, then the American minister to France; met H. K. Brown, who was enroute to Florence; saw something of several English painters; and probably called on Lamartine (Capponi furnished him with a letter of introduction), Gerard, and other French artists and writers. On the whole, however, he was no more pleased with the city than formerly. "The hurry and rush of business," he wrote Powers,

> the overwhelming interest of politics—the ten thousand clever and amusing nothings in the shape of theatrical entertainments raree shows etc leave but little taste or disposition in the public for the quiet and proper appreciation of art. Hence the crowd of pretenders—the shop window exhibitions—the seizing on every passing event that promises a momentary interest and *all for money.*[24]

Late in the summer, still waiting to hear from Louisa, he had decided that if she was no longer planning to return and go with him to Florence, he would go to America in October. When she wrote she evidently said she had decided to stay longer and perhaps transmitted advice from his family and friends that he come home, if for no other reason than to see about the proper placing of the "Washington." On the 28th of September he sailed from Le Havre, on the *Emerald,* for New York.

The Green Land and the Old Battle

The *Emerald* reached its destination on September 22. Announcing his arrival to Henry, Horatio reported himself exhilirated by his first look at "these green woods, this brilliant town, this world of living and acting men."[1] He proceeded to Boston, where he and Louisa stayed for a while with the T. B. Curtises. About the middle of November Horatio and Louisa went to Washington, where during the next five months he was chiefly occupied with the problem of relocating his statue.

He noticed with interest the artistic changes in the city, though he was not altogether pleased by them. The new buildings he pronounced "respectable" and the post office "the handsomest palace in the country," but he thought the "ornamental department of the Capitol," the interior of which had been coated with white lead, "controlled by the demon of bad taste." "The great material interests," he wrote Henry, "absorb the country (as is natural), and the most proper thing for an artist here to do is to keep quiet and exert an indirect and gentle influence in his own sphere."[2]

Soon after his arrival he was asked by Robert M. Patterson, Master of the Mint in Philadelphia, for advice about contemplated changes in the coinage. He had at various times, for his own pleasure, prepared designs for coins, and he sent sketches of three of these designs to Patterson. Apparently the first substituted an "imperial" eagle for that already in use; the second depicted on one side a group of Indian corn (for this he expressed his partiality, partly because this product was a staple from Maine to Georgia) and on the other the figure of Liberty kneeling to the eagle; the third represented "Industry and Plenty—Agriculture and Mechanics" and showed a figure sowing grain. On the reverse side of each coin he apparently preferred that only its value be stated in Roman letters. Though

Patterson admired all Greenough's designs as "truly classical," he felt they departed too radically from the current law, which required the eagle and the figure or bust together with the name of Liberty on almost all coins. Greenough's figure of the sower he feared would be "attacked as a Virginia field-hand" and so precipitate a controversy about slavery. Greenough agreed that changes in such designs had to accompany changes in public taste, but to that part of the law respecting the name of Liberty he took vigorous objection. It was a "barbarous age of art," he thought, quoting a Greek historian, which produced images so vague that the public could not be trusted to recognize them. "They who fancy that real freedom depends in any way upon such puerile adhesion to an antiquated and childish conception," he wrote,

> might get a different notion from a glance at the tower in the Grand Duke's Square in Florence, where that magic word inscribed by republican hands, has been allowed to remain in pure contempt by twenty successive princes; while the bayonets that glimmer below as the guard is relieved by day and night and the rattle of arms presented on the passing of each decorated minion, shews the difference between words written and things done.[3]

The political scene in Washington also dispirited Greenough. He was confirmed in his views of "old-fashioned federalism" as being "only a desire for monarchy or aristocracy, with monopolies, privileges, and all the old-fashioned furniture of old-fashioned governments" and feared that the people might not be "equal to the task of guarding their rights from the mistakes of their friends and the machinations of their foes." He found the number of jobbers "sickening" and the log-rolling of office holders "disgusting." "I think," he wrote Henry,

> the democracy is not pure nor high-minded. It is strong, very strong. If it cannot be enlightened, elevated, and placed on a level

with its position, if it cannot be raised to a sense of its duties, the country will be degraded.

In great contrast to the new politicians were such old ones as John Quincy Adams, on whom he and Louisa called several times. (Adams' Jubilee Oration of a few years before he had pronounced "godlike," "the clearest exposition of true American principles & policy.")[4]

Late in April, all other preparations for the removal of the "Washington" having been completed, he and Louisa moved to Wilmington, Delaware, where he proposed to stay until the pedestal came from Quincy. They left Washington, he said, partly for economic reasons but also to have "the sight of green things." "How lovely are the plains of this region," he wrote a few days after their move,

the verdure, the quiet, the up-going and down-floating sloops and brigs without number! My heart will always yearn after America.[5]

Early in May he visited the annual exhibition of the Pennsylvania Academy of the Fine Arts in Philadelphia, but was disappointed by all he saw. The "temple of Art" itself he felt could not compare "with the shop of a milliner or the office of a broker," both of which were "substantial and handsome."[6]

Late in May he and presumably Louisa made a trip to Boston. He investigated the delay about the pedestal, and the two completed negotiations for the sale of part of the Gore property for some $12,000. While in the city he was elected a Fellow of the American Academy of Arts and Sciences there.[7]

Possibly about this time he made arrangements with John L. O'Sullivan, editor of the *United States Magazine and Democratic Review,* to have two essays of his printed in that magazine: "Remarks on American Art" in July and "American Architecture" in August. Probably the first, like the second, was begun at least as early as 1836 and was among those which

Everett read in 1841. It consisted largely of a protest against artistic academies, whose establishment in America Greenough particularly feared. Their "great evils" for art students were, he wrote,

the insisting upon a routine, the depriving them of all choice or volition, the giving a false preference to readiness of hand over power of thought.

In contrast he described the system of apprenticeship practiced by the Renaissance masters, in which artists "formed one another": "Sympathy warmed them, opposition strengthened, and emulation spurred them on." He was, however, generally optimistic about the future of art in America. Democratic institutions were, he declared, "more favorable to a natural, healthful growth of art than any hotbed culture whatever." In conclusion he referred complimentarily to the National Academy of Design and to Powers.[8]

About this time, too, Greenough discovered that it was necessary for him to return to Europe immediately or wait until the next spring. Probably Louisa was pregnant. They decided to go immediately, and by July 3 Greenough was in Washington preparing for their departure. At this late date Cooper discovered that he was in America and wrote inviting him to Cooperstown. Probably he made no such visit, however. For a month he kept his note acknowledging his election to the American Academy of Arts and Sciences written to the secretary Charles Folsom, hoping they would meet. "It would have given me the greatest pleasure," he wrote Folsom again early in July, "to have . . . spoken with you not only of the past, but of the present and of the *mighty* future." By this time he was prepared to speak with his old faith in the democratic experiment, and he concluded,

I leave my country once more cheered in [page torn] belief that its institutions are working in the main agreeably to the intentions of their founders and eager in my humble walk to leave some trace my [*sic*] birth right as a citizen.[9]

He managed to spend a Sunday—the first in July—with Bryant on Long Island, again reveling in the natural scene. "Oh, the beautiful land!" he wrote Henry a few days later.

I saw bobolinks and fiery hangbirds rain gold among the green boughs; I lay on the velvet knolls and saw the snowball swing and nod in the breeze. It was all glorious.[10]

On July 13 he and Louisa sailed from New York, on the celebrated steamship the *Great Western,* for Liverpool.

A few days before, on the 9th, Allston died. In the day or so remaining to him in America after he heard the news Greenough wrote Josiah Qincy from New York, begging that Quincy use his influence to prevent "tampering" with the works which Allston had left. Several weeks later, writing from Europe, he made the same request of F. C. Gray. He tried to make both men, he said,

feel that works like his are always finished because the first lines that declared his *intention* were a *whole,* and never finished, because the last agony of elaboration was but an approximation to his thought.[11]

In September, when he was in Paris, Greenough received a letter from Richard Dana, evidently announcing Dana's intention of writing Allston's life and asking for recollections to be used in this connection. Greenough promised to write accordingly from Florence, but the project did not appeal to him. He thought it inevitable that Allston had not been fully appreciated in America since

In whatever walk of culture a Genius now labors, he is a Scourge. To the superficial—to the heartless, to the timeserving—to the false, he must be a scourge! In the early ages of art a genius threw open new sources of light and stood in a blaze of his own creation a demi-god; but now . . . even the artist whose mission seems so peaceful, bears a two-edged sword.

America has always acted toward her artists like a hen who has hatched ducklings. She cannot understand why they run to the water instead of thriving upon the dunghill—which only asks to be scratched in order to feed them all!

He blamed no one, yet he thought that "we should withhold our testimony until the nation awakes to a sense of the worth of her noble child." He felt, moreover, that even the best biography could not record Allston as an artist. "It is to the *men* who will be born *of him,*" he explained,

that I look for a fit monument of his career; and hence my sense of the duty of collecting and preserving his unfinished works, because they are full of invaluable instruction to kindred minds.[12]

Not until June 1844 did he write Dana again, and even then he did not produce a very coherent composition. He had set down many reminiscences of Allston, he said, but he had destroyed them all, convinced not only that he could say "nothing worthy his memory" but also that the painter's "works must ever be his monument as a poet." What he now sent was a brief description of Allston's early years, pointing up his independence of neo-classicism and attachment to older traditions; and a general assessment of his achievement, emphasizing his devotion to "Moral beauty" and attributing his slight production to his own will. "His was truly a great and noble example," he concluded.

Was such ever thrown away? Surely never. More even than in his works do I believe that he will live in the awaken'd mind of American art.[13]

Three months later, in September 1844, Greenough wrote a third letter to Dana largely about Allston, in answer to Dana's inquiry for information regarding the painter's association with German artists in Rome. Greenough knew little about this association, but he took up again the subject of Allston's limited popularity, which he now explained in even broader terms. "Allston," he declared,

> was an Idealist, and as the Ideal is a criticism of the actual, he shared the fate of those who in whatever branch of culture, rise where the mass cannot follow.

It was not the "mass" in the sense of the artistically uneducated that he blamed, however. He felt that Allston's influence would have been greater had his works been seen by "the body of the people in the interior," "the country folk," whose unfamiliarity with the "language of art" was "more than balanced by their freedom from the cant, the false taste and the frivolity of self sufficient society." It was this society which was at fault—not only in America but England. The facts seemed "a command to quit the paths of high art and to ornament and amuse society." But he construed them otherwise:

> There is a battle then . . . between what is and what might be, between poetry and fact—between the passions and the tastes of the day and the eternal beauty of Nature. . . . The battle is not merely in Art God knows It is everywhere. Alston is the head the chief—the Adam of American Idealists. He is the first of that noble Spartan band—sure to fall because the hosts of the Persians are overwhelming, but sure to carry with them to the ground whereon they fall not only the sense but the proof of having acted the noblest part that God grants to man, that of sacrificing body to mind—expediency to right—fact to truth—now to here after.[14]

In all three letters to Dana Greenough largely misrepresented the course of Allston's career by leaving out of consideration the painter's psychological difficulties and his peculiar frustrations in the American environment. It was his own state of mind at this time which the sculptor most clearly revealed. As he struggled with his disappointment over the reception of his "Washington," he consoled himself partly by hoping for a better judgment in the future but also by claiming a moral triumph in defeat. In so doing, he enlisted himself on the side of the martyrs in the old battle, which was not, it appeared, to have a new outcome in the new world.

The Water Cure

In Liverpool, the terminal port of their transatlantic voyage in the summer of 1843, the Greenoughs stopped for a short time. Horatio made characteristic observations on the scene and the people (their "groomed neatness" he took to be the "result of police interference"); probably visited nearby ruined Greenhalgh Castle, formerly the seat of the Greenough family in Lancaster; and with Louisa exchanged letters with the George Calverts, who were at Great Malvern in Worcestershire, at one of the newly opened hydropathic establishments there. Receiving an attractive description of the place, the Greenoughs altered their itinerary in order to visit it.[1]

Probably they arrived early in August. Both being impressed by what they saw, Horatio adopted water as his only drink[2] and began to take daily cold baths, and Louisa tried the treatment. Within a few weeks the results were so beneficial—especially to Louisa—that they became complete converts to the hydropathic system.

By no means a new therapy, hydropathy had a few years earlier been revived and systematized with phenomenal success by the Silesian Vincent Priessnitz, under the name of *das Wasser kur*. As administered by him and a horde of imitators in many countries, it consisted generally of repeated external applications of cold water (in the form of baths and wet packings), much walking in the open, and adherence to a bland diet. The water cure became one of the century's greatest fads (along with phrenology and spiritualism, with which its critics sometimes associated it). Yet without doubt it had an efficacious effect on certain functional disorders, and the simple life prescribed with it was conducive to good health.

Neither of the Greenoughs was a faddist, and apparently they were little impressed by what they had probably heard about the water cure from the Calverts (who had tried it previously) in Florence. Yet both were predisposed to favor homeopathic treatment of disease. By this time Louisa had, Frances B. Greenough said, a "horror" of doctors and medicine.[3]

The philosophy inherent in hydropathy, moreover, was calculated to appeal to Greenough. Nature was assumed to be the only curative agency, which the various hydropathic prescriptions merely assisted or imitated, and the natural and simple life was not only the healthiest but the best morally. "The refinements of high civilization," declared John Balbirnie in his *Philosophy of the Water Cure,* "are the most prolific sources of disease." The human body's functioning, pointed out James Wilson, founder of one of the establishments at Great Malvern, was, like that of all organized structures, in obedience to laws of action, and herein the properties of these structures transcended the mere physical or chemical properties belonging to inert matter. "Nature," he wrote, "is merely another word for *God in Creation.*"[4]

After a few weeks at Great Malvern, Horatio, leaving Louisa there, went to London. There he saw Joseph Severn, whom he had known in Rome; Everett, still the American minister, who introduced him to several Englishmen prominent in public affairs; and the architect Charles Barry, who took him to see the new houses of Parliament which Barry was then erecting in the Gothic Revival style. In Greenough's opinion they were "colossal gewgaws." By early September Louisa had arrived in the city.[5]

About the middle of that month the Greenoughs left London for Paris, where they stayed until September 26th. From there they traveled by way of Strasbourg, Munich, and Milan, reaching Florence about the middle of October. With them Louisa brought an Englishwoman, Turner, as housemaid.[6]

After so long an absence from his studio Horatio returned to it with new enthusiasm. Presumably he now saw that the blocking-out of the main figures of his group was begun. With his new modeling mixture he began a six-foot statue of David and by February 1844 had nearly finished it. It represented, according to one report, David leaning on the sword of Goliath; in one of his sketches, possibly a study for it, the head of Goliath rests on the ground. It was very finely conceived and executed, a traveling New Yorker thought, the countenance and bearing of David admirably expressing his "modest pride and subdued exultation" in his victory.[7]

Greenough also began late in 1843 or early the next year the recumbent figure of a St. Bernard dog for Colonel Perkins, presumably that set up a few years later on the Perkins lot in Mount Auburn Cemetery. He thought again of modeling another Venus. For Lowell's statue he executed a pedestal, which he planned to send in the spring.[8] By that time he was reported working "fiercely" on plans for an equestrian Washington. Hearing this news, Crawford sent him a message through Powers:

> Rest a little moment from thy labours dear Horatio, twil do thee good, and remember an over excitement of the mind defeateth much fine attention.[9]

Possibly he executed about this time a bust of Bostonian Charles Tappan; it was exhibited at the Boston Athenaeum in 1846. He may also have begun a bust of Christ.

A typical variety of other activities engrossed him during the fall and winter. Apparently he again considered bringing out a volume of appreciations of his work, to appear in London by arrangement of Wiley and Putnam of New York. He and

Louisa read with delight Prescott's *Conquest of Mexico;* went to court, to Lord Holland's, and most of all to the Mouravieff-Apostols'; and entertained several Americans. To sculptor John Cogdell, who was in Florence about this time with his wife, Greenough offered part of his studio, tools, clay, marble, and other artistic necessaries free for the winter, but the Cogdells, homesick, did not stay. Back in America Cogdell wished he had accepted this "noble offer"; he thought he might then have found Greenough "more warm."[10]

Meanwhile Horatio and Louisa continued to follow the general hydropathic regimen and to be pleased with its results. They abstained from tea, coffee, wine and spices; between the time they arrived in Florence and the end of the following February walked an estimated six hundred miles; and at that stage of the season had not had even a headache. "Imagine my delight," Horatio exulted to Henry,

> who thought I was made with an inherent necessity for periodical winter catarrhs and pocket hankerchiefs! This, then, is no fetich, no humbug, no nine days' wonder. Eureka![11]

Sometime after leaving America Louisa presumably had another miscarriage, of a particularly serious nature.[12] In any case, they had decided by February to go to Priessnitz's establishment at Grafenberg in Austrian Silesia to see the administration of the water cure there, with the particular hope that Louisa might be enabled by it to bring to birth a fully developed child. They left probably about the first of April, taking the English maid, Turner, with them. En route they stopped in Vienna, where the American minister, Daniel Jenifer, entertained them. Horatio was delighted by the "cleanliness and order" of its streets and its "well dressed, cheerful, and polite" population.[13] Probably near the end of the month they reached their destination.

Grafenberg was the name of a high hill, on top of which

Priessnitz's establishment was located. At the foot lay the village of Freiwaldau, where patients were also lodged. The hill was covered with fountains and paths for their use. Accommodations were, in the words of Murray's *Hand-Book for Travellers in Southern Germany* in 1850, "such, that patients should be prepared to rough it." The rooms were meagerly furnished, the fare coarse, and the treatment more severe than elsewhere. (Novelist J. W. DeForest, one of many who went to Grafenberg on Greenough's recommendation, lamented when he went on to the hydropathic establishment at Divonne that in contrast there was "no insanity here in the cure.") Priessnitz, a peasant by birth, was unprepossessing in appearance and manner but endowed with considerable shrewdness and skill and completely devoted to his practice. A unique feature of his administration of the water cure was his provision of various active amusements—shooting matches, outdoor fetes, and balls—for his patients. About the time Horatio and Louisa first went to Grafenberg the clientele numbered some seven or eight hundred and represented some fifteen nations. It was throughout the history of Priessnitz's establishment markedly upper class, though his rates were very low. "Noblemen could be seen chopping wood," remembered Frances B. Greenough, who was there in the 1840's: leaping, and jumping, to quicken their circulation, and high-born women sawing logs together with double-handed saws.[14]

The Greenoughs soon came to respect Priessnitz highly, and their experience with the hydropathic system continued to prove agreeable. After about a month they made a trip to Florence,[15] but they were back to Grafenberg by the first of August, planning to remain until the end of the year. In the meantime, about the middle of July, Louisa became pregnant again.

After their return they had an apartment in a house with an adjoining garden on the square in Freiwaldau. Late in August Horatio went to Vienna to obtain books and other articles for the next three months. He began a serious study of German this fall. By the end of the year they had decided to remain at Grafenberg throughout Louisa's pregnancy. At this time Horatio made another trip to Florence, probably chiefly to discover how the blocking-out of his group for the Capitol was progressing, and probably on this occasion suspended his studio operations.[16]

As they settled more, during the latter part of 1844, into the life of Grafenberg both Horatio and Louisa became increasingly gratified by it. "I would rather," Horatio wrote Robert Winthrop in August,

> have the most dangerous fever here or the small pox in its worst form, than the slightest illness that requires medical aid elsewhere. . . .

The next spring after seeing recoveries from almost all sorts of illness, he enthusiastically declared:

> I have lived in various lands. I have seen many of the great men and things of my time, but what I have here seen surpasses far away in importance all that I have witnessed.

He himself continued to enjoy, as he had ever since adopting water as his drink and daily cold baths, a "health and spirits" which he had supposed "the privilege only of boyhood." For two months that winter the thermometer hovered around zero. "[R]espect an enthusiasm which has survived a winter at Grafenberg!" he wrote a correspondent in the spring; "with my habits & tastes too."[17]

Most important of all, Louisa responded to the treatment. She had a "frightful eruption" in the beginning, by March had been forbidden to write letters, and at last became quite fleshy. On the whole, however, she enjoyed "robust health." She took exercise and at least three baths—sometimes as many as six—daily and the day before her confinement "never looked heartier." It was, on the whole, with great "content and joyful anticipations" that Horatio watched the successful progress of the "experiment" they had made.[18]

Nevertheless throughout the period he experienced qualms about having brought Louisa to Grafenberg. "When I reflect," he wrote Powers in November 1844,

how few persons have a knowledge of this system at home and the most suspicious and quackery-looking physiognomy which the whole affair presents to a superficial observer, I feel that I have run a risk.

The next spring he expressed himself more fully to Robert C. Waterston (whose wife was one of the daughters of Josiah Quincy):

Seven years experience had shown me that I had but to go on consulting *"the most eminent physicians"* in order to see my wife go down to an untimely grave. I was sure that her body had been injured by impertinent and ignorant and presumptuous interference. I resolved instead of letting the plant stay in the green house and calling botany, chemistry &c to explain its drooping, to transplant it to the open field of Nature. . . .[19]

His decision, however, was completely vindicated. On May 11, 1845, Louisa gave birth to a healthy ten-month boy, weighing almost eleven pounds. Priessnitz "carried out the system of stimulation by cold water to the last moment" (he was in the next room during the confinement), and the child was washed in cold water immediately. He was named Henry Saltonstall. "The main object of my journey hither is attained," Horatio announced to Powers two days afterward. "Tell your wife," he continued ebulliently,

that my boy has very dark blue eyes (which he says he means shall change by and by as soon as he can get a little leisure) a famous chest and much more hair on his head than his papa. He has already changed his notes from an even wail to savage yells which are worthy of a young Mohawk. He fights like a devil in the water and seems not to share our belief in Priessnitz at all.

When the announcement he made to his family in America arrived, his sister Louisa said she never knew him "in so happy a frame of mind."[20]

Sometime in July the Greenoughs set out for Florence, taking a wet nurse with them. In Vienna they encountered difficulty about Turner's passport and had to return to Grafenberg, but early in August they were on their way again. From Vienna Louisa wrote Mrs. Powers, requesting that several arrangements be made before their return and reporting that

My boy flourishes, & repays me for all the slopping, sousing, & drenching I have undergone. He coos, laughs, & crows to any extent & of course I look upon him as a perfect wonder.[21]

About the first of September they reached Florence.

They had been absent approximately a year and a half. It was one of the two longest periods Horatio ever spent away from his studio and the longest he was ever cut off from contact with his art. He may have begun a bust of a Count Olgar at Grafenberg and discontinued it because of some misunderstanding.[22] There is no evidence that he modeled anything else. The suspension of activities in his studio further interrupted the progress of his career. "I have every reason to hope," he wrote Powers as he prepared to leave Grafenberg,

that I shall be able hereafter to remain at Florence. I have paid dear for my wife's recovery but not too dear—not too dear, I am sure you justify me.[23]

It was also the longest period Greenough ever spent without a number and a variety of social contacts. "I have been now one year divorced from civilization," he wrote Waterston in March 1845, "and have had scarce a look but the sky and the forests."[24] Delightful as such a look always was for him, there was a limit to what he saw thereby.

During this period he was not, however, intellectually idle. He read, studied German, and wrote. Probably he composed at this time some if not all of the four essays which were printed in February 1846 in the *United States Magazine and Democratic Review* under the group title, "Etchings with a Chisel." There were four: "The Miraculous Picture," an account of the painting of the Annunciation in the church of SS. Annunziata in Florence, said to have been miraculously finished when the artist fell asleep at his easel; "Do Not be Afraid of Grace and Beauty!", largely a commentary on the dancing of the celebrated Austrian Fanny Elssler, who was currently appearing in Florence, Vienna, and other European cities; "Prince Metternich," a description of Greenough's meeting with the Chancellor in Vienna in the spring of 1845, with general criticisms of paternal government; and "By Their Fruits Ye Shall Know Them," a brief contrast of the social effects of republics and empires, particularly in Italy and France. In May 1845, after the birth of his son, he wrote a letter intended for publication to the editor of an American periodical, possibly O'Sullivan, describing typical cures at Grafenberg and defending Priessnitz against the charges recently leveled at him by the English doctor Robert Graham; apparently it was not printed. Two other compositions of Greenough's which have survived were probably written about this time: a description of a church service in an Austrian village (probably Freiwaldau) and a discourse on organized religion in relation to the nature of man. The first was printed after his death in the *Crayon*. His essay on dress, also printed in the same magazine at that time, may also belong to this period.

In the two of these essays concerned with political systems Greenough applauded republicanism and denounced all varieties of tyranny, as he had often done previously. (The monkeys tied to poles in the anteroom at the chancellery in Vienna seemed to him admirable symbols of paternalism.) He now, however, for the first time saw weaknesses inherent in civilized systems. A group of Galician lancers trained to a mechanical perfection, which he saw in Vienna, seemed to him symptomatic of civilization. "There are two ways of governing both man and beast," he wrote at the end of his description of the village church service. "The caress or the bit." Though the latter was effective, it was deadly. Citing the indulgence with which Arabian steeds were treated in old age, he pointed out,

We have excellent horses but they keep the breed. . . . we ask barbarians for pure blood and confess that our system like a withering fire consumes its own elements.[25]

The Spanish civilization, he declared in "By Their Fruits Ye Shall Know Them" (probably reflecting his reading of Prescott), exhibited the fruits of barbarism as the Mexicans themselves did not.

Two other pieces evinced his interest in the Roman Catholic Church, toward which he was always more sympathetic than many of his countrymen. (Among his friends whom Tuckerman made a point of remembering was a Franciscan friar.)[26] He was amusedly skeptical of the legend about the miraculous painting in SS. Annunziata and only mildly critical of the garishness of the shrine it had been made into. He admitted that the Austrian peasants assembled for mass in the village church presented a laughable (and a "mephitic") spectacle (soon to be masked by the fumes from the censer), but he declared:

I assist with pleasure at these shews. The sight of so many human creatures worshipping touches me and when the organ peals and all the people chaunt the tears rush into my eyes. I see the picture of the dying Lord through wreathes of sun lit smoke and the stone building vibrating to the sound seems to thrill and tremble at the real presence. . . . I cannot but feel that in this institution these people have a great blessing. . . .

It is a system and great minds have tried to mend it and have been nonplussed. We must let it alone. Religion said a bishop to a friend of mine must be made thick enough to be felt.

At the same time, his own mind, never strongly influenced by institutionalism, was now exploring the purely naturalistic approach to religion and morality. He recognized, as apparently never before, the claims of man's sexual nature. In "Do Not Be Afraid of Grace and Beauty!" he frankly acknowledged that the dances of Elssler were primarily gratifying to his senses, representing as they did

the full power of womanhood revealing itself to man—strongly, for it is the origin of all strength—gracefully, for it is natural—innocently, because it is just what God made it.

He could but contrast

that drunken thrill to the sober stir of my blood, the soaring of my mind, as I look upon the Apollo. . . . Does all this charm me because it is divine? Surely not; but because it is humanity—humanity not ashamed of itself; which seems to say—Imperfect as I am, show me something better!

The Greeks he now praised for a new reason: "Venus and the [Charites] were not inseparable, yet they were not incompatible." It was an inconsistent civilization that would condemn such a performance as he had seen and condone the immodest female costume of high style. Contrasting the two, he was

tempted to quarrel with civilization. I cry out in my bitterness, Alas! alas! what have ye done with my people?

All efforts to repress human instincts he likened to a dam built across a stream, whose waters were sure to go over or through such an obstruction eventually. (The analogy appeared in other compositions of his about this time.) For the construction of such a dam he largely blamed the hierarchy of the established church. "The theatre in Catholic countries," he somewhat cryptically concluded this essay,

is an opposition to the cathedral. The camp-meeting and the conventicle are theatres. In Austria, there is a poor man's opera-house in every village—with a cross at the top of the spire.[27]

The relationship between organized religion and human

nature is more fully treated in another composition of Greenough's written about this time but apparently never printed. Some three thousand words long, it is loosely organized and lacks a trenchant thesis. It begins with affirmations about man's social character, the kinship between man and the brute creation, and the fallacy of all theories of individual and group superiority. The body of the essay is devoted to broad criticisms of the Christian religion, in which the doctrine of the future life is assailed for being liable to exploitation by the clergy, all religious government is represented as by nature corrupt, and the supposition that sexual desire is evil together with all attempts to suppress it is declared tragically wrong. He defined religion as "the spiritual opposition to mans carnal government," which as soon as it "becomes a government and not an opposition . . . becomes carnal animal and corrupt." "To make a man a fit agent for the continuation of his species," he declared,

yet to be free from desire except as regards one mate at certain times and under certain circumstances would be to make a machine and not a man. The fire that consumes your house is the same fire that cooks your steak, and though its action as regards yourself is hard it has under God and nature only done its duty. . . . If you force him to *celibacy* as a means of ensuring chastity—if you build your whole social pile of the like monstrous propositions you will soon find that nature will do in the moral world what she has always done in the physical world. What is denied a natural & easy outlet will make for itself an irregular for you—a painful one. The fistula you say is a disease. The fistula replies no I am a compromise between obstruction & death.[28]

The view of man presented in these last two essays represents in a general way the influence of Greenough's marriage on his thought. More specifically, it reflects his experience during Louisa's long invalidism and her recovery under the water cure.

Indeed, the influence of that experience may be seen throughout Greenough's writing at this period. The nature of the hydropathic treatment and probably the character of the particular hydropathist who administered it to Louisa induced him to speculate about the whole relationship of the intellectual and the non-intellectual aspects of man and of history and to modify some of his former conceptions of this relationship. Confronted at last with the contradiction implicit in the assumptions which he had long made of the natural goodness of man and of the superiority of the civilized to the primitive state, he struggled to reconcile the two. He was not altogether successful in doing so. In the process, however, he discovered a greater complexity and a deeper meaning in creation than he had previously apprehended. At the same time he approached from another direction the broader view of art which he was taking in these years, in which both primitives and sophisticates had a place.

From the beginning Greenough tended to regard the cures which he saw effected at Grafenberg mystically. He was sorry, he wrote Winthrop in the summer of 1844, to see so many attempts being made by medical men to explain them scientifically. It was just as possible, he declared, "to explain how a tree grows or whence the law of gravitation takes its rise" or "the conversion of bread and meat into men and women." In the spring he described Louisa's health and strength as "a mystery to me," adding, "thank God I have a joyful and not a mournful mystery to deal with." His convictions about hydropathy, he wrote Waterston in a long letter in March 1845, which seemed

at first sight very humbling to our man's pride, after all only removed the crown of wisdom from the schools to place it on the collective head of the race. And it is scarce more than fair—for did not the plough and the spindle—the corn grasses and the alphabet, laws and saws come to us out of darkness? What have we done since records were made to balance what had been done before?

Yet in another sense the truths of the water cure were "the basis of a new philosophy—nay the germ of a new civilization."[29]

During the next few months—especially, it would seem, after his son's birth—he continued to speculate along these lines. Late in May, in the letter addressed to the periodical editor, he made perhaps his most lucid statement of his notion of the water cure as a way of life:

I conceive this system great and valuable as it is to the sick and the suffering to be still more important to the sound and healthy. A system which enjoins labour—which makes it clear that idleness is decay and excess and vice suicide must have important moral results—perhaps the day will come when cleanliness will be preached when decency will consist in showing a wholesome clean and well developed body instead of hiding a dirty sick one. . . . Perhaps it would then be clear that [not] only the soul but the body also is of God and we should learn like the brutes whom we despise to make our passions harmonize with his providence—not like the botanist worrying dissecting and peeping through lenses but like the gardner planting watering and grubbing about letting what some wise ones call Nature have his own way a little and putting trust in him. . . .[30]

Early in July he wrote Waterston again, setting forth a theory of nature, the human race, and the creature man. Both nature and the race, he thought, were divinely sustained through a system of balances, in which death in one sphere was necessary to life in another. "That three blossoms," he illustrated,

should open where one cherry ripens—that 2 babes should die where one man attains the age of maturity seems at first rather a puzzling fact but I am forced to admit that what I call abortive may not really be so & that when the blossom perishes to my eye it but travels a road which I cannot see. When I look upon the heavens at night and imagine the existences moral and intellectual that are burning there, I cannot escape the feeling that intense darkness and ignorance is our portion here. . . .

When he thought of the discrepancy of lot between the serf and Newton or Bonaparte, he was "overwhelmed," but when he saw "culture end in exhaustion and ignorance come in to supply vigor to the worn out soil" he recognized the relationship between parts of a whole. He loved

to look upon the mind of man not as an individual ever repeated in slightly varying patterns, but as one as the waters of the globe are one, one as the air that weighs on the bosom of the planet is one. The fractional portions are nothing apparently. . . . I find a consolation in thus belonging to a great whole; it saves me from my nothingness. . . .

Man being a creature whose animal nature was as divine in origin as his intellectual nature, he thought the great weakness of Christianity was its denial of this unity, its tendency to be "a moral and intellectual and spiritual aristocracy." Though he conceded Christianity to be "the strongest yearning of man after the truth and the most successful," he found in it a "fundamental imperfection"—the admission of the existence of evil. But for "*social* phenomena," he felt, such an admission would never have been made. (Society he described as "a partial, individual, perishable existence.") He felt safer "in hugging to Mother Earth than in theories"; he heard "Gods voice plainer from the clod than from the pulpit."[31]

At no time before or afterward did Greenough engage in so much abstract speculation as he did at Grafenberg in 1844 and 1845. The importance to him of Louisa's condition and the narrowness of the environment in which they lived were clearly accountable for the fact. Possibly he was also influenced by his reading, but precisely what he read then is not known. After they left Grafenberg he took a more detached view of hydropathy. In later writings he criticized social philosophers as vigorously as ever and held up to his countrymen again a highly civilized standard of excellence. Nevertheless his view of man was broadened and his optimism deepened permanently. In more than one sense his experience at Grafenberg brought him to full maturity. In his later writings, moreover, he tended to explore the philosophic and religious rather than the artistic implications of the concept of functionalism.

Soon after he returned to Florence he began on the marble of the male figures of "The Rescue" and put into marble two copies of a bust of Christ. It was one of two designs he executed of this subject, presumably the one with a base of a coiled serpent and cherubs' heads, probably designed as a companion piece to his "Lucifer." It is a study in composure, with an almost mechanical regularity of features and an impersonal aspect which represents the classical conception of a divine nature. To his knowledge, it was the first treatment of the subject by an American sculptor. He agreed that the subject posed peculiar difficulties, but he thought

The prayers and hymns of the most pious are as far unworthy the perfection to which they are addressed, as the lights and shadows of the artist; yet both may be accepted as fervent aspirations after the good and beautiful.[32]

In the fall he sold both copies of the work—one presumably to New Yorker Asaph Stone—and could have sold two more.[33]

For something over a year this was the virtual extent of Greenough's work in his studio, chiefly on account of various circumstances connected with his family. Early in October, a few weeks after he and Louisa reached Florence, Henry and his wife and two children arrived, planning an extended stay on account of Henry's poor health.[34] Horatio and Louisa were anxious for them to share Casa Baciocchi, and they decided to do so until the summer. The joint establishment, however, did not prove satisfactory. There was only one kitchen and one bath, the temperature was uncomfortably low for the visitors from America (Frances sat over a fire with a shawl and "wadded" slippers and sleeves and wished she could bring the thirty-foot ceiling down), the servants clashed (the suitor of

Frances' maid, jealous of Louisa's manservant, arrived one day with a knife to kill her, and slashed several pairs of shoes in the house). After about five weeks Henry and his family took rooms in another house.

The two families were intimately associated, however, throughout most of the time the Henry Greenoughs were abroad—altogether four years and a half. Henry went with Horatio on such expeditions as the one to Serravezza late in 1845, and the two customarily took long walks after dinner, stopping at a cafe and smoking a cigar on their way. Frances and Louisa often dined, had tea, went to the theatre, the opera, galleries and churches, shopped, and took drives in Louisa's carriage. Louisa was, Frances decided, a "remarkable instance" of "indolence becoming industry & carelessness method" through "affection & the strong incentive of maternal feeling"—though she took "treble time for accomplishing anything to what is necessary."[35] Together both couples saw a good deal of the Powerses, the Moziers, the English banker Sloane and his wife, the Camerons, the G. L. Browns, Ives, Kellogg, Jesi, Count Gräberg and his daughter, and entertained various Americans who passed through the city.

Little Henry Greenough made his presence felt increasingly in both families. There was no end, Frances wrote her sister Harriet in the spring of 1846 to the "anxieties & *fusses* (there is no other word) over him" by his parents. He reminded her of the children of a royal family. At half-past twelve one night the chambermaid was called out to amuse him because he was restless, though both his mother and nurse were with him. Louisa had a pair of sandals made for him lest shoes hurt his feet. As for Horatio, he exceeded all Frances "could have imagined of a nursing papa." A year later she recalled,

Horatio, who has never noticed any babies, used to speak of him as a perfect wonder of health & strength! which to us was quite amusing, he did not walk till he was 19 months old! So much for not being a father till one is 40 years old & only having experience in marble infants.[36]

The disturbing fact was that the infant was sickly throughout his early years.

At the approach of the summer of 1846, early in May, both Greenough families set out from Florence for Grafenberg to spend the season there. They traveled together as far as Padua, from where Horatio went by land and Henry by way of Venice and Trieste. By the end of the month they were both at Freiwaldau, in houses on the square five doors apart—Horatio and Louisa evidently in the same quarters they had had before.

Henry had meanwhile been "quite sickened" by Horatio's enthusiastic letters and later talk about the water cure and was at first "quite refractory" about taking it. Soon, however, both he and Frances did so and both were well pleased with the result. Louisa and Horatio promptly wrote home that a "*wonderful* change" had taken place in Henry, of which Frances' "more moderate views" were "that he is benefitted." She thought everything relating to the cure was treated by her brother- and sister-in-law a little " 'en beau.' " "I consider Louisa & Horatio quite *fanatical* on the subject," she wrote her sister Mary. "They seem to think Priessnitz superhuman. He is a very intelligent man certainly with much experience. . . ."[37] By the end of the summer the Henry Greenoughs had decided to stay at Freiwaldau through the winter. Actually, for one reason and another, they remained until the fall of 1847.

Into other aspects of life at Priessnitz' establishment both couples evidently entered with equal enthusiasm. They went to the scheduled entertainments, church services, the theatre, and the circus. On the Casino club list Horatio, who was enjoying perfect health and looking "stout and hearty," was entered as the younger of the two brothers, to Henry's mortification.[38] Late in July Horatio went briefly to Vienna. It was, Frances said, with reluctance that he prepared a few weeks later to return with Louisa to Florence.

They left Freiwaldau about the middle of September, traveling by way of Germany. They stopped briefly at Carlsbad, visited Walhalla on the Danube (the temple recently erected to the Bavarian war heroes by King Louis I), and spent at least the first two weeks in October in Munich, whose general appearance Horatio praised and whose art collections he enjoyed. From there they evidently went by Innsbruck, Verona, Mantua, and Bologna and reached Florence about November 1. William and Arno were waiting for them, several appurtenances of Palazzo Baciocchi had been renovated, various improvements were being made in the city, and Fanny Elssler was there. Yet Horatio was not elated to be back. If he were not tied by his engagements, he wrote Henry, he would

> willingly be elsewhere. The character of this town, after seeing the order, cleanliness, and comfort of Munich, to say nothing of living art, displeases me.

His spirits began to revive, however, with his return to his studio. "I found my David as fresh as a rose," he reported. "He looked as if I had only left him over night."[39]

Risorgimento

Early in 1847 Greenough received the long delayed third installment of his payment for his group for the Capitol and so had his doubts about that commission once more dispelled. Probably partly on this account and partly on account of his new domestic happiness, he experienced a revival of artistic energy. Between the time when he returned to Florence from Grafenberg and the summer of 1851, when he left for America, he finished his group, modeled and partly put in marble eight or ten new pieces, remodeled one, and made plans for at least three or four others. He also built a studio for himself.

Evidently he remodeled his "David," this time representing the subject going to meet Goliath with staff and sling.[1] Late in 1849 he was reported finishing it, though probably not in marble.

By May 1847 he had modeled several bas-reliefs. One represented Castor and Pollux on their horses. A Bostonian had by that time ordered it in marble, and Greenough evidently executed two copies. He modeled it at least twice, achieving more spirit and better balance the last time; in sketches for it he made use of a new drawing method of interlocking circles which he had learned from a book he bought in Munich. The French draughtsman who was drawing "The Rescue" early in 1851 wanted to make a lithograph of this relief. To James Jackson Jarves, who saw it in plaster, the horses were "beautiful creations, full of fire and spirit; steeds of eternity, like those of Phidias." In the opinion of Jarves, all these reliefs which he saw were "replete with the best classical feeling. . . . severely composed, and vital with inward life and graceful action."[2]

Another of them was executed as a gift for Ticknor, in gratitude for the money Ticknor had sent Greenough years before. It depicted a sculptor sitting in dejection before an unfinished work—a miniature of the "Venus Anadyomene"—with a dying lamp which was being replenished by a hand emerging from a cloud. (Thorvaldsen had executed a similar design called "The Genius of Light," of which Greenough may have known.) He evidently modeled it, too, more than once, at first representing the benefactor as a veiled figure. The marble was shipped in the fall of 1849. Ticknor had it placed in the entrance hall of his house, at the head of Park Street, where, he liked to remember in later years, Greenough saw it shortly before his death. The "little assistance" Greenough had needed as a youth was a "trifling" matter compared to this acknowledgment of it, Ticknor felt.[3] Unfortunately the work seems no longer to exist.

About this time Greenough modeled a relief of a bacchante and young faun. Evidently he never put it in marble and apparently it has been destroyed. Judged from a photograph of it, it was one of his most pleasing works.[4] The relaxed figure of the bacchante and the straining of the faun, and the barren and the fruitful vines, suggested a tension beneath the general repose which also gave the design a certain depth.

By June 1847 Greenough had finished what he described as "the Genius for Giusti's . . . monument." According to Tuckerman, this monument to the poet had been erected by 1853 at Pescia, near his birthplace. No record of it, however, seems to exist. Possibly the project was abandoned when the revolutionary movement of these years, in which Giusti was active, was put down.[5]

In the summer of 1847 Greenough was also modeling the bust of Napoleon, using a death mask for his authority. Members of the Bonaparte family in Florence thought it a "fine likeness."[6] Perhaps about the same time he executed a small bust of Napoleon as a boy. He used the Hermes form for the first, appropriately in view of his idealization of the subject.

This summer—in August—he bought from the Commune of Florence a parcel of land at the intersection of Via San Francesco Poverino and Via San Caterina, on the newly laid out Piazza Maria Antonia, on which he began to build a studio for himself. By the next February it was well advanced. That April he bought a smaller adjoining piece, fronting on Via San Caterina. The building was completed by the following spring, and he had moved most of his works into it.[7]

This building still stands, but after Greenough's death it underwent such drastic alterations that its original appearance cannot be accurately determined. It was originally of one story (subsequently two more stories were added); the front is of hammered stone, the windows have pediments and apparently originally had fanlights, and between the windows are pilasters. A stone shield, in which the letter *G* once appeared, surmounts the corner window. The entrance has presumably always been, as now, in Via San Caterina. The basic floor plan consists of a large octagonal room on the corner and two wings at right angles to it. The central room—"a noble rotunda," Tuckerman called it—was "finely lighted from above," G. W. Curtis said, presumably through the fanlights, and "most delicately designed." It was hung with pictures, chiefly the gifts of artist friends of Greenough's. Around it, on a lower level, were smaller workrooms, from which a large work in the central room might be studied. The building also contained, Tuckerman said, presumably in the wings,

> a spacious and admirably lighted exhibition-room . . . the sculptor's private studio, a large apartment for the workmen, a gallery of plaster casts, a vestibule hung with pictures . . . and a charming library.

From the central room a short flight of steps led to a garden. The whole building was full, Curtis noted,

> of beautiful bijoux of a scholar—of choice books, medallions, engravings—everything tempered by the most tranquil taste.

The works by Greenough himself which he saw there he thought most appropriately housed. It was "the ideal retreat of a classical, cultivated, ideal artist." It was by far the most elaborate studio in the city and according to Tuckerman "unsurpassed in Europe."[8]

By the summer of 1849 Greenough had evidently completed studies for an equestrian Washington. One of his sketches presumably for this work depicted a cloaked figure with uplifted hand, another a hatless figure on a rearing horse. Apparently he sent two designs to Edward Everett in June, which Everett

Palazzo Pucci, Florence.
(From a photograph by Alinari.)

Greenough's Studio, Piazza Independenza, Florence,
with upper stories added.
(From a photograph by Talani.)

thought well calculated to win popular approval. He proposed to execute the work in bronze, perhaps to be placed in State Street in Boston, and considered various means of raising the money for the casting. Ticknor offered his assistance, and Everett suggested a raffle be held. Greenough also proposed to take a subscription, but reports of an economic slump early in the fall discouraged him.[9]

In the fall of 1849 he was remodeling his bust of Christ. That which he produced presumably at this time represents the subject as younger and more effeminate than the other one and is altogether a less effective work. By the next summer he had finished the model of another life-size Venus, in the same pose as Lowell's, which he called "Venus Vincitura." In Frances B. Greenough's opinion, it was one of his "most perfect works." Benjamin Gibson, brother of the English sculptor in Rome, praised it extravagantly, and Robert Browning, who had recently settled in Florence with his wife, urged it be sent to the Crystal Palace Exhibition in London in 1851. Greenough wanted to show it in England, along with "The Rescue." It was not put into marble and was broken beyond repair during its transportation to America in 1853.[10]

Also in the early fall of 1850, Greenough modeled two bas-reliefs, entitled "The Genius of Poesy" and "The Genius of Italy."[11] Apparently neither was put in marble, and both have been destroyed. Among his sketches is one which may represent the first of these works. It is the figure of a nude youth seated with his head resting on one arm and the other holding an object resembling a stylus. The second relief, judged from a photograph of the model,[12] was one of his most ambitious, though less successful than others. It depicted a nude youth, representing Italy, clasping a lyre in one hand and a wreath in the other, standing between two seated and partially-draped figures: one with a sword, representing the military; the other, bearded, with a shepherd's crook, representing the church. The military figure, in profile, was designed in Greenough's best classical style. But the figure of Italy, though rendered immature probably on purpose, was not especially engaging and the face of the figure of the church bore a curiously quizzical expression.

At this time he made plans for another heroic figure, to be called "Apollo the Avenger," probably in allusion to the god's directing the arrow of Paris against Achilles. In October he sent Henry a sketch, but evidently did nothing further with these plans.[13]

By May 1851 he had conceived the plan of a monument to record the treason of Benedict Arnold, the capture and death of John André, and the fate of Nathan Hale. He proposed that Arnold's figure be represented veiled to the waist, the last words of André and Hale be written beneath their statues, and presumably the relief work consist of the arrest of André by the three rangers. He wrote William Cullen Bryant of the plan and, being then on the point of departing for America, proposed, if Bryant, Paulding and Cooper approved it, to "go straight to the people for the means to do it, and lecture and stump it, till I get the wherewithal."[14]

Sometime after 1846 he also made sketches for a group consisting of Samson and Delilah. In all of them both figures are reclining and in some the woman holds shears. In a few the pose of the male figure resembles that of Michelangelo's Adam in the Creation scene in the Sistine Chapel. A related sketch appears to depict Hercules and Queen Omphale. Altogether these sketches represent a notable allegorizing of Greenough's experience during the years of artistic inactivity which he spent at Grafenberg with Louisa. No executed work of his had so personal a character. This aspect of them may explain why nothing further seems to have come of either of these group conceptions.

Other sketches of Greenough's, presumably for statues or reliefs, which seem to belong to this period include several of a satyr and a faun, two of a maiden (probably Atalanta) with an apple, one of a centaur and a nymph, and several of three figures intended for Electra, Orestes, and Pylades. His small bust of Homer, modeled from one of the antique treatments of this subject, and a work called "The Graces," which Tuckerman described as an ideal bust, but which could conceivably have been a relief,[15] may have been done about this time.

By 1851 he had invented a process to be used in lithographic work. As he described it to Henry,

A copy being carefully made out on paper is placed under a square of thin, white ground-glass, and the drawing stumped and deepened with lead-pencil; the high lights are put in with white *gouache*. It works evenly, rapidly, and bears any amount of tooling and erasure, of course.[16]

The Frenchman who made a drawing of "The Rescue" at this time used this process and was pleased with it.

During the first of these years Greenough was often concerned about the well-being of his family. In the spring after they returned from Grafenberg an epidemic broke out in Florence, which he first called spotted fever but later thought was cholera. Louisa fell ill, and for a while he despaired of her life. Evidently little Henry was also ill, and Horatio had fever late in April. He proposed to take the whole family to Grafenberg if they did not recover strength rapidly, but the journey was not necessary. By the first of May they were at Pratolino, a rural neighborhood a few miles out of Florence, where Louisa spent most of the summer and Horatio went often from Florence. By the fall little Henry had gained weight, and in December he at last walked. Yet his father continued to be apprehensive. "Poor Horatio!" Frances wrote her sister Harriet B. Loring early in 1848,

I really pity him, his little boy cannot have a common cold or a heaviness of the eye lids, without alarming him and making him wretched. He says he was very happy till he was 40 yrs old! but that since the birth of the baby, he has been on a bed of thorns! Partly in consequence of such attention the child was "wilful and noisy," she thought.[17]

At the end of September 1847 Henry and his family returned to Florence. For two weeks they were again at Casa Baciocchi (Frances was prepared to stay longer, "in the true John Wells spirit," if they found nothing better), and then they took rooms in Casa Pucci in Via Larga, a block or so away. The following October they moved to the apartment of the Moziers, who were then out of the city, in Casa Pegua on the Piazza Maria Antonia, across from Horatio's new studio. Here they stayed for at least a year and probably until they left Florence.[18]

Late in 1847 both Louisa and Frances became pregnant. It was decided that Louisa would remain in Florence, but she took baths assiduously and in the spring had her bath woman come from Germany. In May she went again to Pratolino, where she stayed until time for her confinement. At her and Frances' request, the American Dr. John Gorham, a friend of Frank Boott's, came from Rome late in July to give them ether. To the last Horatio worried. As Louisa began labor he wrote a hasty note asking Powers to be ready to witness that the child was born alive "if such should be the case"; the matter was important in connection with the estate. His fears, however, were not realized. Louisa gave birth on July 25 to a daughter, who was named Mary Louise. Frances' child, born ten days later, was a boy. He was washed with cold water twice daily for three weeks, as no doubt his cousin was also.[19]

A few months later, in October 1848, Horatio and Henry went to Austria to accompany Frances' German maid, who had become ill, and Louisa's bath woman part of their way home. Outside Vienna the brothers were delayed several days because of a revolutionary outbreak in the city, and at Monselice they were taken for spies, arrested, and confined for half an hour. They returned to Florence about the middle of November.[20]

The next month they all had influenza, and little Henry was so ill that Louisa took him to Leghorn, presumably to benefit from the sea air. They stayed until the middle of February 1849. By this time Frances regarded the "Florentine scion" as unworthy his name. He was "*the* most disagreeable child I have ever seen," she wrote Harriet,

and I fear will prove a source of trouble to his parents. Henry says they are bringing him up just as his mother did John. An awful warning!

On her return from Leghorn Louisa occupied a villa at Fiesole for a while. In the summer she and her son spent two weeks at the Baths of Lucca, where Frances and her children were staying, but fearing the air for him there she took him back to Pratolino. He nevertheless (to his uncle Henry's amusement) took whooping cough. A few weeks later Louisa was at the sea resort of Viareggio. Both Horatio and Henry stayed in the city through this summer, but usually went to their families weekly.[21]

In the fall of 1849 Horatio and Louisa moved to Villa Brichieri Colombi on the hill of Bellosguardo, a mile outside the Porta Romana, to benefit, he said, from fresher air and greater opportunity for exercise.[22] The house, which dated from the fifteenth century, had twenty-two rooms; adjoining were large stables and a garden; and the whole estate commanded a magnificent view of the valley of the Arno and the mountains southwest of the city. Frances and Louisa now saw more of each other than when they were neighbors, and Henry customarily walked or rode out with Horatio each evening as far as the gate.[23] A feature of Horatio and Louisa's entertainment now became the opportunity of viewing the sunset from their terrace.

Several other members of the family circle returned to Florence in these years: late in 1847 Frank Boott, recently widowed, with his infant daughter Elizabeth (as before, he entertained Horatio and Louisa with his singing, accompanied by her at the piano); early in 1850 John and Richard Greenough and Richard's wife and mother-in-law. By this time Horatio thought "highly" of Richard's "capacity" as a sculptor and predicted, "With time, he will do much."[24] After about a year Richard moved to Rome.

Other American artists passed a season or so in Florence during the late 1840's, among them Christopher Cranch (brother of John), Story, and Chapman. Through the winter of 1848–49 the Greenoughs, the Cranches, the Storys, and Boott often went to the opera and to dinner together.[25]

One of the American travelers at this time who most appreciated her associations with Horatio and Louisa was Margaret Fuller, who was in Florence for a short time in the fall of 1847 and, with the Marquis Ossoli, for several months in 1849 and 1850. She brought a letter to Louisa from Mrs. Calvert, which was the means of her enjoying, she said, much "refined and exhilirating intercourse." Moderately satisfied with Horatio's sculpture, she exulted over his republican spirit. He was "one of the few Americans," she wrote in a letter printed in the New York *Tribune* in the fall of 1847,

> who, living in Italy, takes the pains to know whether it is alive or dead, who penetrates beyond the cheats of tradesmen, and the cunning of a mob corrupted by centuries of slavery, to know the real mind, the vital blood of Italy. . . .

She was particularly grateful to him (in the fall of 1849) for interceding personally with Prince Corsini, the Tuscan Secretary of State, to get permission for her and Ossoli to remain in the city after the police had ordered them out.[26]

Meanwhile political events all over Italy moved toward the revolutionary activities of 1848 and 1849, during which the yoke of Austria was temporarily thrown off in scattered states, but lasting victory was not won, chiefly because of the failure of the insurgents to unite their efforts. Greenough's sympathies lay all along with those who desired Italian independence, and evidently he was at least acquainted with radicals Guerrazzi and Berti.[27] His closest Italian friends were, however, like himself, moderates. In any case, he refrained from becoming involved in Italian politics, as he wrote Edward Everett in 1848, for reasons both of policy and of principle.[28]

The political events of these years nevertheless affected him and his family. In 1847 and 1848 certain reforms were coercively obtained from the Grand Duke, among them the organization of the National or Civic Guards. This event was celebrated in Florence on September 12, 1847, with a parade, on which occasion a flag was reportedly made by Louisa with the help of other ladies and carried by Horatio.[29] A month later through Horatio's arrangement the Marquis Baciocchi put the courtyard of his palace at the disposal of a society for military drill, presumably volunteers of the Civic Guards.[30]

Leopold granted Tuscany a constitution in the spring of 1848, and Capponi became the prime minister, but by fall this government was in danger. About this time, with a typical gesture, Leopold commissioned all professors in the Academy of Fine Arts, presumably including Greenough, captains in the Civic Guards.[31] In February 1849 Leopold fled his post, and a provisional government was set up, of which Guerrazzi became the chief executive. All over the city the royal insignia were torn down, liberty trees were planted, and houses were illuminated in honor of the event. Greenough refused to illuminate his house or to pay tax for the trees; in consequence his windows were broken by those calling themselves "Patriots."[32]

Their victory, however, was short-lived. In the middle of April altercations in Florence between a deputation of six hundred Leghornese and some Florentines almost precipitated a riot. On this occasion some thirty soldiers entered Henry's house on the Piazza Maria Antonia shortly after dinner, purportedly to help defend the city, ordered the entrance fastened, went to the second floor, and fired a few shots from the windows. At nine they left—furnished with cigars by Henry.[33] The situation was quickly gotten in hand, but partisans of Leopold took advantage of it to turn the tide of popular feeling. The next day he returned. The liberty trees were cut down, houses were illuminated to celebrate the restoration (now Henry's windows were broken because they were dark), and a month later some twenty thousand Austrian troops entered the city, ostensibly to protect Leopold. When Horatio found several of them quartered in his stables, he wrote immediately to Binda for a diplomatic office which would spare him such impositions, and by June had been appointed vice-consul of the neighboring town of Porto San Stefano—though without any duties to perform.[34]

The regime thus restored in Tuscany was soon more bitterly resented than ever, and minor breaches of the peace were common. After the Greenoughs moved to Villa Brichieri, chickens and miscellaneous objects from the coach house were several times stolen and they themselves were twice accosted for money at midnight in the neighborhood. They were repeatedly frightened and at least twice injured on the Bellosguardo road by players of *ruzzola,* a Tuscan game in which wooden disks to which strings were attached were rolled down hill. When complaints about all these matters to the guard outside the Porta San Frediano brought no results, Greenough addressed a letter early in 1851 to the Prefect of Florence, listing them and concluding that unless something was done he would be obliged to find another place to live where the law was better enforced.[35] "His love of freedom and education in a land of liberty," as Frances put it later, "made foreign despotism in his second home a daily annoyance" and even in a measure destroyed the charm of this home. He found the study of Austrian character in Italy, she noted wryly, "far less interesting than in Austria."[36] On this account alone he began to think again of returning to America to live.

Yet as he did so, the problem of the artist in America—especially such an artist as he had become—rose again to trouble him. He looked forward "with anxiety to the future," he wrote Cogswell in the fall of 1850,

partly on account of the complications of European politics and partly from the fear that my being so long out of sight will put me equally out of mind with the public of America.

. . . .

After being so long employed on works of a high order it is not possible for me to play the shopman and cut fancy work for furniture or cultivate the vogue of the day. I have chosen my path and if the state of the national taste does not afford me support I must wait and arm myself with courage for the consequences.[37]

Most profoundly disturbing of all during these years was the state of Greenough's mental health. The tensions created by the abortive Italian revolution, Louisa's uncertain health and the birth of their children, the long delay of his payment and of the marble for his group, the diminution of his reputation after the public rejection of his "Washington," his forced artistic idleness, the increasing competition of other sculptors—these tensions were more numerous than those he had sustained at any other period of his life. Partly no doubt on this account he evidently suffered at this period recurring attacks of dementia. After his death a few years later during such an attack, Powers wrote Everett that though shocked he was not surprised, for

His mind had been affected more or less for years. I have often heard him make strange remarks. . . . We were once together on the bank of the Arno at the Cascine [the large park on the outskirts of the city], talking pleasantly, when suddenly he stared at something before him, and exclaimed: "Did *you* see that?" "What? Where?" "Why just there before us. He rushed across our path and leapt into the river." At this he rubbed his forehead, and presently became as calm and sensible in his conversation as before.[38]

As Henry and Frances prepared to return to America (in the spring of 1850), Horatio talked of his and Louisa's going with them. Henry said little about the matter, fearing, as he wrote their mother, that if Horatio

talks much about it he will get all the enjoyment of a return in his imagination in which case, I find from experience he will not be at the trouble to put his plans in execution.[39]

Louisa was eager to go. But in the meantime she once more became pregnant and had reluctantly to give up hope of doing so. There was also his group for the Capitol to keep Horatio in Florence. Henry and his family left unaccompanied in early May 1850.

Horatio and Louisa's remaining year in Florence was disturbed in many respects, but was happy in others. On September 16 their third child was born, a girl, who was named Charlotte. That fall a young Italian, one of the Falcinis, was working with Horatio as a pupil, "solely for the *vendaggio* . . . of being a son of mine in art," he proudly wrote Henry. Among visitors to the city whom he knew were young Charles Eliot Norton, Cogswell, and DeForest, who preserved a vivid impression of meeting him. DeForest had been sitting in the Caffè Doney, he wrote in *European Acquaintance,* "hobnobbing" with the sculptor Galt over ice cream, when Greenough—

a gentleman of agreeable air, though reserved and commanding, whose features were high and fine, whose eyes were of a stern gray, and whose full beard and mustache gave him all his natural grave manliness of aspect—

entered, sat down, drew "a furred glove from his white taper fingers," and began to talk "with his rich voice and earnest manner."[40]

Among the books Greenough read at this time were some of Emerson's essays. Emerson put himself at a disadvantage, Greenough wrote Landor in the spring of 1851, in using words so weighted with meaning as to express more than could be seen in a given thing. Yet he added,

still "they be prave 'ords." I am sure that the Greek statues, though they are not tormented by an ambition to say all, yet include all. . . .

That summer he read Emerson's *Representative Men,* about which he also expressed reservations.[41]

Meantime he and Louisa made plans to go to the United States. At first they evidently considered making a visit and returning. Horatio thought Florence might look better to him then, and he kept his eye on a studio behind his own for Henry. By the time he had finished the group and begun negotiations for Commodore Morgan to transport it, however, they had decided their move was to be a permanent one. They had certain of their effects packed to be shipped with the group: six cases of books, six of marble busts, two of "plaster" (presumably casts), one each of bas-reliefs, pictures, silver plate, and earthenware. Some items were left in his studio, including the casts of Michelangelo's "Day" and "Night" and of a few arms and legs and the bust of Wilde. In July he and Louisa and their children, together with two young Italian nursemaids, left Florence.[42]

They spent the rest of the summer in Switzerland, at an inn where they saw many of the "higher class of Swiss," whom Greenough liked, and where he had some stimulating conversation with a French philosopher. Soon after their arrival there he learned of Alfred's death, which had occurred in June. "I know not how I could have borne this life of disappointment, anxiety, and inactivity," he wrote Henry in reply, but for the tranquillizing effect of the lovely scenery among which we live. In the presence of these giant hills . . . man and man's doings seem but of little importance.

While there he prepared a rough draft of a proposed monument for a Mr. Dwight.[43]

Late in August the Greenough party steamed down the Rhine to Brussels, a city which pleased Horatio. He had known the American minister, R. H. Bayard, as a senator. He planned to go to Paris for two or three days, if only to see Lamartine and Hugo; "I admire and love these men," he wrote Henry.[44] From the continent the party crossed to England, made a brief visit in London, and on October 4 sailed from Liverpool, for Boston, on the *America*.

6

Yankee Philosopher : 1851-1852

1

Reaching home on October 17, Horatio and Louisa spent a few days in Cambridge (where Henry and his family lived) and then went to the Brattle House in Boston. During the next few weeks Horatio renewed several old acquaintances and met, among others, Longfellow. "A fine, hearty, free, cordial gentleman is Horatio Greenough," wrote Longfellow in his journal shortly afterward.

A tall, handsome fellow he is; full of fire and vigor and excitement. The climate acts on him bravely, and braces him like an athlete.[1]

Greenough intended going to Washington immediately, to see what arrangements had been made for the transportation of his group for the Capitol, but was delayed.

Meantime he made plans for two major works. One was a colossal equestrian statue of Andrew Jackson, with "adjuncts" commemorating Jackson's military, civil, and private careers. He proposed to collect twenty-five cents each from contributors and to be responsible to a committee for the money expended. The other work was a monument to Cooper, who had died a month before Greenough arrived home. He proposed a seated portrait, flanked at the base by figures of Leather-Stocking and Long Tom Coffin, to occupy a niche "in a façade or in the court of some literary institution." Plans had already been launched by other friends of Cooper to erect a monument to him, and Greenough did not wish to interfere with them; if one were located in New York he thought he would put his in Philadelphia or Baltimore. Early in November he wrote William Cullen Bryant describing both his new projects. "I thank God from the bottom of my heart," he concluded this letter,

that I have once more put foot on my own, my native soil and I hope though now arrived to the "mezzo del cammin di nostra vita" to be of some use here both in illustrative art and in structure for here I mean now to stay.

As a returned native, moreover, Greenough promptly assumed a role which he played throughout the remaining year of his life: that of a kind of Dutch uncle to his countrymen. Early in November he wrote two letters to the editor of the Boston *Transcript,* defending the fallen Hungarian revolutionary leader Louis Kossuth, then about to come to America, and flaying Kossuth's American detractors. When Kossuth arrived a few weeks later, Greenough had an interview of an hour with him.[3]

Early in November Greenough went to Washington, where he waited six weeks in expectation of "The Rescue." At the end of that time he learned, indirectly, that it had not yet been shipped. As he reacquainted himself with the city, he was newly appalled by the state of the arts there. With difficulty he found who was Commissioner of Public Buildings. "Well, we don't think it's of much importance who takes care of these things," an official told him; "there ain't much of 'em." "If you wish to give an idea how this was said," he wrote Henry, "speak as if your mouth and tongue were clogged with baked beans. My only answer was a low bow." He was even more discouraged when he met the Commissioner, William Easby, "an Irishman," he wrote Rufus Griswold,

whom I should not trust for one hour in the *presence* of any work of art without having him watched.

"The Mannikin-Pis of Brussells," he observed,

which I take to be the lowest example of a European monument has more care and more efficient care taken of it than all the works at Washington on which so much money has been expended.[4]

Moved to protest about the whole situation, Greenough wrote while in Washington most if not all of five essays which he had printed there as a pamphlet, entitled *Æsthetics at Washington,* probably in December, by John T. Towers. Presumably he had projected a series, for it was designated "No. 1." The title page identified the author as "Horatio Greenough, Sculptor" and bore the motto, *De gustibus disceptandum est* ("concerning taste there is disputing"). The issue was probably small; only five copies of the publication seem to have been preserved.[5] In the title essay he delivered several broad artistic challenges to his countrymen. He deplored the materialistic and Puritanical prejudices of the American public against art (citing the "purblind squeamishness which gazed without alarm at the lascivious Fandango" yet cried out against his "Chanting Cherubs" and "awoke with a roar at the colossal nakedness of Washington's manly breast"); yet he insisted that

> It is the great multitude that has decided the rank of the statesmen, the poets, and the artists of the world. It is the great multitude for whom all really great things are done and said and suffered. The great multitude desires the best of everything, and in the long run is the best judge of it.

Convinced of the vital relationship between "High art" and the trades, he urged the establishment of "Normal schools of structure and ornament" to train designers of manufactured products. In conclusion he set forth anew his architectural theory, this time including among his examples of functional forms the products of artisans and mechanics:

> The men who have reduced locomotion to its simplest elements, in the trotting wagon and the yacht America, are nearer to Athens at this moment than they who would bend the Greek temple to every use. I contend for Greek principles, not Greek things. If a

flat sail goes nearest the wind, a bellying sail, though picturesque, must be given up. The slender harness, and tall gaunt wheels, are not only effective, they are beautiful for they respect the beauty of a horse, and do not uselessly task him.

In his second essay in *Æsthetics at Washington,* "The Washington Monument," Greenough objected to the design for this monument proposed by Robert Mills (a circular structure with Doric colonnade surmounted by an obelisk) chiefly because it combined forms unadapted to each other and in favor of an obelisk wrote that it

has to my eye a singular aptitude in its form and character to call attention to a spot memorable in history. It says but one word, but it speaks loud. If I understand its voice, it says, Here! It says no more. For this reason it was that I designed an obelisk for Bunker Hill, and urged arguments that appeared to me unanswerable against a column standing alone.

In "The Embarcation of the Pilgrims," the third essay, he criticized Robert Weir's painting of that name in the rotunda of the Capitol because the accessories had been treated more carefully than the essential elements. In the next essay, "The Smithsonian Institute," he disparaged this building and the Gothic style in general on political and moral grounds. As he walked about Washington one moonlit evening there had suddenly risen between him and "the white Capitol" "the dark form of the Smithsonian palace."

Tower and battlement, and all that mediaeval confusion, stamped itself on the halls of Congress, as ink on paper! Dark on that whiteness—complication on that simplicity! It scared me. . . . It seemed to threaten. It seemed to say, I bide my time! Oh, it was indeed monastic at that hour!

He was, he hastened to explain, not without appreciation of the Roman Catholic Church, but he feared its doctrine "because it seems to lull and to benumb the general, the average mind, while it rouses and spurs the few," and he hated its politics "because they are hostile to ours." In the final essay of the group, "The Desecration of the Flag," he protested as inappropriate the erection of the national flag on buildings and vehicles other than national ones.

During his first few weeks in the country Greenough had, as he said, seen not only vehicles and engines which embodied his theory of structure but also evidence of pernicious foreign influence at work in American design generally. He therefore decided to seize this time to bring his theory to public attention. He talked to several persons in Washington about it, but they were not interested. Late in December he wrote to Emerson and evidently to Bryant setting it forth and asking Emerson for permission to come to Concord when he returned to Boston and read Emerson what he had written on the subject. "Here is my theory of structure," he put it succinctly.

> A scientific arrangement of spaces and forms to functions and to site. An emphasis of features proportioned to their *gradated* importance in function. Colour and ornament to be decided and arranged and varied by strictly organic laws—having a distinct reason for each decision. The entire and immediate banishment of all make-shift and make believe.

He thought that men were "not wanting" to put this theory into practice; yet, with his inclination to feel martyred, he added that it was "too lovely not to be hated by those who are not loving and strong."[6]

Emerson was delighted by Greenough's letter, which he called "the happiest omen of the new year." The theory which it set forth was in agreement with his own organic theory of art and with many of his strictures on architecture. He looked forward to meeting Greenough again and promised to recall to him then the "day dream" or "night *vigil*" which Greenough had given him in Florence nearly twenty years before about the social nature of art.[7] In the intervening years he had often thought of it and had several times referred in his journal to Greenough—as a mediocre sculptor but a promising intellectual. Perhaps at his suggestion Greenough was made an honorary member of the Town and Country Club, formed in Boston in 1849 for the purpose of bringing together some of the New England intelligentsia and possibly founding a periodical. About the time Emerson received Greenough's letter, he copied into his journal the lines from Ben Jonson,

> These we must join to wake, for these are of the strain
> That justice dare defend, and will the age sustain,

and underneath them the names of twenty-five of his contemporaries, beginning with Greenough's.[8] He showed Greenough's letter to Thoreau, who, though also conceiving of buildings in organic terms, pronounced the substance of it little better than "the common dilettantism."[9]

Meanwhile Greenough made plans for more literary composition. He projected a series of articles on a variety of subjects relative to the national life to be printed in newspapers and presumably wrote a preface for them on the first day of the new year.

Meanwhile, too, he proceeded with his project for a monument to Cooper. On his way to Washington in November he had stopped in New York, met some of the members of the committee formed to erect such a monument, and learned that he was looked to as its sculptor. Washington Irving, the president, had suggested a statue of Cooper with the head modeled from Greenough's bust. Greenough met at least once with the committee. (Probably he had particular association in connection with this project with Fitz-Greene Halleck, who was one of the secretaries; apparently about this time he made a drawing of Halleck, which was subsequently engraved.)[10] About the middle of December it was announced that he was to execute for this group a colossal statue of Cooper in one of the uptown parks of New York. At first Washington was suggested as the site, but after seeing that city again Greenough decided there was "an insuperable objection" to it as the site of "any monument of which the *preservation* is important."[11]

On his way back to Boston from Washington in January 1852 Greenough conferred again in New York with some of the committee members, including Bryant. By early February he had worked out an elaborate plan for a memorial edifice instead of a statue, giving as one of his reasons for preferring an edifice the fact that other artists should be allowed to work on "this truly American task."[12] It might be located, he thought, in University Square in New York. He described it in a letter to Bryant at this time and subsequently in an essay entitled, "The Cooper Monument." It was to be oblong (twenty-four by forty-eight feet, with about a twenty-foot ceiling, he stipulated in the essay), lighted from above, raised on three steps, at the corners of which would stand figures of four of Cooper's characters. There was to be an external frieze, ornamented, he wrote Bryant, with "illustrations of the poetry of the forest and the flood"; which, together with the statues, would "announce the character and purposes of the building." Later he described the frieze as bearing designs "embodying national traits described by the poet."[13] Inside, the walls were to be covered with paintings illustrating scenes from Cooper's novels, and a sculptured portrait of the novelist by him was to stand at one end of the room. To Bryant he added that the ceiling should be blue, with stars, and that there should be a pavement of reticulated iron hexagons, "defying the chewing race for 24 hours and movable for cleanliness." There was to be "no unmeaning flourish or foliage or girigoggoli whatever" anywhere about the building. It was, above all, to embody the genius of Cooper as "the abstract type of the *American ideal man.*" "I count," he wrote in his essay,

upon the soul of this building to impress itself on the body, and if, as I believe, its purpose is great and noble, let no man fear that greatness and nobility will not get utterance through the hands of those who rear and illustrate it, even as the leaden types arrange themselves now at the command of the long buried Shakespeare.

More practically, he proposed that a model of the structure be made before any work was done.

Probably this plan of Greenough's was regarded as too expensive, as he himself seemed to fear. By the end of March a total of only a thousand dollars had been received by the Cooper Monument Association, as the group sponsoring the project was then called. By April Greenough had evidently severed his connection with it. He may have been referring to the failure of his plan to be approved when he wrote to a correspondent that

Neither my habits or my temperament adapt me for managing an undertaking of this kind without the presence of 2 data—1st a desire for the success of the enterprise on the part of the constituency—2nd a preference of my work on other grounds than those of personal influence and electioneering. I have done all that I think I can do without pushing.[14]

No monument to Cooper of any sort was erected by the Association.

About this time Greenough was also concerned about the financial state of Cooper's family and offered to contribute fifty dollars to a fund from which the novelist's debts might be paid.[15] Evidently no such fund was established.

During Greenough's sojourn in New York early in 1852 he met young Mann S. Valentine II, author and art enthusiast, who recorded several conversations the two had, perhaps in the hope of publishing them.[16] A fragmentary composition among Valentine's notes was entitled, "Horatio Greenough An Aesthetic Reminiscence." Greenough was, Valentine wrote, "a person of grand proportions, commanding air, & noble features." The author asked the sculptor's opinion of his book, *Amadeus,* then ready for publication, especially of his conception of the ideal sculptor as one who harbored ideas inexpressible in stone and was aptly represented by a female figure chained to a rock. Greenough was evidently only moderately encouraging. Few men of Valentine's age, he told the youth, really understood "the *Actual,*" which he defined as knowledgeable not only from the world but from the great artists and writers of the past. He disapproved of Valentine's image of the sculptor and argued, characteristically, in favor of accomplishment and practicality. "I do not like him—I hate him," Valentine reported that he said of Ruskin.

> Why does he not do something in his art. . . . I like . . . to have marriage and offspring . . . I love Hazlitt altho he failed the other is despicable—I have no feeling with yr transcendentalists. . . .

They reminded him of a spider placed on a piece of wax in a saucer surrounded by water, who escaped by running out on a thread as he threw it, though its other end was attached to nothing.[17] Greenough's "whole love," Valentine thought, "was his country's eminent distinction," and his "character & influence abroad" were an honor to America. He was "high toned, proud & noble," with "a classic mind," yet "too coldly pure" to be appreciated by his countrymen. Later that year Valentine purchased Hubard's portrait of Greenough.

About the middle of January, receiving word that his and his wife's estate was in danger because of the critical financial position of her trustee Josiah Quincy, Jr., Greenough cut short his stay in New York and returned to Boston. The crisis was soon averted, but Horatio stayed on in Boston for some two months or more. He several times saw Longfellow (his pamphlet contained "a good deal of truth," Longfellow thought, "rather brusquely uttered"); heard Emerson's lecture "Worship"; dined with Emerson and Thoreau at Longfellow's; was consulted by Everett about the best position for his statue of Arno in Everett's library; and interested himself in the Boston sculptor E. A. Brackett, then in straitened circumstances. After attending the exhibition of Brackett's group, "The Shipwrecked Mother and Child," he wrote Richard Dana a letter praising it and proposing to contribute to a fund with which it might be purchased for some institution. The letter was printed promptly in the Boston *Daily Advertiser* and subsequently in the exhibition catalogue of the Boston Athenaeum (when the work was exhibited there), the New York *Evening Post,* and the *Home Journal.* Both of these papers referred complimentarily at the time to Greenough as a judge. He was, declared the *Home Journal*, the "highest artistic authority in the country." In reply to the editor of this paper, Greenough disclaimed any such role, submitting that as a citizen he was merely "one of the jury" and as an artist he was on trial himself. He had, he said, merely tried to do for Brackett what Allston, Morse, and "many distinguished men of letters" had earlier done for him: notice the artist's work in a manner so as to give him more work.[18]

Probably about the middle of March Greenough went again to New York to see about a new monument project just being launched there: the erection of a bronze equestrian statue of Washington.[19] A group of New Yorkers, led by merchant James Lee, hoped to raise $50,000 from a hundred subscribers for such a work. The most subscribed, however, was $34,000, by sixty-eight persons. According to Tuckerman, half this sum was secured by Greenough's "personal applications."[20] For this sum a contract was made about the first of April with Greenough and H. K. Brown, then living in Brooklyn, who had had some experience with bronze and who had at his service a group of French workers in this material. Greenough was to design the statue and Brown to superintend its casting. Greenough wrote two letters to the New York *Evening Post* about the project late in April and early in May, enclosing with the latter a list of the subscribers; by that time the number had decreased to fifty-two.

The statue was to stand in Union Square, the site where Washington drew rein upon entering the city after its evacuation by Sir Guy Carleton. It was to be fourteen feet high, exclusive of the pedestal, and the figure of the General was to be clad in the military dress of the Revolution. Evidently Greenough decided on the dimensions and had done so by early April.[21] By early May he had conceived a set of accessory figures: four statues of subordinate generals to stand at the angles of the pedestal and in the rear the figure of Benedict Arnold, veiled to the waist. He thought that as the talents of Arnold had been great, his crime had been a major threat to the success of the Revolution, and that it was

as if Judas were excluded from the *Cenacolo,* when our constellation of patriots appear shorn of this damned contrast.[22]

Those with whom he conferred about these figures, however, objected to the representation of Arnold. By July he had evidently set up a studio at 151 Atlantic Street in Brooklyn.[23] By the end of the summer he had presumably modeled the horse for the figure of Washington.

By that time, however, the partnership between him and Brown had been dissolved. Probably Greenough's desire to elaborate the design together with the uncertainty that all the subscribers could be depended upon made the joint enterprise infeasible. The painter Walter Gould had wondered in the beginning how the two would "get along together."[24] In September a contract was made with Brown alone, whereupon seven more subscribers withdrew. The next year Brown began work on the statue, and in 1856 it was set up. Tuckerman and Calvert thought that Greenough had suggested what was original in the work, and Tuckerman wrote an article in a New York newspaper making that claim. Brown, however, assumed complete credit.[25]

In the spring and summer of 1852 Greenough worked on another piece which he intended to put in bronze: a colossal bust of Cooper. Matthew Brady furnished him with a daguerreotype as authority. Late in July the model was reported finished. At that time he proposed to erect the bronze at his own expense on a granite shaft, near the old mill in the vicinity of Newport, Rhode Island, where part of Cooper's *Red Rover* was laid, if this site were given over to public use. The model was not cast and has evidently been destroyed. Judged from a print, it resembled his earlier treatment of the subject but was more rugged.[26]

During these months Greenough became interested in other uses of metals and in metals other than bronze. Calvert remembered that he liked to go into foundries and that when he came out he would make drawings of iron fences, bedsteads, and stoves. Late in May he was trying to launch the project of erecting a fire-proof hotel in New York. Two hotels having just burned, he "beat while the iron was hot," he jokingly wrote Henry. Disturbed, especially after long familiarity with stone edifices, by finding combustible materials still so commonly used in American building, he heard with interest architect Richard Upjohn talk about introducing cream-colored brick into New York.[27]

In May, recognizing his theoretical as well as practical concern with art, some of the "leading men of letters" in New York broached him about filling a professorship of art in a university "on a grand scale."[28] He was invited to meet a committee in order to discuss the matter but was out of town at the time. Nothing further seems to have been done about it.

Meantime the middle Greenough child—four-year-old Mary Louise—had become ill, and by the latter part of May Horatio had taken his whole family to Newport for the benefit of the sea air. Throughout the summer they remained there, and he shuttled between this city, New York, and Boston. In one of his exhilirated moods soon after reaching Newport, he wrote Henry that the scent of some sweetbriar near their house "seemed to unlock old, closed-up cavities in the brain and lungs and added ten years' vitality to my frame," and exclaimed, "God is great and Newport is His abode." The Calverts were permanent residents of the city, and the Longfellows, Bancroft, G. W. Curtis, Tuckerman and other friends of the Greenoughs were there during the summer. The men often dined and swam in the surf together. Greenough had delayed choosing a place of residence in the United States, pending the outcome of the several projects he was considering, but now he decided to settle here. About the first of September he bought two lots on the hill above the city, on which he planned to build a residence and a studio. He was full of sculptural projects. According to Tuckerman, he had at this time partially sketched studies for twenty years' work.[29]

He was also full of ideas on subjects other than art, to be expressed through other than artistic media. Tuckerman noted a change in him, possibly produced by his "domestic ties":

As he had once talked of art he now talked of life. His affections had led him to reflect upon human destiny; and I found him as eloquent and as ingenious in the discussion of the religious sentiment and educational theories as he was wont to be when intent upon the vocation of the artist.

In some of these speculations Tuckerman thought him "imaginative," though "remarkably in earnest and reverent of nature as the true mother."[30]

In May and June he wrote three letters to the editors of the *Home Journal,* ostensibly concerned with artistic subjects but essentially moral in nature. They were in answer to an anonymous critic, probably G. W. Curtis, who had written disparagingly in the New York *Tribune* of A. B. Durand and Bryant, asserting that neither had obeyed the "stern claim" made upon every artist, the "terrible law" calling for him continually to grow and surpass his own best achievement.[31] Greenough's second letter, entitled "The Stern Claim and the Terrible Law," contained the crux of his argument. The "man of genius," he declared, was "pre-eminently the servant of a God whose service is perfect freedom," acting under pressure from within not without, belonging to the future more than to the present. It required "the collective heart of man to make a quorum to judge the broad, the deep, the genial soul." Yet therein lay a tragedy:

> The man of vast power of mind is like the fortress full of armed hosts, with spears glittering over the turret, with pointed artillery and burning match. We set down to sketch it and glorify it more cordially, when the portcullis chain is broken, the guns are spiked, and the ivy and the owl have possession of its towers.[32]

To this letter the critic replied, though only to defend his original position. Subsequently his identity became known to Greenough, and in a passage appended to the text of his three letters printed in his book later in the year Greenough disclaimed any personal implication in them.

Throughout the first nine months after his return to America, Greenough wrote a good deal: at least some fifteen or twenty essays and an assortment of aphorisms in addition to *Æsthetics at Washington*. He showed many of these pieces to some of his literary friends, who "united," Tuckerman said, "in admiration of their freshness, beauty, and acumen."[33] By the summer of 1852 he had decided to bring out a volume composed of some new and some old pieces. Early in August the manuscript was in the hands of G. P. Putnam, the New York publisher.[34]

In the middle of that month, on August 18th, Greenough at last went to Concord and stayed a day and a night with Emerson. Emerson was captivated. "An extraordinary man," he wrote in his journal of his visitor,

> a man of sense, of virtue, and of rare elevation of thought and carriage. One thought of heroes,—of Alfieri, of Michael Angelo, of Leonardo da Vinci. How old? "Forty-seven years of joy I have lived" was his answer. He makes many of my accustomed stars pale by his clear light. His magnanimity, his idea of a great man, his courage, and cheer, and self-reliance, and depth, and self-derived knowledge, charmed and invigorated me, as none has, who has gone by, these many months. I told him I would fife in his regiment. The grandest of democrats. His democracy is very deep, and for the most part free from crochets—not quite,—and philosophical.

He also recorded several of Greenough's opinions expressed on this occasion—on the unity of humanity and of human activity, on function in relation to beauty, on England. It was "a most memorable visit," Emerson wrote Henry Greenough years later.

> Until that day I had no knowledge of the power of his genius, or the wealth of his mind. His ingenuity his variety of knowledge, his eloquence, his power of illustration, his high moral demands, his ideal democracy, &, through all, the perpetual presence of the Artist, were an incessant surprise & delight to me.[35]

While Greenough was at Emerson's George P. Bradford, one of his college classmates, also called and was equally delighted and astonished at Greenough's discourse. A few days after Greenough's visit Emerson wrote his brother William, who was planning to build a new house on Staten Island, suggesting that Greenough be consulted about the design.[36]

In the summer word of Commodore Morgan's decision not to load "The Rescue" reached Washington. Throughout the summer and the fall Greenough corresponded with government officials there about his overdue payment for it, and late in September he was in the city again, presumably in connection with his claim.

About this time—"a few weeks" before his death, Louisa said—a daguerreotype was made of him, possibly by Brady. In April, when he gave Greenough the daguerreotype of Cooper, Brady had wanted to take Greenough's picture, but Greenough had asked that the process be postponed until he had shaved. The likeness which was made was "speaking," Louisa thought. It reveals a great deal of tension and weariness, and seems to be that of a man much older than Greenough, then forty-seven.[37]

2

Throughout the month of August Putnam's advertised Greenough's book among its forthcoming publications. By the second of September he had received copies of it, presumably unbound. During the remaining few months of his life he considered, largely on the advice of Emerson, making various revisions in the text, but there was no other printing. Only a few copies were distributed, and only two are known to have been preserved.[1]

The volume bears the title, *The Travels, Observations, and Experience of a Yankee Stonecutter,* and gives the name of the author as Horace Bender (adopted perhaps partly in recognition of the literary bent of Greenough's mother's family). Its 222 pages are divided into eighteen chapters, a Preface, and a Con-

HORATIO GREENOUGH, 1852.
(From the daguerreotype in the author's collection.)

clusion. A quotation from Schiller—"We are never so truly in earnest as when at play"—appears on the title page, and a print of Mills' design for the Washington Monument forms a frontispiece. Four of the chapters had been previously printed: "Remarks on American Art" (the original ending referring to Powers is omitted in the book), "American Architecture," "Æsthetics at Washington" (all the essays in the pamphlet), and "The Stern Claim and the Terrible Law" (all three letters to the *Home Journal,* with a short postscript). The rest were evidently written, like the last two, after he arrived in America in 1851. Half the total number deal with artistic subjects. The other half—of which four were collections of aphorisms—are expressions of his personal prejudices on a variety of social, moral, and political subjects. A blank page follows Chapter Sixteen, and the last two chapters lack numbers, seeming to have been appended. The words "End of Part I" appear on the last page, with the explanation:

The foregoing pages, intended as contributions to a newspaper, have been put into this form the better to test their capacity to obtain a hearing. I now close this first part, that I may not waste my words until I know if I can have an audience.[2]

As a whole, the book lacks unity. The subjects of the non-artistic chapters bear little relation to those of the others or to each other; the title is not particularly pertinent; the frontispiece is misleading; the point of view is part intellectual gentleman and part common sense philosopher. It is uneven both in substance and style. At best Greenough wrote in a vigorous, affirmative and metaphorical vein, expressing sound and penetrating artistic judgments and excelling in giving examples of his points. He tended, however, to indulge his fondness for foreign and slang words, to belabor small issues, and to be captious, especially in the social and political spheres. The text abounds, moreover, in misspellings and errors of punctuation and typography, for which Greenough was at least partly responsible. Altogether the volume reflects his increasing distraction throughout 1852.

Greenough's *Travels* is, nevertheless, a book remarkable for the range of interests, the liberality of views (with the notable exception of his view of the Negro), and the independence of mind which it exhibits. To a great extent it exemplifies the organic or functional theory applied to literary expression, as he himself recognized. ("If I seek another form, another dress than that with which my thought was born, shall I not disjoin that which is one?" he inquired.) Whereas Greenough's letters generally echo eighteenth-century rhetorical patterns, his essays—especially the later ones—are, in their loose construction, sudden transitions, and unfinished effect, related to new traditions. They also belong to a distinctively American tradition: the expression of personal opinion on an assortment of subjects in an often blatant tone by a Yankee character type. In one sense it was a particularly inappropriate role for him: with the Yankee as rustic, peddler, and mechanic he had nothing in common. Yet in his venturesomeness and self-reliance and on the international scene especially—where he consistently played Brother Jonathan to John Bull and defended the democratic faith and the Puritan ethic against their Old World enemies—he did indeed represent a native type. His book is, finally, unified to a remarkable degree by the functional point of view, which dictates judgments in almost every chapter.

In the Preface, Greenough represented his motive in writing as being largely the desire of a notionate New Englander for self-expression. But he also owned another motive, which was more indicative of his essential character and, as it proved, prophetic:

. . . I am arrived at that *"mezzo del cammin,"* that half-way house, where a man sees, or thinks he sees, both ways. . . . I begin to love to sit alone—to look upon the skies, the water and the soft green—the face of the mighty mother! I feel that she thus sweetly smiles on me . . . because she means to call me home to her own bosom. I would not pass away and not leave a sign that I, for one, born by the grace of God in this land, found li[f]e a cheerful thing, and not that sad and dreadful task with whose prospect they scared my youth.

Of the hitherto unprinted chapters in the book, five are concerned with artistic subjects: "The Cooper Monument," "A Place for Everything," "The Stonecutter's Creed," "The Shin Piece," and "Relative and Independent Beauty." "A Place for Everything" and "The Shin Piece" are of little consequence: in the first he recorded his pleasure in seeing that the unnecessary figurehead of a steamer in the New York harbor had lost both arms and one leg; in the second he described a visit he made to the Trumbull Gallery in New Haven and defended Trumbull's "The Declaration of Independence" in the rotunda of the Capitol. More than half "The Cooper Monument," containing a description of the edifice which he had proposed earlier in the year, is devoted to the exposition of general principles of structure considered in relation to function. He now emphasized more than in any earlier exposition the importance of industrial design. The "American trotting wagon" he cited as proof of the fact that

The redundant must be pared down, the superfluous dropped, the necessary itself reduced to its simplest expression, and then we shall find, whatever the organization may be, that beauty was waiting for us, though perhaps veiled, until our task was fully accomplished.

Far from calling the style of mechanics "cheap," he pronounced it

the dearest of all styles! It costs the thought of men, much, very much thought, untiring investigation, ceaseless experiment. Its simplicity is not the simplicity of emptiness or of poverty, its simplicity is that of justness, I had almost said, of justice.

"The Stonecutter's Creed" and "Relative and Independent Beauty" reflect a more distinct development in Greenough's thought: a turn toward philosophy and religion. His creed had been prepared, he said, for his young son, who had asked him what God was. "Three things, my child," he replied,

have I seen in man worthy of thy love and thought. Three proofs do I find in man that he was made only a little lower than the angels—Beauty—Action—Character.

By beauty I mean the promise of function.
By action I mean the presence of function.
By character I mean the record of function.

The glory of beauty is the faith of future action.
The honor of action is the hope of future character.
The divinity of character is the charity that giveth itself to God, in sacrificing self to humanity.

These three do I find, and the greatest of these is charity. Go thou, my child, into the thoroughfare, test these my words, and if they be clever statements of a lie, say to them, *retro Satana!* But if they be feeble lines of truth, come to me once more, and we will pull these threads and seek to know where their other end is fastened.

He illustrated these articles of belief by describing the life cycle of a leaf from April to November. There was, he declared, not a deity for each season, but one for all, whom he thus addressed:

Thou who dost not grope as I, but seest, who art not dumb as I, who have dabbled in jargons till I have lost my vernacular, and gained no tongue, but speakest, say of man, say of nations, say of creeds, say of every juxtaposition of parts for an end what I have tried to say of the leaf; what thou feelest I struggle after, even as the drowning man clutches, vainly, and if it be not true, there must be more Gods than one.

In "Relative and Independent Beauty" Greenough developed the formula set forth in "The Stonecutter's Creed." Since the "normal development of organized life" was from beauty to action to character, he reasoned, any attempt to prolong the first phase could only be "through non-performance; and false beauty or embellishment must be the result." This result could be seen in "THE INSTINCTIVE EFFORT OF INFANT CIVILIZATION TO DISGUISE ITS INCOMPLETENESS, EVEN AS GOD'S COMPLETENESS IS TO INFANT SCIENCE DISGUISED." The conception of independent beauty—"the grand conservative trap"—came from man's perceiving in nature "a sensuous beauty, not organically demonstrated" to him because of his limitations. To assert that anything was beautiful per se was "to arrogate godship." Yet he was convinced that

there is not one truth in religion, another in the mathematics, and a third in physics and in art; but that there is one truth even as one God, and that organization is his utterance.

In terms of the human creature, this meant that both its lower and its higher requirements had to be satisfied. "The brute man," he put it, "clings to the higher man, he loves him even as himself, he cannot be shaken off, he must be assimilated and absorbed."

Of the essays which composed the other half of Greenough's book the most ambitious and provocative was "Fourier et hoc Genus Omne," in which he most fully set forth his antipathy for theoretical thought. He pictured the typical theorist as a man perched on "an income which is a dead branch of the living tree of industry," spouting "generalities" irrelevant to the needs of the day.

He hath said in his heart that God's world till now hath been but rough draft on slate, and saith that he hath a sponge. No so, brother! This is a fight, come down and take thy side. . . .

In his opinion, the ideas of Aristotle, Bacon, Machiavelli, Rousseau, Alfieri, and Wilberforce would have been "mere masturbations of the brain" had they not gotten into "the brains and arms of men who knew not how to write. "[S]tudy thou thy anatomies!" he exclaimed.

it is well! still shalt a Silesian peasant cure while thy utmost book only sufficeth to kill; study thou thy electricities and chemistry in thy Institut and Royal College, yet shall one American painter alone, report thee to the antipodes, another row thee thither. . . .

He urged Henry James, Sr., to read his *Lectures and Miscellanies* "in German beerhouse" or before a group of Irish immigrants to discover the impracticality of the ideas in it. (In April of this year he recommended this volume to Henry as containing "some sharp criticism of nonsense.")[3] He found the ideal man in Shakespeare,

not only because he is genial, warm and real, not only because he is substantial, hath an *avoirdupois,* a perfume and a taste, but because he is multiform, elastic, not procrustean, not monomaniacal.

In two essays, "Abolition" and "Development" (assembled, significantly, with "Fourier et hoc Genus Omne" to form one chapter), Greenough expressed his violent prejudice against the Negro. "I am not partial to negroes," he began the first.

I dislike their neighborhood even in a menial capacity. I prefer doing many tiresome, and some very disagreeable things for myself rather than be very near a black man.

. . . .

I turn my back on him, as all animals spurn their own ordure.

. . . .

I could sleep on the same straw with a horse, I love him! On the same straw with a negro, or a low, white man, never!

Though he conceded the low-white might be enobled, he was sure the black perished in the process of civilization. He compared the "abolition mania" to

a child's sucking its thumb, or a puppy tearing in pieces whatever falls in its way. It is an instinctive effort to relieve a certain *demangeaison* or uneasiness produced by the teeth pushing through the gums.

As a substitute he suggested that

the philanthropist of the north might find a very pretty coral plaything in the question of prostitution for instance, which might occupy their gums for a while. . . .

"The Virtue of Chastity" contains the same general argument on this subject which Greenough had advanced in some of his writing in the 1840's. At best, he thought, chastity was a negative virtue. The notion that it was anything more, he declared,

comes from very far east and is very old—I am, however, from very far west and forming part of the chain that holds this young country, calling aloud for offspring, I am disposed to look narrowly into the matter.

He questioned especially the practice of celibacy among the Roman Catholic clergy, pointing out its usefulness as a political policy, the violations of it, the tragedy of young men who too early submitted to it. "With all the energy of my soul," he concluded,

do I spurn the wretch, whether he wear a gilded coat or a black one, who, thinking to read my nature by the light of his own perverted consciousness, seeks to poison my peace with the fear that my love of woman is not as near what my Maker intended it, as my body is to the normal type of manhood. . . .

In "Bank Note Typography," "Soup and Sleeping," and "Filth" he protested unduly about minor issues: his experience of inadvertently attempting to pass a Springfield, Illinois, bank note in Massachusetts and having it rejected; Webster's remark —undignified under the circumstances, Greenough thought— after hearing that he had lost the Presidential nomination, that he was going to bed and to sleep; the failure of Brooklyn to dispose properly of its refuse and sewage. His aphorisms, too, were for the most part ineffective. The most successful were sympathetic judgments of the Roman Catholic Church.

On September 2 Greenough sent a copy of his *Travels* to Emerson, calling attention particularly to "The Stonecutter's Creed" and "Relative and Independent Beauty" and asking for Emerson's criticism. Now that he saw these chapters again, he felt sure they were not fit for publication, though he was convinced the views were sound. "I care not," he wrote, "for the slovenly *opus,* but I am sensitive about the *materia.*"

Again Emerson responded promptly and enthusiastically. Greenough's was, he thought,

> a very dangerous book, full of all manner of reality & mischievous application, fatal pertinence, & hip- and thigh-smiting personality, and instructing us against our will.

He questioned its success on the popular level, pointed out that Greenough had been "unpardonably careless" in proofreading, and deplored the fact that "it should confound things on the negro question, & put weapons from a most unexpected quarter into the hands of the base & greedy partisan." But he declared that

> it contains more useful truth than any thing in America I can readily remember; & I should think the entire population well employed if they would suspend other work for one day & read it. As long as they do not, you may be very sure a few of us will profit by the secret & deal it out to them little by little.

It raised in his mind "the old question, Why not a journal in this country that will combine the sanity & talent of really liberal men," and he felt "tempted to go out into the highways & drum the *rappel,* now that I see this new strength." In a postscript he added that "the splendor of statement" was "better than Canning."[4]

On the same day Emerson wrote his brother William again, enclosing a letter of introduction to Greenough and urging William to read Greenough's book when it appeared.[5]

Greenough, prepared for more severe criticism, was delighted by Emerson's praise. He decided to distribute only a few copies of the volume, "in order to get light and help," and to issue a revised edition. He asked Emerson to mark the particular passages which Emerson thought needed revision, yet he defended at length his attitude toward the Negro and slavery.[6]

In reply Emerson recommended that Greenough dispense with a pseudonym, correct a certain "want of perspective" in the work as a whole, omit all possible names and personalities and some colloquialisms ("some less low, but some intolerable, like *nincompoop*"). Again he remonstrated about Greenough's attitude to the Negro ("Ah no, Slavery is a poor hoggish thing, with which you & I have nothing to do") and suspicions of England. But he urged that the book be printed. Ellery Channing and Thoreau agreed with him about its "importance": "Its radical good sense, its reality, & its strong American flavor captivated them also." A few weeks later Emerson sent Greenough some lines from Martial, in which the poet urged Faustinus to issue his writings to the public.[7]

On October 25, after his trip to Washington, Greenough went again to visit Emerson in Concord, having meanwhile developed somewhat further, he said, his views of structure and organization. This time he stayed a day. As before, the two men talked of a variety of subjects—Fourier, England, sex, Puritan esthetics, diet, ornament, the Elgin marbles, foreign influence in America—and Emerson recorded Greenough's opinions in his journal at even greater length than on the earlier occasion.[8]

A few days later Emerson made further suggestions about Greenough's *Travels* in a letter to him. On looking the volume over once more, Emerson had not found any chapter which he wanted to suppress:

The brush with the Tribune is the one I had first marked: but that contains good sense, &, with a little dropping of the compliments, on which I must insist, that may stand. The chapter on Webster's night-cap, of course, cannot now stand, unless with some grave & generous preamble inserted [Webster had died a few days before]. For that on chastity, you must judge for yourself. I like it well enough. That on abolition, I have told you, is bad: if you print it, we will roast you. The Illinois bank-note, again, whether you keep these lighter craft, must depend on how much soldier matter you may find in your portfolio. Some or all of the Preface, I could willingly spare,—if it came to particulars,—for instance, the first page.

But again he advised,

Rather than not publish, if the sponge & interpolation take too much time, print away, good & bad, with all my heart; and suddenly.

"You have done me a world of good by a pair of conversations," he added. "May I often see you!"[9]

Greenough was pleased with Emerson's suggestions, which he promised to adopt in their entirety. With his reply he enclosed another piece on the Negro, asking Emerson as the "man midwife of my babe" to point out its weak points. "I will fight this fight to the end of all time," he declared, "for I believe we are after all, together." The new piece Emerson thought had its merits, but was

very splendidly wasted powder, & all makes only more flagrant this new example of genius spent in a bad cause.[10]

Early in November Greenough prepared to deliver two public lectures in Boston on some of his ideas, in order, he said, "to get the means to print." He meant to make his theory "live according to the strictest rule of demand & supply.[11] According to Tuckerman, he wrote out both lectures, but he also planned to read from his *Travels*. Having no copy, he sent to borrow Emerson's.

About this time Greenough read Sumner parts of his "book on the Beautiful," as Sumner called it, including at least one essay (on Burke) not in the printed volume. In Sumner's opinion, no European artist had excelled him with the pen.[12] Among those who received a copy of the volume was Tuckerman, who was agreebly reminded by it of the author's conversation.[13]

At his death Greenough left a number of unpublished essays and shorter pieces and "copious notes"[14] for lectures besides the two which he had delivered. Tuckerman thought there was sufficient material, including some correspondence, to fill more than one volume. Louisa planned eventually to publish all Greenough's manuscripts. Yet she felt there was "much in his writings to provoke discussion," and considering his derangement at the time of his death she wished for a good while afterward "to avoid every thing of the sort."[15] With her approval, selections from his published and unpublished writings were included with the biography of him by Tuckerman and several tributes in *A Memorial of Horatio Greenough,* brought out under Tuckerman's name in 1853. Ten of the pieces in Greenough's *Travels*—mostly those of artistic or esthetic nature—and three new ones appeared in the later volume. They were, Louisa thought, "prudent—perhaps judicious" selections. Yet she felt they did not give "altogether a just idea of the elevation and strength of his character."

On the essays by Greenough reprinted in *A Memorial of Horatio Greenough,* a good deal of editorial work was done, presumably by Tuckerman. Obvious errors were corrected, the punctuation revised extensively, and much of the phraseology altered, being generally refined and often weakened. "The Cooper Monument" was made into two essays. Probably the three essays here printed for the first time were edited in similar fashion. They were entitled "Burke on the Beautiful," "Criticism in Search of Beauty," and "Fashion." All were probably written in 1852.

In the essay on Burke, Greenough aligned himself with the

relativists in the eighteenth-century dispute between them and the absolutists over the nature of the beautiful. In "Criticism in Search of Beauty" he expressed more distinctly organic concepts than in any other composition. Reviewing several other definitions of beauty besides his own, he insisted that all were false because its creation in art was not a "scientific synthesis" but "a welling up from the depths of the soul." It was an expression of life, which could "only be obtained by *living*." Moral and political applications followed:

To follow blindly the dictates of sense and instinctive craving—that is, to be a brute and not a man; to deny the promptings of sense and instinctive craving, that is to perish. Behold the absolute. Between these lies human life—an existence for which no revelation will ever afford a mechanical rule or absolute dogma, without its immediate translation from time to eternity. . . .

Because the American people tended to eschew such absolutes, because they were "one vast interrogation," he felt they were the "advanced guard of humanity." In the short piece about fashion Greenough defined this phenomenon as "the instinctive effort of the stationary to pass itself off for progress." Yet insofar as it denoted "a lurking want not clearly expressed," a "protest against finality," he thought it raised hope of better things.[16]

Tuckerman's volume brought the best of Greenough's essays to public attention, and generally the comment on them was favorable. The reviewer for the New York *Evening Post* quoted the passage on the ship from "American Architecture" and perspicaciously associated Greenough's "exceedingly severe" taste with his theory of structure. Yet both this reviewer and the one for the *Herald* regarded Tuckerman as a better writer than Greenough. John Bigelow thought that Greenough's perception of analogies was remarkably acute and felt that he might have become as eminent a master of literary as of plastic art. "He was," Charles Eliot Norton wrote Arthur Hugh Clough of Greenough,

a man perhaps not of the highest genius, but full of that originality in combining and creating which forms so large an element in what we mean by genius. These writings of his look rude, unfinished, but vigorous, fresh and full of his own nature, unfinished like Michel Angelo's Brutus, not from deficiency, but from excess of power.[17]

Two years later three other pieces by Greenough were printed for the first time, in the *Crayon,* a periodical devoted to artistic concerns. They were an untitled fragment beginning with a description of a Chinese ivory ball within a ball (an example of a mere mechanical achievement, having "no fruit or result")[18]; "Dress" (in which he found modern clothing objectionable in relation to temperature, to motion, and to taste); and "A Sketch," the description of a church service in an Austrian village. Probably they were all composed in the 1840's.

Altogether six literary compositions of Greenough's were thus published posthumously. Probably he left little else in other than the form of notes and fragmentary sketches. Only one unpublished essay has apparently been preserved—that on religion and man's nature, probably written at Grafenberg.

As reflected in all the writing he did at the time, the general drift of Greenough's thought during the last decade of his life is clear. It became both broader and more abstract. As he earlier passed from the practice to the theory of art, he became at last a moral philosopher. In this role, too, he exhibited affinity with both old and new schools. For all his hostility to the Transcendentalists, he was in many ways one of them. He attributed to mercenary interests most of the ills of society as well as the bad taste in art. His repeated references to the process of generation reflected his distinctly organic concepts of phenomena, and his relativism was in keeping with the evolutionary spirit. This relativism, however, was held in check by his concept, typically deistic in details, of a powerful absolute. Compared to other moral philosophers of his day, he was perhaps most distinguished for his recognition of the importance of man's sexual instinct. Indeed, his idealization of enlightened and cultivated social states was to a great extent saved from insubstantiality by this recognition. Yet he regarded man, for all his kinship with the brutes, as having been created supremely for intellectual and moral action.

3

Throughout the year after Greenough's return to America in 1851 the number and variety of his activities was remarkable. As symptomatic of his mental state at this time, however, they were alarming in these same respects. Stimulated on the one hand by the new environment, frustrated on the other by the delay in the transportation of "The Rescue" and the final payment for it, he became increasingly keyed up. Though probably not the original cause of his final collapse, these circumstances seem to have precipitated it. Apparently his family and closest friends felt them to be chiefly responsible.

Tuckerman emphasized the effect of the change of environment on him. "Greenough's temperament," he wrote,

> was both sanguine and nervous—a combination more favorable to a receptive and sympathetic, than a self-possessed and tranquil character. . . . Artist-life in Italy, so calm, absorbing, and undisturbed, was fitted to his nature. . . . The restless, bustling, ever changeful existence that infects the very atmosphere of this country were sometimes oppressive and irritating. He felt the absence of that equability and routine, that keeps brain and heart so well balanced in the old cities of Europe. He missed the gradations by which the temperature seems to adapt itself to the sensitive frame. . . . It seemed as if the genius of enterprise around had

infected his mind with a tendency to action at once impulsive and uncertain. He constantly broached new plans; and sought to attach others to his own aims. . . . He caught the spirit of the times, and was eager to throw his energies into the stream of popular activity. There was soon obvious not so much an inconsistency of thought as a want of correspondence between his avowed sentiments and purposes and his actions. It was evident that his mind had become unduly excited, as is so often the case with the novice in American life.[1]

Others recognized the long history of and the important hereditary element in Greenough's condition. "The most there heard said," R. H. Dana, Jr., wrote Sumner two days after Greenough died,

is that nervous excitability is constitutional with him and hereditary, and has been growing upon him for several years, aggravated lately by change to our exciting climate, failure of all occupation, and some anxiety and discouragement arising out of the manner in which his statue has been neglected by our government.[2]

In the fall Henry and one or two of his intimates noticed that he was "under a little too great nervous excitement." About that time he changed his mind once more about his residence and decided to return with his family to Florence permanently the following June.[3] The fact was evidence of his increasing instability.

Until his collapse, however, he seemed to nearly all who saw him in perfect health. "I never knew," Dana wrote Sumner, "the case of a man so full of health and vigorous manly beauty, so soon struck down." Tuckerman, visiting him at Newport early in the fall thought that he never appeared "more full of noble aims, more kindled by the inspiration of nature and society, and more abounding in intellectual sympathy." They passed a rainy evening together, Greenough working on a crayon head and discoursing on a variety of topics. "With the skill of a consummate *improvvisatore,*" Tuckerman recollected afterward,

he had told a story in the dramatic and artistic way peculiar to him . . . he had analysed, with tact and discrimination, several characters of our mutual acquaintance; he had ably discussed a question of public concern, and he had evolved several *bon-mots. . . .*[4]

On November 21st, a few days before his final illness, Greenough was a guest at the dinner Emerson gave for the English poet Clough, at the Tremont House in Boston. Other guests were Hawthorne, Longfellow, J. R. Lowell, Theodore Parker, Sumner, Samuel Ward, and Ellery Channing.[5]

A day or so later, Greenough called on Bronson Alcott and left a card of admission for his first lecture. Later he returned and spent the evening with Alcott, discussing "art—the symbolism of man's body, particularly," Alcott recorded in his journal. So impressed did Alcott become by Greenough's conversation, lectures, and probably his essays, that he listed the sculptor as the subject of one of the six "conversations" he proposed to conduct in Boston a year later.[6]

On November 24 Greenough read the first of his two lectures, on "Art as Related to Life," in the Lecture Room of the New Music Hall on Winter Street, at four-thirty. Tickets were available at Ticknor's and Munroe's bookstores and at the door. The audience was, the *Transcript* reported, "highly gratified." Frances and presumably Henry were there. Alcott pronounced it "An admirable essay, and far too metaphysical and fine for the few who came to hear." R. H. Dana, Jr., however, referred to both lectures as "the first work of an unbalanced mind." On the 27th it was announced that the first lecture would be read again, the time and place to be determined later.[7]

On the 29th Greenough read his second lecture, in the same room as the first, at a quarter to four. Again the audience was small. Only $14 was realized from the sale of tickets for both lectures. On the occasion of the second, according to the record made at McLean Asylum in Somerville when he was entered as a patient there soon afterward,[8] what he said was "a curious *mixture* of *incomprehensibleness*," which nevertheless did not surprise his audience, they supposing it to be only his style. T. B. Curtis was convinced that he was mentally disturbed and advised his return to his family. The following day—the 30th—Greenough spent the morning with Alcott, discoursing, Alcott wrote in his journal,

> sagely on art and artists, to my great surprise and profit. He amazes by the subtlety and mysticism of his distinctions, no less than by his great American sense and solidity of perception.[9]

That night he dined at Henry's. "Not well," Frances wrote in her journal, though she did not indicate to whom she referred. The next day Henry went with Horatio to Newport.[10] That day Henry also procured at Horatio's request a letter of credit for $2000 from Curtis to settle Horatio's account with his Florentine bankers.[11] In Newport Horatio soon suffered an attack of "violent mania," as the McLean record put it, which rendered him completely irrational.

On the 4th Henry brought him, in a closed carriage, back to Cambridge and on the same day he was taken, in a strait jacket, to McLean's. Here he survived two weeks. According to Tuckerman, his sufferings were slight and his "delusions" "of a gay rather than a despairing nature."[12] He continued in a state of excitement, at first standing and gesticulating though not noisy, later sleeping for short intervals, talking "constantly," R. H. Dana, Jr., said, mostly if not entirely in Italian. He took food but most of the time had no natural elimination. On the 10th he was wearing lead straps. On the 18th he "sunk" suddenly, and at six o'clock in the morning he died. He was visited twice by

Dr. George F. Bigelow, but apparently no treatment was attempted. The cause of his death was given in the Cambridge Death Records as "nervous derangement" and in most other accounts as "brain fever."

During these two weeks Louisa was seriously ill at Newport. A few hours before word arrived of Horatio's death, it was dramatically prophesied by her two Tuscan women. Finding a large owl, which had descended the chimney, in the parlor, they declared it was an omen that the "*Padrone* would surely die."[13]

The funeral was held on December 21 at Henry's, conducted by the Rev. Dr. James Walker, President of Harvard. Longfellow was one of the few present. It was "Rather private," he wrote in his journal. "Dr. Walker officiated solemnly. Mournful day!"[14] Interment was in Mount Auburn Cemetery. Louisa, who came from Newport, returned there the following day.

Greenough left no will. In the settlement of his estate his assets were valued at $5851.97, of which $5830 was owed him by the government. The remaining amount consisted chiefly of the sum received from the sale of the lecture tickets. When all the claims against the estate were in except the final hospital bill (which Henry paid) and the expenses of the administration, they came to nearly $8700.[15]

On December 6, while Horatio was at McLean's, news reached Boston of John Greenough's death in Paris late in November. Only Henry and Richard among the brothers were left. He had, Henry wrote Powers in the spring, lost three brothers in a year, "the last the nearest & dearest tie I had to Earth, excepting only my own wife and children."[16]

Throughout 1853 Louisa corresponded with the poet and spiritualist Mrs. Sarah Whitman, attended seances, and read a good deal about spiritualism, in the hope of establishing communication with Horatio, but she never felt that she did.[17] (Mrs. Browning reported that she received a message from him.)[18] She soon had the name of her son changed to Horatio. She lived until 1891, much of the time, like her children Horatio and Charlotte (Mary Louise died two years after her father), in Europe.

At the time of Greenough's death the newspapers in Boston, Newport, and New York carried long obituaries of him. Possibly Bryant wrote that in the *Evening Post,* in which it was said that a day passed in Greenough's studio or wandering in the fields with him was one to be remembered. That in the Newport *Mercury* may have been written by Calvert. Calvert composed an elegy, "Monody on the Death of Horatio Greenough," in which he defined the "highest man" as one

> Whose dreams die not—in whom the ideal,
> Surging for ever, makes life real,
> Ending where it began,
>
> In visionary deeds,

and invoked mourning for Greenough because he was such a man:

> Then mourn, my country! Shed
> Deep tears from thy great lids, and borrow
> Night's gorgeous gloom to deck thy sorrow;
> Greenough, thy son, is dead.

When the news of Greenough's death reached Rome early in 1853, all the American artists in the city, together with John Gibson and others, met at the home of Thomas Crawford and passed memorial resolutions, recognizing Greenough as "the Pioneer of American Sculpture," who "lived and shone not merely for success, but to elevate Art," and also as "eminently a gentleman . . . and high-minded man."[19]

In most of the private eulogies of him, too, Greenough was

praised more as a man than as an artist. "He was a noble, gallant fellow, so full of life!" Longfellow wrote in his journal on learning that Greenough had died. The "best thing about him," Charles Eliot Norton wrote Clough shortly afterward,

was his liberal, unjealous, generous heart. He was never scrimping or narrow in his praise of men whose reputation as artists were growing while his own was rather falling from its height.

Emerson, who was lecturing in the west at the time, did not hear immediately of Greenough's death. He was in Cincinnati, he recalled, writing to Henry eleven years later, when he

learned what an end had come to all my joy & exultation. It was the more deplorable, that he appeared to be in the perfection of manly power & beauty. I must think that the country has never met so great an intellectual loss as in that life; and I say it in the recollection of his extraordinary conversation, which seemed to me to cast all his works of art with all their excellences into shade.

"Our few fine persons are apt to die," Emerson wrote Carlyle in April 1853.

Horatio Greenough, a sculptor, whose tongue was far cunninger in talk than his chisel to carve, and who inspired great hopes, died two months ago at forty-seven years.

In July he made the following entry in his journal:

I do not think of any American in the century who would make so good a subject for a lecture as Greenough. But oh to hear again his own eloquent and abounding discourse!—but he passed away suddenly like the brightest of mornings.

I account that man, one product of American soil (born in Boston), as one of the best proofs of the capability of this country—[20]

As a man, Greenough made, indeed, an extraordinary impression on Emerson, which remained with him throughout the rest of his active life. Evidences of the fact are scattered through his journal, his essays, and his lectures.[21] Probably partly because of his failing strength, he did not accede to Louisa's request in 1869 that he write Greenough's life.[22]

There was, however, one notable member of Greenough's generation who, without having any personal acquaintance with him to be influenced by, accorded him his due as an artist. This critic was James Jackson Jarves. "We were as fortunate," Jarves wrote in *The Art-Idea,* published in 1864,

in having Horatio Greenough for a pioneer in this direction [sculpture] as Allston in the sister-art. Both were true artists, in advance of their times, inspired by the best examples of the old schools, though in execution unequal to their conceptions. Like Allston, also, Greenough's ambition prompted him to a high range of art. His aesthetic feeling was eminently lofty and pure. We cannot point out any masterpiece, as showing an entirely satisfactory fulfillment of his own desires, but his whole career was an example in the right direction.

He lamented that American sculpture as a whole had disregarded its first practitioner and been "speedily seduced into the facile path of realism by the national bias to the material and practical," but he felt confident that,

As we rise to the level of his sympathies and knowledge, so shall we better understand him and appreciate his efforts.[23]

As his greatest admirers and as he himself apparently realized, Greenough was not a great creative artist. He was most successful in his less ambitious pieces of sculpture, and he barely ventured to embody in edifices his theory of architecture. Yet, as Jarves recognized, his conceptions of the nature of art and architecture and of the character of the artist and his relation to society were vital conceptions. His major talent and his chief legacy were intellectual ones, as Emerson bore witness. Yet it was above all essentially an art-idea which he promulgated, as Emerson, with his limited artistic sensibility, did not fully appreciate.

To Greenough art was the supreme expression of man, the affirmation of his physical and his spiritual, his individual and his social nature. It was the great reconciler, the major link not only between the real and the ideal, but between the common and the enlightened classes, the democratic and the heroic principles, the present and the past, the New and the Old Worlds. To him all these forces, potentially antagonistic to each other, were parts of a whole, which it was the task of man and of nations to unite. To him the union was not only symbolized but practically achieved by the transformation of rude and disparate elements of nature into beautiful and useful forms for men.

Plates

Sculpture and Sketches for Sculpture

Drawings

Of the fifty-five or more works of sculpture by Greenough which have been located—nearly half the total number he executed and probably more than half the number still in existence—thirty-seven appear in the following plates. In addition, photographs of or studies for fifteen others appear. Altogether, all his original statues, groups, and bas-reliefs which are known to exist or of which depictions are available, together with typical specimens of his male, female, and children's portrait busts and his ideal busts are represented.

Relatively few of the large number of drawings which Greenough produced seem to have been preserved. He customarily made studies in ink or pencil for his sculpture; especially as a student drew from the antique, the nude, and anatomical parts; made several finished drawings for presentation to friends; and sketched a great deal, often in a vein of whimsy or caricature, for his own amusement. Except for his finished drawings, none of which has been found, all these types of his drawing are represented in the following plates.

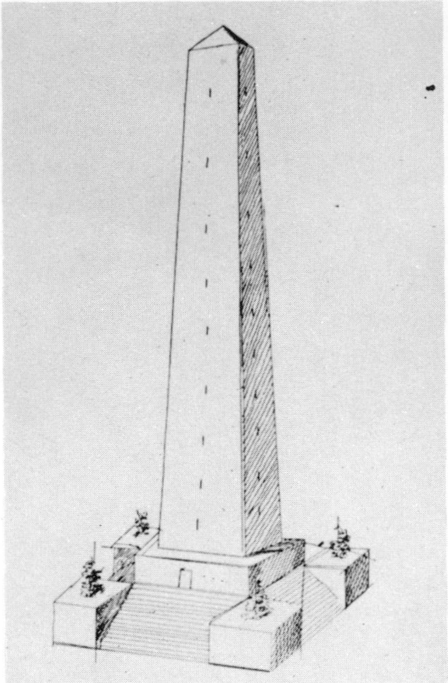

Drawing for the Bunker Hill Monument.
(From G. W. Warren, *The History of the Bunker Hill Monument*.
Boston, 1877.)
Tracings of drawings for accessory statuary.
(Inscriptions in Henry Greenough's hand.)
(Author's collection.)
1825.

JOSIAH QUINCY, SR. 1826–1829.
(Courtesy of Mr. Edmund Quincy and the Massachusetts Historical Society.)

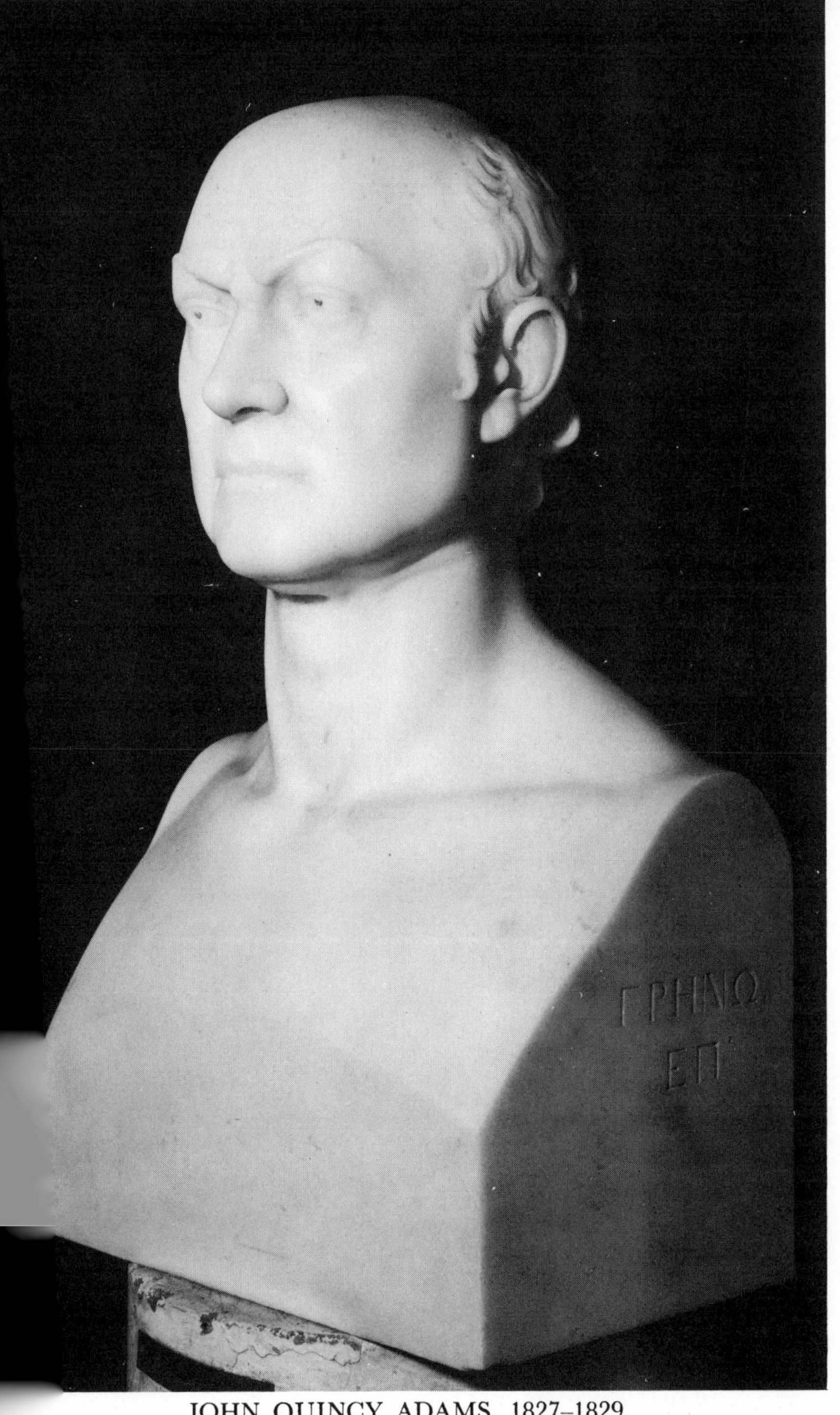

JOHN QUINCY ADAMS. 1827–1829.
(Courtesy of the Boston Athenaeum.)

JOHN ADAMS.
(Courtesy of the Boston Museum of Fine Arts.)

SARAH R. LADSON GILMOR. 1828–1829.
(Courtesy of Mrs. Grover Cleveland Edwards, Inman, S.C.)

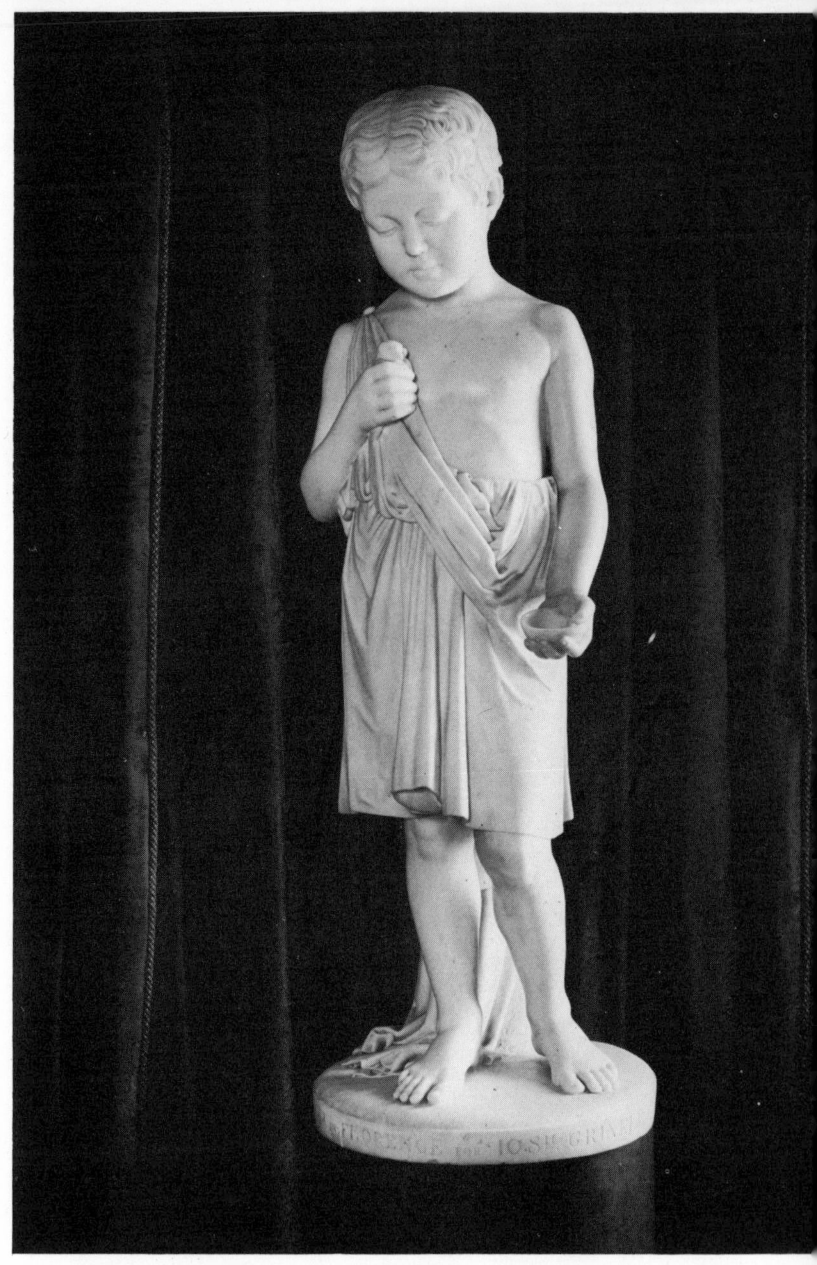

CORNELIA GRINNELL. 1830–1832.
(Courtesy of Mrs. William Burnham, Brookline, Mass.)

THOMAS COLE. 1831.
(Courtesy of Mrs. Florence Cole Vincent, Catskill, N.Y.)

SAMUEL F. B. MORSE. 1831.
(Courtesy of the National Collection of Fine Arts, Smithsonian Institution, Washington.)

MEDORA. 1831–1833.
(Courtesy of Mrs. Sumner A. Parker, Baltimore.)

GEORGE WASHINGTON. c1830–1834
(Courtesy of the Boston Museum of Fine Arts.)

MARIE JOSEPH PAUL YVES ROCH GILBERT
DU MOTIER, MARQUIS DE LAFAYETTE. 1831–1834.
(Courtesy of the Pennsylvania Academy of the Fine Arts, Philadelphia.)

JAMES FENIMORE COOPER. 1831–c1833.
(Courtesy of the Boston Public Library.)

Sketch of THE GENIUS OF AMERICA. 1832–1833.
(From S. I. Prime, *Life of Samuel F. B. Morse,* N.Y., 1875.)

NATHANIEL PARKER WILLIS. 1832–c1834.
(Courtesy of Mrs. William Burnham, Brookline, Mass.)

WASHINGTON. 1832–1841.
(Courtesy of the National Collection of Fine Arts, Smithsonian Institution, Washington, D.C.)

ELIZABETH CABOT. 1832–c1833.
(Courtesy of Dr. George C. Shattuck, Brookline, Mass.)

ANGEL AND CHILD. 1832–c1833.
(Courtesy of the Boston Museum of Fine Arts.)

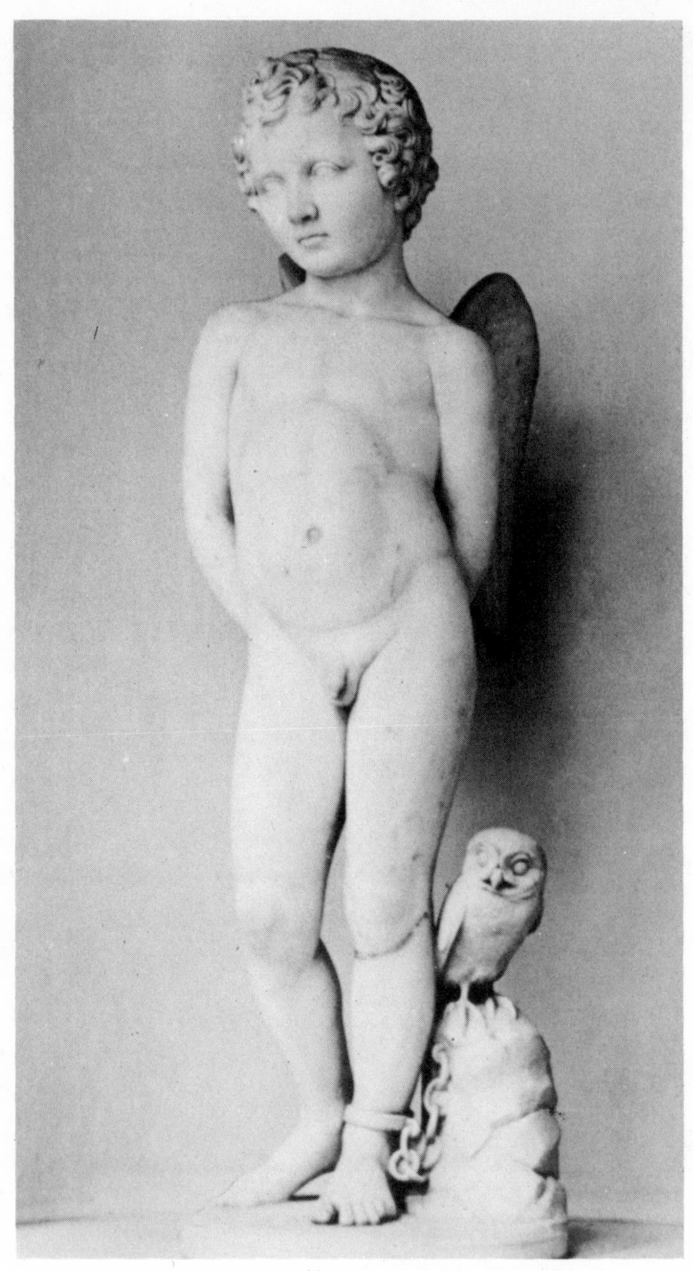

LOVE CAPTIVE. c1834–1835.
(Courtesy of the Boston Museum of Fine Arts.)

MARY FRAZIER CURTIS. c1833.
(Courtesy of Mrs. Louis Curtis, Brookline, Mass.)

JAMES FREEMAN CURTIS. c1841.
(Courtesy of Miss Mary Curtis, Hamilton, Mass.)

FOREST CHILDREN. 1835–1837.
(Grace and Knyvet Winthrop Sears.)
(Courtesy of the Massachusetts Historical Society, Boston)

DAVID SEARS. c1834–1835.
(Courtesy of the Somerset Club, Boston.)

ELLEN ADAIR WHITE. c1833–1834.
(Courtesy of the Mary Buie Museum, Oxford, Miss.)

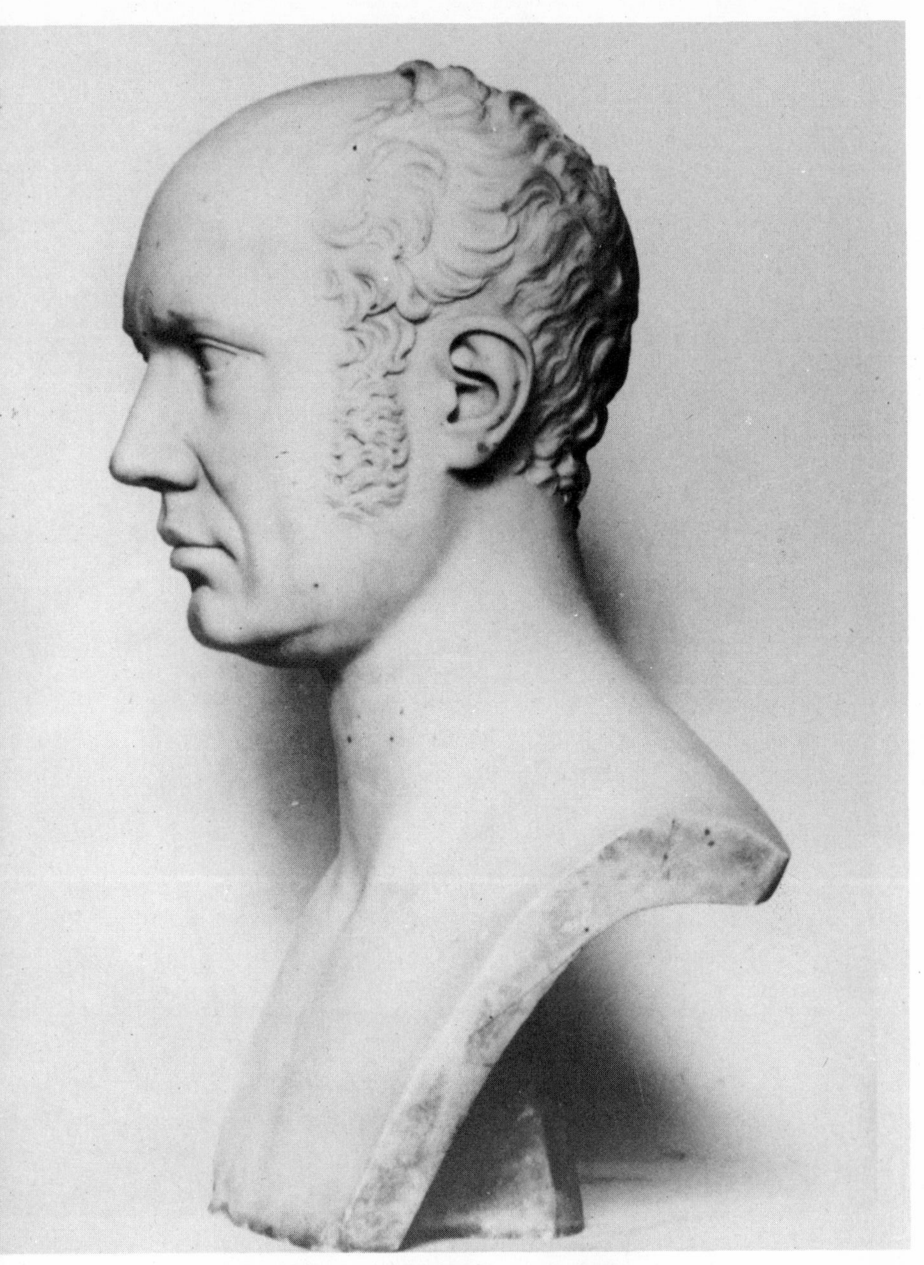

JOSEPH M. WHITE. c1834–1835.
(Courtesy of the New York Historical Society.)

SAMUEL APPLETON. 1836–c1838.
(Courtesy of the Fogg Museum of Art, Harvard University.)

EMILY MARSHALL OTIS. 1836–c1844.
(Courtesy of the Boston Athenaeum.)

ELIZABETH TODHUNTER THOMAS.
(Courtesy of the Maryland Historical Society, Baltimore.)

EVAN PHILIP THOMAS. 1837.
(Courtesy of the Maryland Historical Society, Baltimore.)

Drawing of the rejected design for the group for the east front of the Capitol. 1837. (?)
(Author's collection.)

THE RESCUE. 1837–1851.
The U. S. Capitol, Washington.

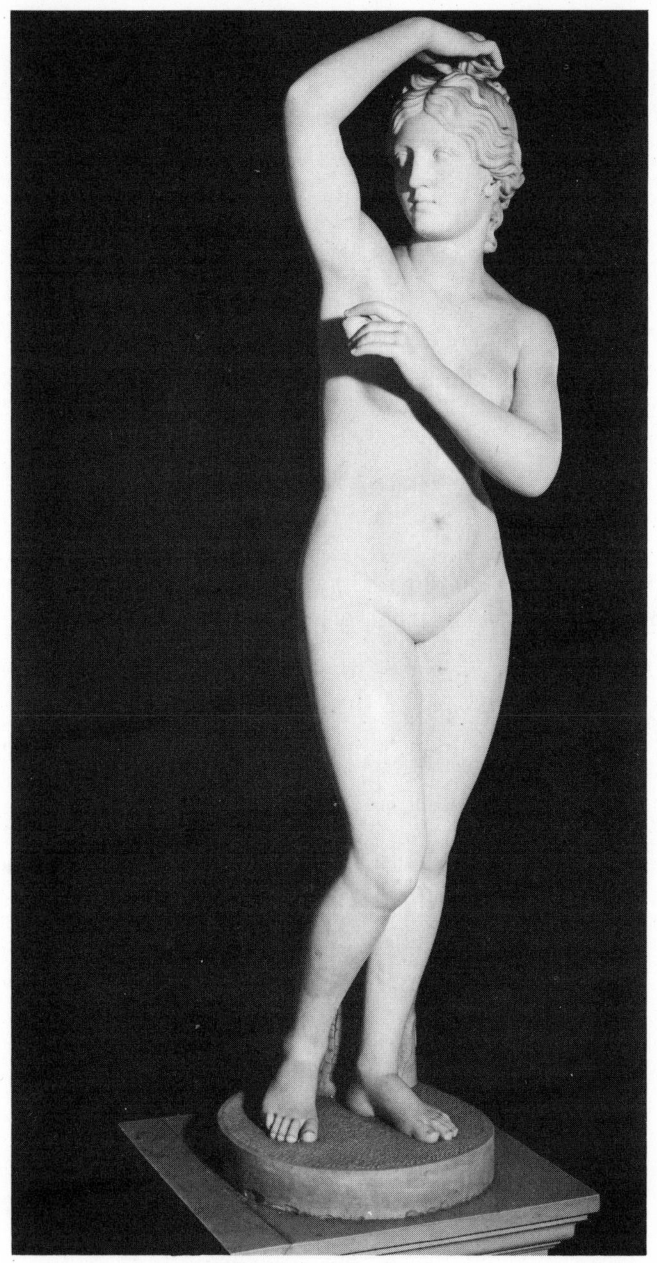

VENUS. 1837–c1841.
(Courtesy of the Boston Athenaeum.)

ABDIEL. 1838–1839.
(Courtesy of the Yale University Art Gallery.)

ST. JOHN AND THE ANGEL. 1838–c1841.
(Courtesy of the Yale University Art Gallery.)

JOHN WARREN. c1838–1839.
(Courtesy of the Fogg Museum of Art, Harvard University.)

MEMORIAL TO GEORGE AND MARY GIBBS. c1839–1842.
St. Mary's Church, South Portsmouth, R. I.

LUCIFER. 1841–1842.
(Courtesy of the Boston Public Library.)

CHRIST. c1845–1846.
(Courtesy of the Boston Public Library.)

ARNO. c1838.
(Courtesy of Gerald Horrigan, Quincy Adams, Mass.)

ST. BERNARD DOG. c1844.
(Perkins family lot, Mt. Auburn Cemetery, Cambridge, Mass.)

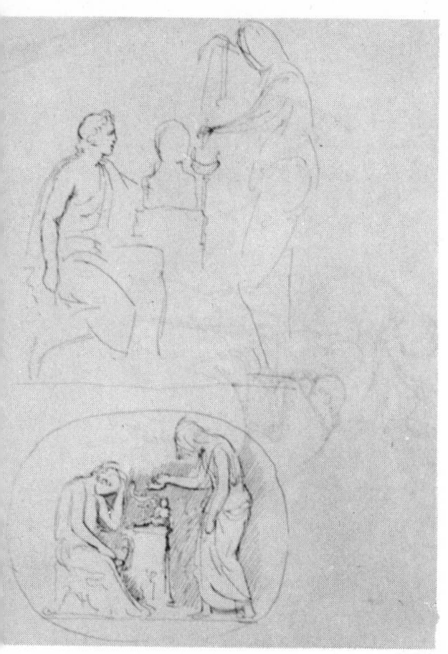

Drawings for
ARTIST WHOSE LAMP IS BEING REFILLED, 1847–1849;
Samson and Delilah group, c1847 (not executed);
ADA REVICZKY, 1840–1841 (?);
equestrian Washington, c1851 (not executed).
(Author's collection.)

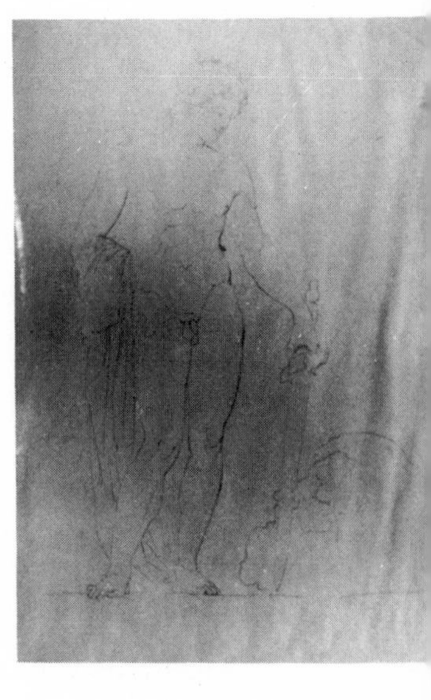

Drawings for
Electra, Orestes, and Pylades relief (?), c1847 (not executed);
THE GENIUS OF POESY, 1850 (?);
DAVID, c1844.
(Author's collection.)

CASTOR AND POLLUX. c1847–1851.
(Courtesy of the Boston Museum of Fine Arts.)

THE GENIUS OF ITALY. 1850.
(From a photograph in the author's collection.)

BACCHANTE AND YOUNG FAUN. c1850.
(From a photograph in the author's collection.)

HOMER. 1847–1851?
(Author's collection.)

Nude figure from Roman sketchbook.
Lake Nemi; the Colonna Castle on the left. 1826.
(Author's collection.)

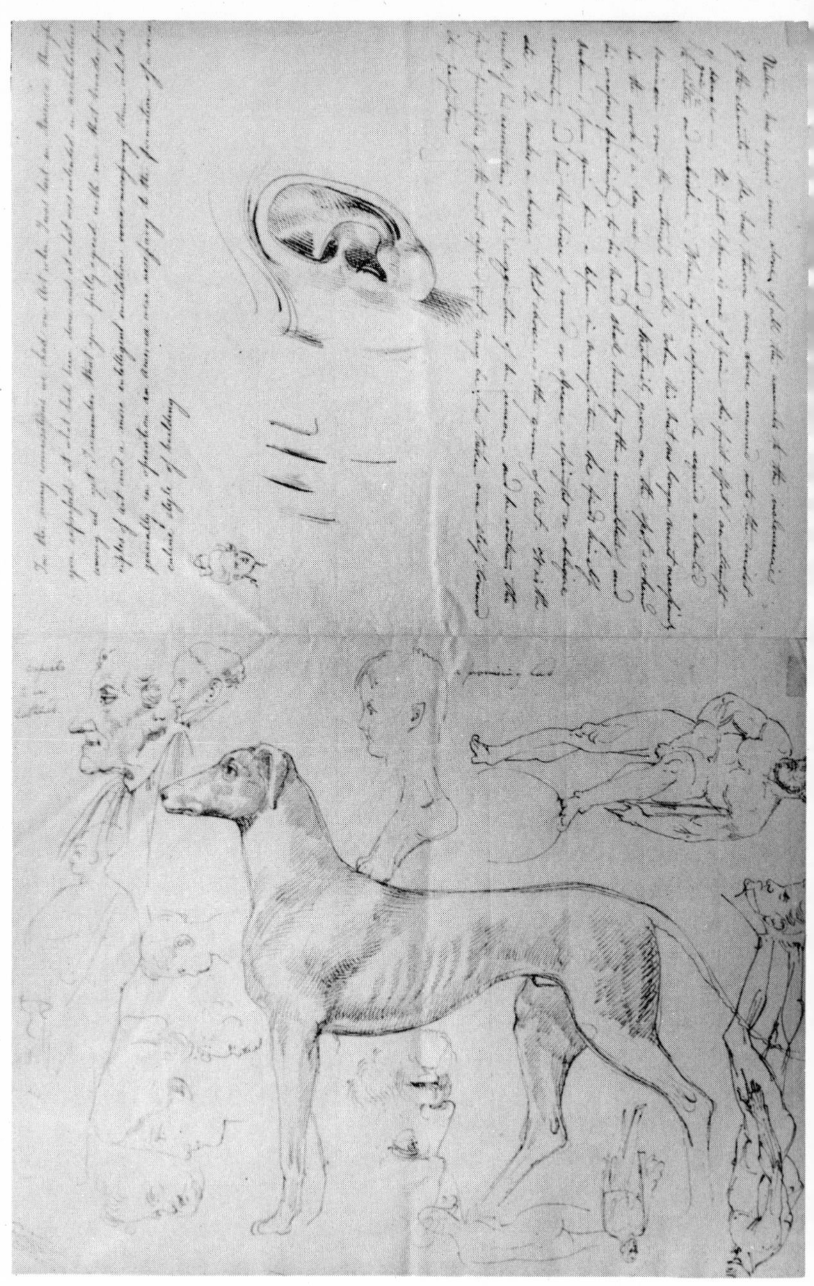

Draft of letter to Washington Allston, Oct. 1831.
(Among the sketches are profiles of Samuel F. B. Morse, with the notation, "expects to be lathered"; probably Paul Cooper, with the notation, "a promising lad"; and Albert Brisbane.
(Author's collection.)

David playing to Saul.

Helios restraining Phaeton from mounting the sun chariot.
1832.
(Author's collection.)

Athena interposing between Achilles and Agamemnon. 1832
(Author's collection.)

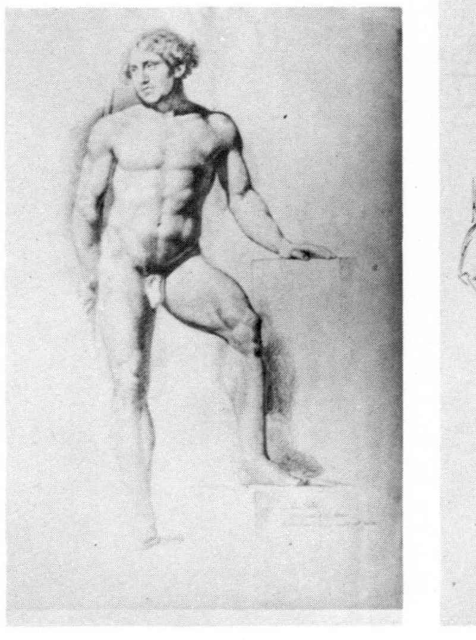

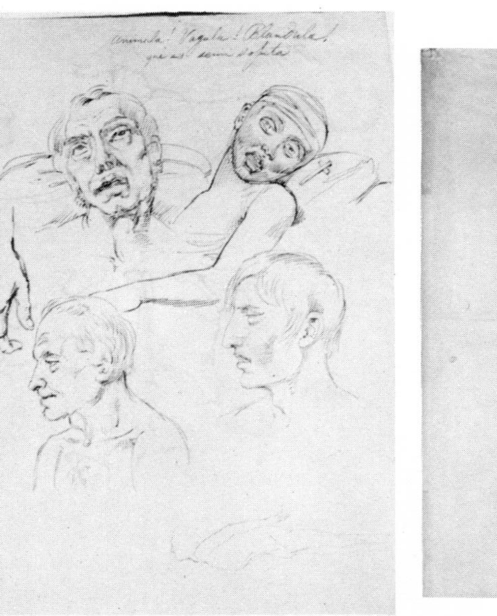

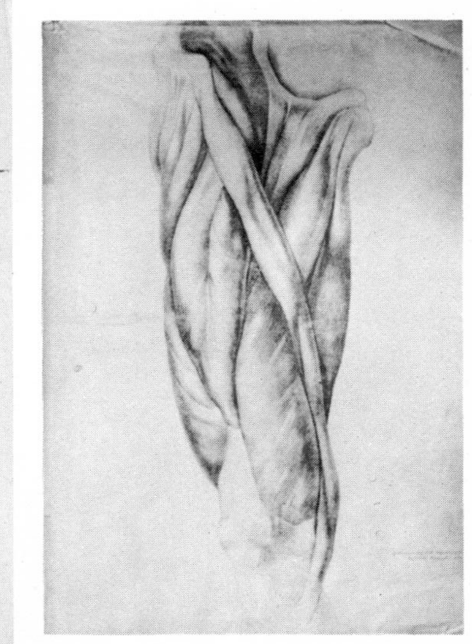

Nude model; "Dec 1830 First week of the Nudo begun Tuesdy evg—could not finish".
Hospital patients; "Animula! Vagula! Blandula! qui es semi sopita". c1835.
Thigh muscles; "Copied from a study at the Hospital of S. M. Nuova By Giuseppe Bezzuoli—1832—".
(Author's collection.)

Joseph Russell?　　Louisa Ingersoll Gore?

1836?

(Author's collection.)

Four portraits.

Upper left : c1831.
Lower left : 1831.
(Henry Greenough?
inscription in Henry's hand.)

Upper right : 1847–1851?
Lower right : 1845–1850?
(Frances B. Greenough?)

(Author's collection.)

Four *cappriciosi.*

Upper left : c1831. Upper right : 1830's?
Lower left : c1847. Lower right : 1847–1851?

(Upper right, courtesy of Miss Alice Thorndike, Manchester, Mass.; others, author's collection.)

Notes

GENERAL SOURCES

The fullest account of Horatio Greenough's life heretofore published is that by Henry T. Tuckerman in *A Memorial of Horatio Greenough* (New York, 1853), which also contains essays by Greenough and tributes to him. This book and *Letters from Horatio Greenough to his Brother Henry* (Boston, 1887), edited by Henry's wife Frances, are the chief printed sources drawn upon in the present biography. The manuscripts of the letters in the latter volume—seventy to Henry and three to other persons—have (except for that to Robert Winthrop) probably been destroyed. Evidently they were not among the family papers inherited by Frances' grandchildren. The fact that Horatio's wife was displeased by Frances' publication may have had some bearing on the disposition of these letters. (See Frances to Louisa G. Greenough, Sept., 1891, not sent; in the possession of David Richardson, Washington, D. C.).

The chief primary manuscripts which have been used are 207 letters or portions of letters from Greenough to various persons, in scattered locations. These and twenty-eight known only in printed or quoted versions are all the other letters of his which have been located. Few letters received by him seem to have been preserved. Only four other manuscripts of his have come to light, all essays, three of which were printed in the *Crayon* in 1855 (all in the possession of Henry G. Nickerson, Dedham, Mass.).

A sizable collection of Greenough's papers and drawings belonged after his death to his wife and later to his daughter, Charlotte Greenough Du Quilliou. At Mme. Du Quilliou's death, at her residence in Vevey, Switzerland, about 1919, it was discovered that most of these papers, which were contained in a trunk, had been virtually destroyed by mildew and the remains were discarded. (This account was given the author by Mrs. Marguerite Wagnière Horton, whose mother, Laura Wagnière-Huntington, Mme. Du Quilliou's first cousin, was present when the trunk was opened.) Other effects of Greenough's were in a box which at that time was brought to Mme. Wagnière-Huntington's house at La Tour de Peilz, but the contents being unknown the box remained unopened until July 1954. (For an account of its being opened, see the author's "A Small Miracle at Petit Sully," *Manuscripts,* VIII (Fall 1955), 42–43.) It contained three of Greenough's portfolios, 139 sheets and a marble slab of drawings and a few drafts of letters by him, an expense account in his hand for his statue of Washington, photographs of some of his sculpture, his diplomas from three artistic societies, copies of his marriage certificate and death record, engravings of his "Lafayette" and his statue of Washington, and several miscellaneous items not directly associated with him, including a few drawings by his brothers John and Richard. (The entire contents, with the exception of one drawing of Greenough's owned by John D. Hatch, Lenox, Mass., are now in the author's collection.) Few other drawings by Greenough seem to have been preserved, chiefly those in his Roman sketchbook (author's collection). Sketches attributed to him are in the Baltimore Museum of Art, the Free Library of Philadelphia, and the collection of Thomas Brumbaugh, Emory, Ga.

The chief study of Greenough's sculpture is Thomas Brumbaugh's "Horatio and Richard Greenough : A Critical Study with a Catalogue of their Sculpture" (Ph.D. dissertation, Ohio State University, 1955), to which the present study is often indebted. The catalogue of Greenough's sculpture herein incorporated is largely based on Mr. Brumbaugh's. Of the total number of Greenough's works here listed—125 to 140, nearly half—55 to 58 (including five duplicates)—have been located. At least 25, many in plaster only, have probably if not certainly been destroyed. Most of the remaining number would be portrait busts.

The chief secondary sources used in the present volume are letters and journals (mostly in manuscript) and travel books written by Americans who visited Florence while Greenough was there and American newspapers during the period of his adulthood. Especially valuable for the years after 1837 are the letters to and from Hiram Powers (most of which are part of the Powers estate in Florence, the property of his descendants) and for the middle 1840's the letters written by Frances B. and Henry Greenough from Europe (David Richardson) and Frances' journal (in the possession of Miss Alice Thorndike, Manchester, Mass.).

ABBREVIATIONS

Dunlap : William Dunlap, *History of the Rise and Progress of the Arts of Design in the United States* (N. Y., 1834), 2 vols.
HG : Horatio Greenough.
Letters: Letters of Horatio Greenough to his Brother Henry, ed. Frances B. Greenough (Boston, 1887).
MHS : Massachusetts Historical Society.
Travels: Horatio Greenough, *The Travels, Observations, and Experience of a Yankee Stonecutter* (N. Y., 1852).
Tuckerman : Henry T. Tuckerman, *A Memorial of Horatio Greenough* (N. Y., 1853).

UNFOOTNOTED LOCATIONS

For the location of HG's letters and sculpture, see Index.

Letters received by HG and letters written by Frances B. and Henry Greenough are in the possession of David Richardson, Washington, D. C., unless otherwise noted.

Letters from members of the Greenough family to Hiram Powers and his wife and all existing sketches by HG referred to are in the author's collection unless otherwise noted.

The letterbooks of Hiram Powers and unless otherwise noted letters to him and his wife and letters from her are part of the Powers estate, Florence.

The diary and letterbooks of Edward Everett are in the MHS.

Part I

1

Boston Boy : 1805-1825

Greenoughs and Benders

The chief facts about the Greenough family are contained in John H. Sheppard, "Genealogy of the Greenough Family," *The New England Historical and Genealogical Register,* XVII (April 1863), 167–169; *Colonial Families of America* (N. Y., n.d.), VI, 118–124; Oliver A. Roberts, *History of . . . The Ancient and Honorable Artillery Company of Massachusetts* (Boston, 1895–1901), I, II, *passim; Massachusetts Soldiers and Sailors of the Revolutionary War* (Boston, 1896–1908), VI, *passim;* Chandler Robbins, *A History of the Second Church . . . in Boston* (Boston, 1852), *passim.* The papers of Thomas Greenough (HG's great-grandfather) are in the MHS. Letters from and to John Greenough (HG's grandfather) are in the MHS and the Boston Public Library; accounts of his early career are in various histories of Cape Cod.

Facts about the career of David Greenough are contained in *A Report of the Record Commissioners . . . Containing the Statistics of the United States Direct Tax of 1798 . . .* (Boston, 1890), pp. 213, 333; . . . *Minutes of the Selectmen's Meetings, 1811 to 1817, and Part of 1818* (Boston, 1908), pp. 114–115, 161–162; . . . *Boston Town Records, 1814 to 1822* (Boston, 1906), pp. 95, 127–128; . . . *Minutes of the Selectmen's Meetings from September 1, 1818, to April 24, 1822* (Boston, 1909), pp. 72, 122; "Original Bank Circular, 1809," *Proceedings of the MHS,* Ser. 1, XI (April 1878), 307–308; Andrews E. Ford, *History of the . . . Town of Clinton Massachusetts* (Clinton, 1896), pp. 151–153; L. Vernon

Briggs, *History of Shipbuilding on North River . . . Massachusetts* (Boston, 1889), p. 193; Suffolk County Registries of Deeds and Probate, Boston; Norfolk County Registry of Deeds, Dedham; Boston City Directories; Harvard College Papers, X, 26, Ser. 2, I–IV, *passim* (Harvard Archives). David and Elizabeth Bender Greenough are described by Frances B. Greenough in *Letters,* pp. 13–14.

No history of the Bender family has been published. Facts about the early Benders in Boston and Marlborough are contained in Lucius Marsh and Mrs. Harriet F. Palmer, *Bronsden and Box Families* (Lynn, Mass., 1902), p. 64; Charles Hudson, *History of the Town of Marlborough* (Boston, 1862), pp. 319, 325; *Vital Records of Marlborough, Massachusetts* (Worcester, 1908), *passim;* records of Trinity Church, Boston; Middlesex County, Southern District, Registries of Deeds and Probate, Cambridge; Boston City Directories. Elizabeth Bender Greenough is described by her granddaughter Laura Wagnière-Huntington in *From Dawn to Dusk* (Vevey, Switzerland, [1929?]), p. 13.

1. *Travels,* p. vii.
2. These portraits are reproduced in Lawrence Park, *Gilbert Stuart* (N. Y., 1926), III, 214, 215, erroneously identified as those of Mr. and Mrs. David S. Greenough II. (David S. Greenough I was a half-brother of David's father.) Another portrait of Elizabeth Bender Greenough attributed to Stuart is in the possession of Miss Alice Thorndike, Manchester, Mass.
3. The fullest descriptions are Samuel A. Bent, "Colonnade Row," *Boston Society's Publications,* Ser. 1, XI (1914), 9–57; and Frank C. Brown, "The First Residential 'Row Houses' in Boston," *Old-Time New England,* XXXIII (Jan. 1947), 60–69.
4. Caleb Snow, *A History of Boston* (Boston, 1825), p. 328.
5. HG to Cooper, July 30, 1836; to Wilde, Aug. 18, 1836.
6. *Occasional Verses* (Privately printed, n.d.), p. [13] (copy in the Boston Public Library).

7. Frances B. Greenough to Harriet B. Loring, Jan. 10, [1846].
8. HG to Morse, April 23, 1832.
9. References to the David Greenoughs during the years they lived in Jamaica Plain (and during a few other years) are contained in the account books of David S. Greenough I and the diary of David S. Greenough II (MHS), both of whom lived there at that time. For the Greenough references in the records of the First Congregational Society, Jamaica Plain, I am indebted to Mr. Clifford Bond, of that city, and for other assistance in tracing the Greenoughs there to Mrs. Herbert Boyd, Arlington, Mass.

The Statue in the Garden

Unfootnoted details in this section and the next two sections come from Dunlap, II, 413–415, 421–422, and Tuckerman, pp. 11, 13, 15–19.

1. Hannah Farnham Lee, *Familiar Sketches of Sculpture and Sculptors* (Boston, 1854), II, 132.
2. *The Letters of Raph Waldo Emerson,* ed. Ralph L. Rusk (N. Y., 1939), I, 119; Vivian C. Hopkins, *Spires of Form* (Cambridge, 1951), p. 79.
3. *Letters,* p. 16.
4. Harriet M. Whitcomb, *Annals and Reminiscences of Jamaica Plain* (Cambridge, 1897), p. 55.

Classical Academics

1. Dunlap, II, 413.
2. C. C. Carpenter (comp.), *Biographical Catalogue of . . . Phillips Academy Andover 1778–1830* (Andover, 1903), p. 71.
3. *Letters,* p. 17. The chief account of this academy is in Abijah P. Marvin, *History of the Town of Lancaster, Massachusetts* (Lancaster, 1879), pp. 521–535.
4. *Travels,* p. 16.
5. Dunlap, II, 415, 421.

6. Jared B. Flagg, *The Life and Letters of Washington Allston* (London, 1893), p. 252.
7. [John Bigelow], "Nuces Literariae," N. Y. *Evening Post,* Aug. 22, 1853.
8. Records of the Immediate Government, X, 70; the Conference is also listed in the Order of Performances for the occasion (Harvard Archives).
9. Harvard College Papers, Ser. 2, II, 115 (Harvard Archives).
10. For an identification of them, see the author's "Horatio Greenough's Borrowings from the Harvard College Library," *Harvard Library Bulletin,* IX (Autumn 1955), 406–410.
11. [Bellows], "Horatio Greenough," *The Knickerbocker,* VII (April 1836), 346; "Sculpture," *The New-England Magazine,* V (Dec. 1833), 483.
12. [Bigelow].

The Master

1. Tuckerman, pp. 16–17.
2. Dunlap, II, 421, 412; HG to Dana, June 11, 1844, Sept. 21, 1843.

The Argument for the Obelisk

The chief facts about the activities of the Bunker Hill Monument Association come from George W. Warren, *The History of the Bunker Hill Monument Association* (Boston, 1877) and from its unpublished records in the MHS.

1. The ms. letter is among the records of the Monument Association; it is printed in Warren, p. 159. The model submitted with the letter and drawings by HG of his proposed monument seem not to have survived. One of his drawings of the shaft, contained in his letter to Morse, [c April, 1832], is reproduced in S. I. Prime, *Life of Samuel F. B. Morse* (N. Y., 1875), p. 214. Others or copies of others are reproduced in Samuel Swett, "Horatio Greenough, the Designer of the Bunker Hill Monument," *The New England Historical and Genealogical Register,* XVIII (Jan. 1864), 60; and Warren,

opp. p. 162. A tracing of a drawing by HG for one of the pieces of sculpture is also reproduced in Swett, p. 60. The original of this tracing and tracings of drawings by HG for the other three pieces of sculpture, all made by one of Henry's daughters, are in the author's collection, together with a letter from Henry to Swett, Aug. 31, 1863, relative to them.

2. Swett, p. 63.
3. H. M. Pierce Gallagher, *Robert Mills,* (N. Y., 1935), pp. 204–207.
4. Minutes of the Association, May 21, 1825; HG to the Association, 1825 (described in *Autograph Letters and Historical Manuscripts belonging to the late J. Wingate Thornton. To be sold . . . Oct. 15th and 16th, 1878.* Boston : C. F. Libbie; and evidently in *Catalogue of the Kellogg Collection of Rare Autographs . . . to be sold by auction on Monday, May 2d, 1887.* Boston : C. F. Libbie).
5. Prime, p. 213. "*Parigina*" in this passage is probably a misprint.
6. *Extracts from the Diary and Correspondence of the Late Amos Lawrence* (Boston, 1855), pp. 338–339.
7. Dunlap, II, 415.
8. Dec. 8, 1833.
9. *Travels,* p. viii.

2

Student Abroad and Critic at Home : 1825-1828

Unfootnoted details in this chapter come chiefly from *Letters,* pp. 20–23, 25–41; Dunlap, II, 391–394, 415–418, 422; Tuckerman, pp. 11–12, 22–23; Irene Weir, *Robert W. Weir, Artist* (N. Y., [1947]), *passim.*

On Holy Ground

1. *Letters,* p. 21.
2. In later years Weir said that he and HG lived opposite Lorrain's, between the houses of Poussin and Rosa, but this description does not accurately locate these houses. (Cf. Dunlap, II, 392 and *Letters,* p. 24.)
3. Dunlap, II, 392.
4. *Ibid.*
5. May 9, 1826. Unfootnoted quotations in the rest of this section come from this letter.
6. HG to Allston, Sept. 19, 1829.
7. Dunlap, II, 422.
8. *Ibid.,* p. 416.
9. Among the portraits from life are several of Turkish types, probably made at Gibraltar.
10. Allston to Gulian Verplanck, Jan. 31, 1828 (copy, MHS).
11. HG to Allston, Nov. 17, 1829.
12. HG to Morse, May 15, 1828.
13. March 7, 1831.
14. The facts about his stay in Naples are contained in the following letters in the State Archives in Naples : Minister of Foreign Affairs to Prefect of Police, Jan. 17; Alexander Hammett to Minister of Foreign Affairs, Jan. 22 (copy); Minister of Foreign Affairs to Minister Secretary of State of General Police, Jan. 23; Minister Secretary of State of General Police to Prefect of Police, Jan 25; Prefect of Police to Minister Secretary of State of General Police, Jan. 31; Minister Secretary of State of General Police to Minister of Foreign Affairs, Jan 31; Minister Secretary of State of General Police to Prefect of Police, Feb. 3; Prefect of Police to Minister Secretary of State of General Police, March 22; Minister Secretary of State of General Police to Prefect of Police, March 22, 1827 (Archivo del Ministero di Polizia, 2° Ripartimento, Espediente n. 57).
15. McLean Asylum (Somerville, Mass.) Cases, 1852–54, p. 211.

Promethean Man

1. R. H. Dana, Sr., to Gulian Verplanck, April 2, 1830; see also Dana to W. C. Bryant, Nov. 15, 1827 (both in the New-York Historical Society).
2. Roman Sketchbook. On the same sheets with the Washington heads he drew the Infant Hercules struggling with the serpents, the subject of one of the reliefs on the chair of his "Washington."
3. Edmund Quincy, *Life of Josiah Quincy of Massachusetts* (Boston, 1868), p. 550.
4. III (March 1828), 115–116.
5. Quincy to Adams, Jan. 27, 1828 (MHS); Allston to Morse, Jan. 24, 1828 (Historical Society of Pennsylvania); Dana to Verplanck, March 12, 1828 (New-York Historical Society); Allston to Verplanck, Jan. 31, 1828 (copy, MHS).
6. Minutes of the National Academy of Design, May 7, 1828; *National Academy of Design Exhibition Record 1826–1860* (N. Y., 1943), I, 196–197.
7. *Letters,* pp. 25, 29, 34.
8. Adams, Diary, Feb. 20, 21, 23, 25, March 3, 1828 (MHS).
9. *Ibid.,* March 30, 1829.
10. *Ibid.,* Oct. 22, 1829; see also July 2, 3, 17, 18, 1829.
11. HG to Waterston, March 25, 1845.
12. [Letters of Chief Justice Marshall], *Proceedings of the MHS,* Ser. 2, XIV (Nov. 1900), 335. See also Marshall to Joseph Story, May 1, 26, 1828 (MHS).
13. HG to Allston, Sept. 19, 1829.
14. John Neal, *Observations on American Art* (State College, Penna., [1943]), pp. 38, 24.
15. *Ibid.,* p. 25.
16. *Letters,* pp. 29, 40.
17. HG to Morse, May 15, 1828.
18. HG to Gilmor, May 17, 1828.

3

Art Colonist : 1828-1886

Quarries of the Renaissance

1. HG to Gilmor, May 17, 1828; Dunlap, II, 417; HG to Gilmor, Feb. 25, 1829; HG's passport, issued June 28, 1828 (MHS).
2. HG to Allston, Oct. 10, 17, 1828; to Gilmor, Feb. 25, 1829. One of his experiences presumably at Carrara this fall is recorded in his "Etchings with a Chisel," *The United States Magazine and Democratic Review,* XVIII (Feb. 1846), 120.
3. HG to Allston, Oct. 10, 17, 1828; to Henry, Sept. 16, 1829; to Gilmor, May 16, 1829.
4. HG to Allston, Oct. 10, 17, 1828.
5. *Ibid.*
6. George Calvert, *Scenes and Thoughts in Europe* (N. Y., 1855), I, 141.
7. Dunlap, II, 416.
8. J. Q. Adams, Diary, July 2, 1829 (MHS); Mabel Swan, *The Athenæum Gallery, 1827–1873* (Boston, 1940), p. 141.
9. April 18, 1829.
10. HG to Allston, Oct. 10, 17, 1828. Unfootnoted quotations in the next two paragraphs come from this letter.
11. HG to Allston, Sept. 19, 1829.
12. HG to Gilmor, May 16, 1829.
13. Edward Everett, "American Sculptors in Italy," *The Boston Miscellany of Literature and Fashion,* I (1842), 5.
14. HG to Allston, Sept. 19, 1829.
15. Frances A. Longfellow, *Mrs. Longfellow* (N. Y., 1956), p. 31.
16. HG to Allston, Sept. 19, 1829.
17. HG to Allston, Nov. 17, 1829.
18. HG to Allston, Oct. 10, 17, 1828.

19. HG to Gilmor, April 12, 1831.
20. "Etchings with a Chisel," p. 125.

"Glorious Fenimore"

Unfootnoted details in this section come from *The Letters and Journals of James Fenimore Cooper,* ed. James F. Beard (Cambridge, 1960), I, II, *passim;* Dunlap, II, 419, 425; HG to Cooper, Jan. 7, March 5, 15, April 10, Dec. 6, 20, 1830, Feb. 17, March 7, 26, June 21, 1831, Jan. 14, 1832; and Susan Cooper, "The Chanting Cherubs," *Putnam's Magazine,* n. s., V (Feb. 1870), 241–242.

1. HG to Gilmor, Feb. 25, 1829.
2. HG to Susan Cooper, Aug. 11, 1852; S. I. Prime, *Life of Samuel F. B. Morse* (N. Y., 1875), p. 218.
3. *The Letters and Journals of . . . Cooper,* I, 412.
4. HG to Allston, Sept. 19, 1829.
5. Dunlap, II, 425.
6. HG to Gilmor, Feb. 25, 1829.
7. Dunlap, II, 422; HG to Cooper, June 21, 1831.
8. HG to Gilmor, Jan. 13, 1832.
9. Peale, "Reminiscences. Painters and Sculptors," *The Crayon,* I (March 14, 1855), 162. The next quotation comes from the same page.
10. HG to Cooper, Dec. 20, 1830 (draft).
11. The copies of Raphael's cherubs in high relief on the gravestone of the Finnish painter Baron Auguste de Mannerheim, a contemporary of HG's in Florence, who died in 1876 and was buried in the English Protestant Cemetery there, may be evidence of a small vogue created by HG's group.
12. HG to Allston, Sept. 19, 1829. When a few years later he considered making copies of the group, he proposed to charge $400 each *(The Letters and Journals of . . . Cooper,* II, 245).
13. Dec. 17, 1831.
14. *The Letters and Journals of . . . Cooper,* II, 335.
15. *Ibid.,* pp. 53–54.

16. Boston *Transcript,* May 18, 1831; N. Y. *Commercial Advertiser,* Nov. 26, 1831; *Morning Courier and New-York Enquirer,* Nov. 17, 1831; *Letters,* p. 71.
17. *The New-England Magazine,* I (July 1831), 25–26; "The Editor's Table," *The American Monthly Magazine,* III (April 1831), 67; Boston *Advertiser,* April 22, 30. The Boston *Advertiser, Courier,* and *Transcript* had several notices.
18. Jared B. Flagg, *The Life and Letters of Washington Allston* (London, 1893), p. 252; HG to Cooper, June 21, 1831. See also *Letters,* p. 70.
19. Boston *Transcript,* May 18, 1831 (see also May 16); Boston *Courier,* May 11, 1831; N. Y. *Evening Post,* May 17, 24, 1831. See also *Niles Weekly Register,* June 18, 1831.
20. Oct. 1831. See also HG to Gilmor, Jan. 13, 1832; Bickford Cooper, "Sculpture in America," *The Journal of American History,* I (Jan.–March 1907), 165. HG's "truculent reply" to the critics of the "Cherubs" on Dec. 1, 1833, referred to by Bickford Cooper, has not come to light.
21. See especially the *American,* the *Commercial Advertiser,* the *Evening Post,* and the *Morning Courier.* A leaflet was issued containing extracts from a letter of Cooper's relating to the work first printed in the *American* ("Greenough's Marble Group of Chanting Cherubs Now Exhibiting at the American Academy of the Fine Arts. . . ." [copy in the Harvard Library]). Poets Bryant and William Leggett were shortly afterward dubbed "the chaunting cherubs of the *Evening Post*" (Allan Nevins, *The Evening Post* [N. Y., c 1922], p. 139).
22. *Correspondence of James Fenimore-Cooper* (New Haven, 1922), I, 252. There were evidently plans to issue an engraving of the work, perhaps through the Academy (William Dunlap to Cooper, June 15, 1831 [Yale]).
23. Crawford to Charles Sumner, June 12, 1842 (Harvard); Frazee to Gulian Verplanck, Feb. 18, 1832 (New-York Historical Society).

24. *Correspondence of . . . Cooper,* I, 264.
25. N. Y. *Commercial Advertiser,* Nov. 26, 1831.
26. *Letters,* p. 75.
27. N. Y. *Commercial Advertiser,* Nov. 26, 1831; HG to Cabot, Nov. 12, 1832.
28. Thomas S. Cummings, *Historic Annals of the National Academy of Design* (Philadelphia, 1865), p. 126; *American Academy of Fine Arts and American Art-Union,* ed. Mary B. Cowdry (N. Y., 1953), II, 159; *The New-York Mirror,* XIV (April 8, 1837), 328; Edward Everett to Louis McLane, Feb. 18, 1834 (Paul F. Cooper, New York); A. Storrs to Cooper, Aug. 3, 1848 (Yale). The Mrs. Stevens mentioned in Storrs' letter, who had apparently purchased the "Cherubs," was the wife of the celebrated yachtsman John C. Stevens. Among the works of HG bequeathed to the Boston Museum of Fine Arts by his wife, who died in 1891, was a plaster group of two small male figures, possibly the "Cherubs." It has apparently been destroyed.

A House of Brothers

1

1. HG to Cooper, March 7, 1831; *Letters,* p. 54.
2. HG to Henry Greenough, Sept. 16, 1829; to Allston, Nov. 17, 1829; Robert Gilmor, Diary, Feb. 8, 1830 (Maryland Historical Society); HG to Allston, Sept. 19, 1829; to Gilmor, July 25, 1833, Sept. 7, 1830.
3. *Letters,* p. 55.
4. HG to Allston, Nov. 17, 1829; John Ware, *Memoir of the Life of Henry Ware, Jr.* (Boston, 1846), II, 80.
5. HG to Allston, Sept. 19, 1829.
6. HG to Gilmor, Sept. 7, 1830.
7. HG to Gilmor, May 16, 1829, Sept. 7, 1830; Boston *Courier,* May 16, 1831.

8. [John Bigelow], "Nuces Literariae," N. Y. *Evening Post,* Aug. 22, 1853.
9. Tuckerman, p. 26; John Locke, Letter from Florence, May 7, 1847, Savannah *Daily Republican,* June 18, 1847.
10. HG to Allston, April 18, Nov. 17, Sept. 19, 1829.
11. May 16, 1829.
12. HG to Morse, Jan. 5, 183[2].
13. April 18, Nov. 17, 1829.
14. HG to Gilmor, Feb. 25, 1829.
15. Nov. 17, 1829; March 7, 1835.

2

1. HG to Allston, Sept. 19, 1829. The portrait is in the possession of Fred Richardson, Boston. Peale referred to HG in his *Notes on Italy* (Philadelphia, 1831), pp. 242–243.
2. HG is referred to in this novel. See also Henry's "Letter from Italy," *The American Monthly Magazine,* II (Aug. 1830), 345–348 *(Letters,* p. 66).
3. For a sketch of him, see the author's "John Greenough, an American Artist," *Old-Time New England,* L (Fall 1959), 43–52.
4. *A Boston Portrait-Painter Visits Italy. The Journal of Amasa Hewins, 1830–1833* (Boston, 1931), p. 48.
5. Chapman to the Trustees of the Athenaeum, July 6, 1832 (Boston Athenaeum).
6. Receipted bills of Morse's, March–May, 1831 (Library of Congress).
7. Prime, pp. 213–214.
8. Among HG's sketches are several nudes made about this time, one dated December 1830.
9. HG to Cooper, Dec. 17, 1831; Cole to HG, Feb. 16, 1832 (New York State Library). Cole's sketchbook is in the Detroit Institute of Arts. His drawing of HG has been reproduced in *Thomas Cole, 1801–1848* (Hartford, 1949), plate X, no. 56.

10. HG to Cooper, Jan. 14, 1832, Dec. 15, 1835; Prime, p. 217; HG to Cooper, Jan. 14, 1832; Prime, p. 213.
11. [Letters of Mrs. John T. Kirkland], *Proceedings of the MHS,* Ser. 2, XIX (Dec. 1905), 448.
12. Joseph Grinnell, B. A. Gould, and William Rollins to the Trustees of the Athenaeum, Jan. 17, 1832 (Boston Athenaeum); [Letters of Mrs. John T. Kirkland], p. 448; HG to Rollins, [c Aug. 1831].
13. Receipt in HG's hand, April 24, 1830 (Mrs. William Burnham, Brookline, Mass.)
14. Sophia to Mrs. Nathaniel Peabody, July 13, 1832 (New York Public Library).
15. HG to Cooper, April 10, 1830; to Morse, Jan. 5, 183[2]; to Cooper, March 26, 1831; Roosevelt to HG, Oct. 4, 1831; N. Y. *Commercial Advertiser,* Dec. 6, 1831; N. Y. *Gazette,* Dec. 5, 1831; *Letters,* p. 66; HG to Cooper, Jan. 14, 1832; to Morton, March 27, 1832.
16. *The Letters and Journals of . . . Cooper,* I, 404; HG to Cooper, March 5, 1830, Dec 18, 1832.
17. HG to Cooper, Dec. 20, 1830.
18. HG to Cooper, March 7, 1831, incorporating a sketch.
19. N. Y. *American,* Dec. 1, 1831.
20. March 7, 1831.
21. The facts about this project come from the following New York papers: *Evening Post,* Nov. 29, Dec. 2, 1831, Feb. 24, 1832; *Daily Advertiser,* Dec. 2, 1831; *Gazette,* Dec. 2, 10, 14, 15, 1831; *Commercial Advertiser,* Dec. 3, 1831.

3

1. HG to Gilmor, May 17, 1828; to Cooper, March 5, 1830; to Gilmor, April 25, 1830.
2. April 12, 1831.
3. Tuckerman, p. 22.
4. HG to Gilmor, Jan. 13, 1832; to Cooper, [Dec.] 8, 1831; [R.

H. Wilde?], "The Arts and Artists in Italy," Washington *Daily National Intelligencer,* April 26, 1836.

5. *The Complete Works of Ralph Waldo Emerson,* ed. Edward Waldo Emerson and Waldo Emerson Forbes (Boston, 1909–1914), V, 5.
6. HG to Cooper, [Dec.] 8, 1831; to Gilmor, June 10, 1832; Thomas H. Cabot, Diary, March 10, 1833 (MHS); HG to Cooper, May 15, 1833; to Gilmor, July 25, 1833.
7. HG to Gilmor, Sept. 7, 1830; July 25, 1833.
8. Alfred Greenough to Gilmor, Oct. 3, 1833 (New-York Historical Society).
9. Boston *Mercantile Journal,* Dec. 2, 1833.
10. H. S. Canby, *Thoreau* (Boston, 1939), pp. 337–338.
11. Boston *Courier,* Dec. 12, 14, 1833.
12. N. Y. *Evening Post,* Nov. 11; N. Y. *American,* Dec. 17; Boston *Independent Chronicle,* Dec. 7; Boston *Transcript,* Oct. 31 (see also Oct. 7); Boston *Daily Advertiser,* Nov. 9 (see also Oct. 25); Boston *Courier,* Oct. 29, 1833; "Sculpture," *The New-England Magazine,* V (Dec. 1833), 484–485.
13. Gilmor's annotation on HG to Gilmor, June 10, 1832; Alfred Greenough to Gilmor, June 28, 1834 (New-York Historical Society).
14. Edward Everett, Diary, March 11, 1833; HG to Gilmor, Nov. 28, 1835; Gilmor's annotation on HG to Gilmor, Oct. 10, 1831; "Mrs. B. I. Cohen's Fancy Dress Party," *Maryland Historical Magazine,* XIV (Dec. 1919), 354.
15. HG to Gilmor, Jan. 13, June 10, 1832.
16. HG to Gilmor, May 16, 1829; Sept. 7, 1830; April 12, 1831; June 10, 1832; July 25, 1833. See also HG to Gilmor, May 17, 1828.

4

Unfootnoted details in this section come from *Letters,* pp. 77–90; Dunlap, II, 423–425; *The Letters and Journals of . . . Cooper,* II, 44, 336; HG to Cooper, Dec. 6, 1830, to Allston, Oct. 1831.

1. HG to Cooper, Dec. 6, 1830.
2. HG to Cooper, Feb. 17, 1831.
3. HG to Allston, Oct. 1831; *Letters,* p. 84.
4. HG to Morse, April 23, 1832; to Cooper, Dec. 18, 1832.
5. Page from the dictionary, in the Morse Papers, Vol. X (Library of Congress).
6. *Letters,* p. 86; HG to Allston, Oct. 1831; Prime, p. 213.
7. HG to Peale, Nov. 8, 1831.
8. Copies are in the possession of Lafayette College, Easton, Penn., and in the author's collection.
9. HG to Peale, Nov. 8, 1831; to Allston, Oct. 1831; to Morse, Jan. 5, 183[2].
10. HG to Morse, May 31, 1832.

5

1. HG to Cooper, Dec. 17, 1831.
2. N. P. Willis, *Pencillings by the Way* (Auburn, N. Y., 1854), p. 223.
3. HG to Cooper, Dec. 17, 1831; June 28, 1832; see also *The Letters and Journals of . . . Cooper,* II, 167, 267.
4. Prime, p. 212; HG to Morse, April 23, 1832; to Cooper, May 28, 1832; to Morse, May 31, 1832; information about Miss Douglas' sketchbook furnished by Angus Davidson, Roylston, England; HG to Cooper, Dec. 18, 1832; to Morse, April 23, 1832; Prime, p. 214; HG to Morse, May 31, 1832.
5. Philadelphia *National Gazette and Literary Register,* July 24, 1834; HG to Cole, May 19, 1832; to Roosevelt, [Dec.] 8, 1831; Prime, p. 213; HG to Morse, April 23, 1832; to Cooper, Dec. 18, 1832; *Letters,* p. 87.
6. HG to Cole, May 18, 1832; to Cooper, May 28, 1832; to Morse, May 31, 1832; Prime, p. 215.
7. HG to Cooper, June 28, 1832; *Letters,* p. 91; Beers, *Nathaniel Parker Willis* (Boston, 1885), pp. 120–121; Tuckerman, pp. 21, 57; HG to Cooper, Dec. 18, 1832.
8. HG to Morse, April 23, 1832.

9. HG to Morse, Jan. 5, 183[2]; to Niles, June 12, 1832; to Cooper, [between Jan. 14 and March 8, 1832]; Prime, p. 212.
10. HG to Morse, April 23, 1832; to Cooper, Aug. 22, 1832; to Morse, April 23, May 31, June 3, 1832.
11. HG to Cooper, Dec. 18, 1832, Jan. 29, 1833; Henry T. Tuckerman to HG, Oct. 25, Dec. 5, 1834; H. W. Longfellow to G. W. Greene, June 5, Sept. 12, 1836 (Harvard); George Ticknor, Journal, Nov. 15, 1836 (Dartmouth). Casa Ximenes was formerly the Oratory and College of the Jesuit Fathers.
12. Samuel Cabot, Diary, Oct. 21–Nov. 19, 1832 (see also March 9–12, 1833); Thomas H. Cabot, Diary, Oct. 27–Nov. 20, 1832 (see also March 9–15, 1833) (both in the MHS); HG to Cabot, Nov. 12, 1832.
13. Boston *Transcript,* Nov. 17, 1834; HG to Cooper, Dec. 18, 1832, Jan. 29, 1833; to Cabot, Nov. 12, 1832; *Letters,* pp. 104–105.
14. Tuckerman to HG, Dec. 5, 1834; Boston *Courier,* Dec. 4, 1832; Hillard, "Mr. Greenough's New Group of Statuary," *The New-England Magazine,* VIII (Jan. 1835), 43, 44; C. F., "The Ascension of a Child Conducted by an Infant Angel" (from the Boston *Evening Gazette,* Nov. 29, 1834) (MHS); "Remarks on Greenough's New Marble Group of Children" (Boston Public Library); Allston, "On Greenough's Group of the Angel and Child" (from the Boston *Daily Advertiser,* Dec. 30, 1834) (Yale); "Lines by Dr. and Mrs. Follen on Greenough's Groupe" (MHS); "To the Same," Tuckerman, pp. 239–240; H. W. Jr., "Greenough's Statues of the Cherub and Child," *Memory and Hope* (Boston, 1851), pp. 1–2; *Life, Letters, and Journals of George Ticknor* (Boston, 1876), II, 76.
15. HG to Cooper, Dec. 17, 1831; to Cabot, Dec. 17, 1832.
16. *The Complete Works of . . . Emerson,* V, 5; HG to Cooper, May 15, 1833; *The Letters and Journals of . . . Cooper,* II, 384; HG to Cooper, May 28, 1833; *Letters,* p. 93.
17. Hiram to Elizabeth G. Powers, Jan. 31, 1835; *Life and Letters of Thomas Gold Appleton* (N. Y., 1885), pp. 178 ff.;

Letters, p. 101; Theodore Fay, "The Minute-Book," *The New-York Mirror,* XII (Jan. 10, 1835), 220.

18. *Letters,* pp. 97–100; HG to Morse, Aug. 24, 1834; Mason to Cole, Aug. 28, 1834 (New York State Library).
19. T. H. Perkins, Diary, May 11, 1835 (MHS); Boston *Transcript,* Aug. 19, 1835; *Letters,* p. 109.
20. *Letters,* p. 106.
21. Perkins, Diary, May 11, 1835.
22. *Letters,* pp. 111, 117.
23. HG to Gilmor, Nov. 28, 1835; to Allston, March 7, 1835; Frances Appleton, Diary, May 15, 1836 (Longfellow House, Cambridge).
24. Everett, *Orations and Speeches on Various Occasions* (Boston, 1868), II, 399; Hoffman, Diary, May 14, 1834 (New York Public Library); Channing to HG, Dec. 23, 1835 (MHS). In May 1836 Frances Appleton saw what she called two Venuses boxed in HG's studio, but they were evidently not his work (Diary, May 15, 1836).
25. Everett to HG, Dec. 15, 1834; HG to Quincy, July 14, 1835; Greene to Longfellow, Jan. 1, 1836 (Harvard); HG to Cooper, Jan. 14, 1832; to Morse, April 23, 1832; Everett to HG, June 8, 1835; HG to Cooper, Dec. 15, 1835.
26. *Letters,* p. 109.
27. [John Bigelow], "Nuces Literariae," N. Y. *Evening Post,* Aug. 22, 1853.
28. HG to Greene, [c Feb. 1836]; Greene to Longfellow, Feb. 2, 27, 1836 (see also Longfellow to Greene, March 25, 1836) (Harvard).
29. *The Complete Works of . . . Emerson,* V, 5–9; *The Letters of Ralph Waldo Emerson,* ed. Ralph L. Rusk (N. Y., 1939), IV, 272; *Journals of Ralph Waldo Emerson,* ed. Edward Waldo Emerson and Waldo Emerson Forbes (Boston, 1909–1914), III, 115–117; John Forster, *Walter Savage Landor* (Boston, 1869), p. 472.

30. Tuckerman, pp. 21–22, 24–25.
31. *Letters,* p. 93; HG to Cooper, Dec. 18, 1832; *Letters,* p. 94; HG to Cooper, April 10, 1833; Henry Greenough, *Ernest Carroll* (Boston, 1858), pp. 223–225; Martha B. Amory, *The Wedding Journey of Charles and Martha Babcock Amory* (Boston, 1922), I, 176; Perkins, Diary, May 12, 1835; Dewey, *The Old World and the New* (N. Y., 1836), II, 34; *Letters,* pp. 101, 107.
32. May 4, 1832.
33. HG to Allston, Dec. 8, 1833.
34. Dunlap, II, 412, 421.
35. HG to Gilmor, July 25, 1833; *Letters,* p. 92; HG to Allston, Dec. 8, 1833; *Letters,* pp. 107, 102.
36. *Letters,* p. 111.
37. Longfellow to Greene, June 5, Sept. 1, 1836 (Harvard); Ticknor, Journal, Nov. 5, 1836.
38. *Letters,* pp. 239, 112.

Death Masks

1. Calvert, *Scenes and Thoughts in Europe* (N. Y., 1855), I, 140; Powers to Elizabeth G. Powers, June 21, 1836.
2. New Haven *Daily Herald,* March 9, 1840; Clay to C. E. Lester, Sept. 26, 1845 (MHS); *Niles National Register,* March 21, 1840.
3. R. H. Wilde to Robert Gilmor, Jr., June 17, 1839 (Historical Society of Pennsylvania); John S. Cogdell to Powers, Feb. 27, 1844.
4. July 30, 1836.
5. *Extracts from the Diary and Correspondence of the Late Amos Lawrence* (Boston, 1855), pp. 338–339.
6. HG to Wilde, Aug. 18, 1836; to Loring, July 5, 1839; *Letters,* pp. 113, 116, 121, 130, 170.
7. Sept. 23, 1836 (Brown).
8. *Letters,* p. 122.

9. Henry T. Tuckerman, *Book of the Artists* (N. Y., 1867), p. 587; HG to Curtis, [c Sept. 1836]; Ralph L. Rusk, *The Life of Ralph Waldo Emerson* (N. Y., 1949), p. 244; HG to Wilde, Aug. 18, 1836; to Palfrey, Oct. 3, 1836.
10. HG to Cooper, Sept. 23, 1836.

Part II

4

Spokesman for the Nation

All documents written to or by government officials cited or quoted in the first two sections of this chapter are, unless otherwise noted, in the National Archives, Washington, in the departments and document groups specified. None of the letters written by these officials to HG seems to have been preserved; references are to copies retained in Washington.

"The Birth of My Thought"

1. Jarvis to Allston, May 15, 1834 (MHS); *Letters,* p. 64; R. H. Dana to Gulian Verplanck, April 2, 1830 (New-York Historical Society); *The Letters and Journals of James Fenimore Cooper,* ed. James F. Beard (Cambridge, 1960), II, 233–235.
2. *Twenty-Second Congress, 1st Session. House Journal* (Washington, 1832), p. 342.
3. Edward Everett to HG, April 12, 1832.
4. State Dept., Domestic Letters.
5. Livingston to George McDuffie, March 14, 1832 (State Dept., Report Book 4); Everett to HG, April 12, July 29, 1832.
6. *The Letters and Journals of . . . Cooper,* II, 235–236; S. I. Prime, *Life of Samuel F. B. Morse* (N. Y., 1875), p. 212; *The Letters and Journals of . . . Cooper,* II, 244–245; HG to Cooper, May 28, 1832.

7. HG to Morse, May 31, 1832; to Cooper, May 28, 1832; Prime, p. 215.
8. HG to Morse, June 3, 1832; to Niles, June 12, 1832.
9. HG to Cooper, Sept. 18, 1832.
10. HG to Cooper, Aug. 22, Dec. 18, Sept. 18, 1832.
11. Livingston to Jackson, Dec. 19, 1832 (State Dept., Report Book 5); to HG, March 30, 1833 (State Dept., Domestic Letters); HG to Cooper, May 9, 28, 1833; to Livingston, July 24, 1833; *Letters,* p. 83.
12. Prime, pp. 215, 217; HG to Cooper, Jan. 29, 1833.
13. Prime, p. 219 (see also HG to Cooper, May 9, 1833); [R. H. Wilde?], "The Art and Artists in Italy," Washington *Daily National Intelligencer,* April 26, 1836; HG to Forsyth, June 6, 1837; Dunlap, II, 422; "Statue of Washington," *27th Congress. 1st Session. House Documents* (Washington, 1841), No. 45, pp. 5–6. The villa is now known as Villa San Paolo and is owned by the Barnabites who operate the Collegio della Querce. It has been entirely reconstructed.
14. Alfred Greenough to Livingston, Nov. 9, 1832, March 16, 1833 (State Dept., Domestic Letters); HG to Cooper, Dec. 18, 1832; "Statue of Washington," pp. 5–6 (see also Alexander to the President of the Athenaeum, Nov. 11, 1833 [Boston Athenaeum]); [Wilde?].
15. Prime, p. 219; "Account of Expences in making the Model of the Statue of Washington. 1834, –5, –6" (ms. in HG's hand, author's collection); HG to Vail, June 26, 1840; to Allston, March 7, 1835; *Letters,* pp. 108–109. HG's letter to Vail, June 26, 1840, gives the dates on which all the processes in the statue's execution were begun and ended. See also HG to Forsyth, June 6, 1837.
16. Everett to HG, July 29, 1832.
17. HG to Cooper, Sept. 18, 1832; *The Letters and Journals of . . . Cooper,* II, 368; HG to Cooper, May 15, 1833; Prime, p. 219; HG to Livingston, Jan. 28, 1834.
18. [Wilde?].

19. Jan. 28, 1834.
20. Boston *Mercantile Journal,* Feb. 6, 1834.
21. R. W. D. Conner, *Canova's Statue of Washington* ([Raleigh, N. C.], 1910), p. 24.
22. *Diary of William Dunlap* (N. Y., 1930), III, 777; Chapman to Morse, Dec. 3, 1841 (Library of Congress); Washington *Daily National Intelligencer,* Dec. 6, 1841.
23. The excerpt from HG's letter was printed on March 11; King's letter, dated March 24, appeared on April 2. HG's reply to Morse, dated May 24, was printed in the N. Y. *American* on Aug. 4, 1834. See also *Letters,* p. 99.
24. Louis McLane to Allston, May 15, 1834; Allston to John Vanderlyn, May 27, 1834 (copy) (both in the MHS); HG to Allston, Dec. 8, 1833; Jarvis to Allston, June 6, 1834; Allston to Jarvis, June 17, 1834 (both in the MHS).
25. Everett to HG, Dec. 15, 1834; HG to Allston, March 7, 1835; [Wilde?]; Parke Godwin, *A Biography of William Cullen Bryant* (N. Y., 1883), I, 310.
26. HG to Allston, March 7, 1835; to Forsyth, Feb. 27, 1835; Forsyth to HG, April 17, 1835 (State Dept., Bureau of Accounts, Letters Sent); HG to Gilmor, Nov. 28, 1835.
27. HG to Gilmor, Nov. 28, 1835; Stout to Constantine A. Pise, Feb. 25, 1843 (Georgetown University); HG to Cooper, Dec. 15, 1835.
28. *Letters,* p. 106; HG to Forsyth, Feb. 27, 1835; to Allston, March 7, 1835.
29. HG to Forsyth, June 6, 1837; "Memorial of Horatio Greenough, Praying the Removal of the Statue of Washington . . . ," *27th Congress. 3d Session. Senate Documents* (Washington, 1843), No. 57, p. 1.
30. Alfred Greenough to Levi Woodbury, May 15, 1837, March 30, 1838 (Treasury Dept., Miscellaneous Letters Received); HG to Forsyth, Nov. 15, 1837; Forsyth to HG, July 11, 1838 (Dept. of State, Bureau of Accounts, Letters Sent). The dates of appropriation and payment and the amounts of all the

sums expended by the government for the "Washington" are printed in Glenn Brown, *History of the United States Capitol* (Washington, 1900), I, 110.

31. HG to Forsyth, June 6, 1837; to Vail, June 26, 1840; to Cooper, Dec. 15, 1835; [Wilde?]; *Letters,* p. 121; Boston *Transcript,* July 7, 1838.

32. *The Letters of Charlotte Brinckerhoff Bronson* ([Cambridge], 1928), III, 408; HG to John Greenough, [c summer 1839]; to Greene, Sept. 15, 1839; to Loring, July 5, 1839; to Sumner, Oct. 24, 1840; to Webster, March 12, 1841; copies of the engraving in the author's collection (see also Everett to HG, Feb. 26, 1844, letterbook).

33. HG to Forsyth, June 6, 1837; Charles Sumner to HG, Nov. 8, 1839 (Henry Luhrs, Shippensburg, Penn.); HG to Sumner, Nov. 16, 1839.

34. HG to Lady Bulwer, [c April 1841].

35. HG to Sumner, Nov. 16, 1839; *Letters,* pp. 134–135; Lady Bulwer, "Modern Art and Artists in Italy," *The Court Journal,* May 8, 1841, pp. 1186–1187; Landor to HG, April 11, [1851]; Perkins, Diary, May 11, 1835 (MHS); Boston *Transcript,* June 20, 1836; Ticknor, Journal, Nov. 11, 1836 (Dartmouth); Cogswell to Dr. John Francis, Jan. 8, 1837 (photostat in copy of *Life of Joseph Green Cogswell as Sketched in his Letters*[Cambridge, 1874] [Harvard]); Edward L. Pierce, *Memoir and Letters of Charles Sumner* (Boston, 1878–1893), II, 111, 174; Sumner to HG, Nov. 8, 1839; Fay, "The Minute-Book," *The New-York Mirror,* XII (Jan. 10, 1835), 220; Sedgwick, *Letters from Abroad to Kindred at Home* (London, 1841), p. 128; Everett, "American Sculptors in Italy," *The Boston Miscellany of Literature and Fashion,* I (1842), 6–8; Jewett, *Passages in Foreign Travel* (Boston, 1838), II, 296; Calvert, *Scenes and Thoughts in Europe* (N. Y., 1855), I, 142–143; Tuckerman, pp. 242–243; Nathalia Wright, "Richard Henry Wilde on Greenough's Washington," *American Literature,* XXVII (March 1956), 556–557;

HG to Wilde, March 6, 1839; [Wilde?]; Appleton, Diary, May 15, 1836 (Longfellow House, Cambridge).

36. *Gazetta di Firenze,* Feb. 18, 1841; [B. Spence], *The Lions of Florence* (Florence, 1847), p. 8; *Guida per la Città di Firenze* (Firenze, 1852), p. 257; Everett, Diary, Jan. 7, 1841; HG to Capponi, [Jan. 8, 1841]; Everett to C. F. Adams, April 29, 1841 (letterbook); Florence *Giornale del Commercio,* March 3, 1841.
37. HG to Lady Bulwer, [c April 1841]; *Transactions of the Apollo Association for the Promotion of the Fine Arts in the United States, for the Year 1840* (N.Y., n.d.), 10–11.
38. Nov. 16, 1839.
39. Feb. 8, 1840.
40. HG to Greene, July 15, Sept. 15, 1839.
41. Vail to HG, May 22, 1840 (State Dept., Domestic Letters); Alfred to Woodbury, Sept. 5, 1840 (Treasury Dept., Miscellaneous Letters Received).
42. HG to Vail, June 26, 1840.
43. June 28, 1840.
44. July 12, Oct. 24, 1840.
45. Forsyth to HG, Sept. 4, 1840 (State Dept., Domestic Letters); HG to Forsyth, Jan. 5, 1841.
46. The chief facts about the transportation of the statue come from Paulding to HG, Dec. 8, 1840 (Navy Dept., General Letter Book 28); "Statue of Washington," pp. 11–15; *Papers of Isaac Hull* (Boston, 1929), pp. 320–328; Hull's Report for May 1841 (Navy Dept., Mediterranean Squadron); Hull to Paulding, July 22, 1841 (Navy Dept., Captains' Letters).
47. HG to Webster, May 12, 1841; Everett, Diary, May 24, 27, 29, 1841.
48. HG to Webster, May 12, 1841.
49. *Letters,* p. 137; Henry Greenough to Fletcher Webster, April 15, 1841 (Treasury Dept., Miscellaneous Letters); HG to Adams, Dec. 12, 1842.
50. June 2, 1841.

51. HG to Webster, March 12, 1841; "Statue of Washington," pp. 5–6.
52. Brown, I, 110.
53. HG to Webster, March 12, 1841.
54. "Statue of Washington," pp. 15, 16.
55. Upshur to Preston, June 10, 1842 (State Dept., Miscellaneous Letters).
56. The chief facts about the preparation of the foundations for the statue come from Mills to Paulding, Sept. 10, 1840 (Navy Dept., Miscellaneous Letters); "Foundation for the Statue of Washington," *26th Congress, 1st Session, House Documents* (Washington, 1841), No. 124.
57. Washington *Daily National Intelligencer,* Oct. 22, Dec. 2, 17, 1841; Boston *Transcript,* Aug. 5, 1841; Preston to Powers, March 10, 1842.
58. Washington *Daily National Intelligencer,* Dec. 23, 1841; Preston to Powers, March 10, 1842; Wilde to Powers, Aug. 11, 1842 (author's collection); HG to Preston, Dec. 16, 1842.
59. See for example Washington *Globe,* Dec. 1; Washington *Daily National Intelligencer,* Dec. 10, 18; Philadelphia *North American and Daily Advertiser,* Dec. 3, 7; Philadelphia *National Gazette,* Dec. 3; N. Y. *Commercial Advertiser,* Dec. 3; N. Y. *Evening Express,* Dec. 7; N. Y. *Evening Post,* Dec. 6; Boston *Courier,* Dec. 6; Boston *Evening Journal,* Dec. 16, 1841.
60. Yates, "Greenough's Statue of Washington," *The Northern Light,* II (April 1842), 12–13; Dakin, "Lines on the Statue of Washington at the Capitol," *The Knickerbocker,* XX (Sept. 1842), 281; Everett, "Greenough's Statue of Washington," *The United States Magazine and Democratic Review,* XIV (June 1844), 618–621. See also George Watterston, *A New Guide to Washington* (Washington, 1841), pp. 51–54, frontispiece and cover.
61. Washington *Union Democrat,* Dec. 28; N. Y. *Herald,* Dec. 6; N. Y. *American,* Dec. 6; Boston *Transcript,* Dec. 13, 1841;

see also Boston *Daily Advertiser,* Dec. 14, Boston *Courier,* Dec. 15, 1841.

62. May 21, 1842.
63. May 13, 1842.
64. N. M. Rothschild & Sons to Everett, Dec. 30, 1841; to HG, Dec. 31, 1841; to Everett, Oct. 6, 1842; to HG, Oct. 14, 1842; to Walter Forward, U.S. Secretary of the Treasury, Oct. 21, 1842; McClintock Young to the Rothchilds, Nov. 8, 1842 (copies of letters from the Rothchilds and original letter from Young in the Rothchild Archives, London). For a description of the correspondence in the Rothchild Archives relative to HG's payment for both the "Washington" and "The Rescue" *(vide infra,* p. 337), I am indebted to Mr. Edmund de Rothschild, London.
65. Louisa G. Greenough to Elizabeth G. Powers, July 8, 1842.
66. Jared B. Flagg, *The Life and Letters of Washington Allston* (London, 1893), p. 325; Perkins to Higginson, Nov. 30, 1842 (MHS).
67. HG to Adams, Dec. 12, 1842; to Higginson, Nov. 13, 1842; *The Letters of Ralph Waldo Emerson,* ed. Ralph L. Rusk (N. Y., 1939), III, 122.
68. *Letters,* pp. 147, 144; N. Y. *Evening Post,* Jan. 31, 1843; *The Letters of . . . Emerson,* III, 121.
69. *The Letters of . . . Emerson,* III, 120, 122.
70. Adams, Diary, Jan. 3, 1842 (MHS).
71. "Memorial . . . ," pp. 2–5.
72. "Removal of Greenough's Statue of Washington," *27th Congress, 3rd Session, House Reports* (Washington, 1843), No. 219.
73. The chief facts about this operation and HG's account with the government in connection with it are contained in four packets of papers in the records of the General Accounting Office: Report Nos. 87.480, 87.977, 105.115, and 105.220; and in HG to Spencer, July 3, 1843 (Treasury Dept., Miscellaneous Letters).

74. HG to Winthrop, Aug. 1, 1844; *Niles National Register,* July 22, 1843.
75. *The Diary of Philip Hone* (N. Y., 1889), II, 216; [Caleb Atwater?], *Mysteries of Washington City* (Washington, 1844), p. 121; S. T. Wallis, *Glimpses of Spain* (N. Y., 1849), pp. 81–82.
76. *Congressional Globe,* May 25, 1844.
77. Nov. 26, 1844. In July 1846 HG addressed a letter to the Secretary of State about removing the shelter but this letter does not seem to have been preserved and its contents are not known (State Dept., Index to Letters Received).
78. Samuel Longfellow, *Life of Henry Wadsworth Longfellow* (Boston, 1891), II, 179; Everett to HG, Dec. 25, 1848; Charles Eaton to Powers, April 18, 1853.
79. Jan. 25, 1847.
80. May 7, 1851.
81. *Letters,* pp. 230–231.
82. Everett, *Orations and Speeches on Various Occasions* (Boston, 1868), IV, 156.
83. HG to Bryant, May 7, 1851.
84. *The Home Journal,* Dec. 13, 1851; Washington *Daily National Intelligencer,* Dec. 19, 1851 (HG's letter was dated Dec. 13).
85. *Travels,* pp. 25–26.
86. Washington *Daily National Intelligencer,* Nov. 11, 22, 1853; Washington *Union,* Nov. 16, 1853.
87. H. M. Pierce Gallagher, *Robert Mills* (N. Y., 1935), p. 156; Charles E. Fairman, *Art and Artists of the Capitol* (Washington, 1927), pp. 143, 191.
88. See for example Lorado Taft, *The History of American Sculpture* (N. Y., 1903), p. 51, and the syndicated column of Frederick Othman in the Scripps-Howard newspapers on Feb. 22 in the 1940's. and 1950's.
89. *Orations and Speeches on Various Occasions,* IV, 156.

Rescue by History

1. W. U. Hensel, "An Italian Artist in Old Lancaster," *Papers Read before the Lancaster County Historical Society . . .,* XVI, (1912), 71–81.
2. Persico to the Commissioner of Public Buildings, Feb. 1837; Articles of Agreement between Van Buren and Persico (Treasury Dept., Miscellaneous Letters, Series K).
3. State Dept., Domestic Letters.
4. State Dept., Index to Letters Received by the Secretary of State.
5. HG to Allston, Feb. 18, 1838; *Letters,* p. 129.
6. Persico to Forsyth, Dec. 14, 1838; Alexander Hammett to Forsyth, Dec. 22, 1838 (both in State Dept., Miscellaneous Letters).
7. Vail to HG, Oct. 22, 1838 (State Dept., Domestic Letters).
8. The copy returned by HG is in the Records of the General Accounting Office, Report of the First Auditor, No. 109.184 (Feb. 7, 1853), Item NLJD. 54–116.500CR; that which he retained is in the possession of David Richardson, Washington.
9. Greenough expected it would be advanced at the time the contract was sent. See N. M. Rothschild & Sons to HG, July 19, 1839 and to S. Pleasanton, July 24, 1840 (copies, the Rothchild Archives, London); Henry Greenough to Forsyth, April 5, 1838 (State Dept., Miscellaneous Letters); to Woodbury, May 29, 1839 (Treasury Dept., Miscellaneous Letters); Alfred Greenough to McClintock Young, May 29, 1839 (Treasury Dept., Miscellaneous Letters). The dates of appropriation and payment and the amounts of all the sums expended by the government for Persico's and HG's groups are printed in Brown, I, 111.
10. *Letters,* p. 129; HG to Paulding, Dec. 14, 1839; *Letters,* p. 131; HG to Forsyth, Feb. 8, 1840; to Greene, Feb. 6, Aug. 18, 1840; to Sumner, Oct. 24, 1840.

11. Pierce, II, 111.
12. *The Prairie* (N. Y., [1895–1900] Iroquois Ed.), p. 217.
13. Forsyth to HG and to Persico, Feb. 28, 1839 (State Dept., Domestic Letters); Persico to the Secretary of State, May 13, 1840 (copy, Treasury Dept., Miscellaneous Letters, Series K); HG to Forsyth, Jan. 5, 1841, March 16, 1841.
14. Everett to Adams, Jan. 12, 1841 (letterbook).
15. Cogdell to Powers, June 14, 1844, April 30, 1845.
16. Frances B. to Elizabeth B. Greenough, Dec. 28, [1845].
17. George Calvert, "Greenough, the Sculptor," *Putnam's Magazine,* I (March 1853), 320.
18. HG to Winthrop, Nov. 26, 1844; to Powers, May 13, 1845; Alfred Greenough to Robert Walker, Aug. 20, 1845; T. B. Curtis to St. Clair Clarke, Nov. 11, 1845 (last two letters in the Treasury Dept., Miscellaneous Letters); Frances B. Greenough to Charlotte G. Parker, Jan. 11, 1847; HG to Bancroft, Jan. 9, 16, 1847.
19. "Our Artists in Florence," *The Literary World,* VI (Feb. 16, 1850), 157; *Letters,* p. 232; HG to Cogswell, Sept. 26, 1850; to Balmanno, Oct. 29, 1850.
20. HG to Forsyth, March 16, 1841; Florence *Giornale del Commercio,* March 3, 1841; Pierce, II, 111; Everett to J. Q. Adams, Jan. 12, 1841 (letterbook); Bryant, *Letters of a Traveller* (N. Y., 1850), p. 236; Hillard, Journal, Nov. 16, 1847 (MHS); Hillard, *Six Months in Italy* (Boston, 1877), p. 115; *Life of Joseph Green Cogswell as Sketched in his Letters,* p. 257; Taylor, *Views A-Foot* (N. Y., 1848), p. 294; Ossoli, *At Home and Abroad* (Boston, 1856), p. 371; *Letters,* pp. 229, 225. In 1874 the New York Lithographer Heinrich Schile issued a colored lithograph copying the design of "The Rescue," with the title "Daniel Boone Protects his Family." A photograph of it appears in John Walton, "Ghost Writer to Daniel Boone," *American Heritage,* VI (Oct., 1955), 10. (Lithograph in author's collection.)

21. Quoted from *Bulletin of the American Art-Union,* Sept. 1851, pp. 96–98.
22. *Letters,* pp. 223, 228, 230.
23. *Letters,* pp. 229, 231–232; T. B. Curtis to Daniel Webster, May 10, 1851 (Navy Dept., Office of the Secretary of the Navy, Letters from Federal Executive Agents).
24. Bill of Lading, Capt. G. Tar, *Atar Gull,* April 25, 1853 (Records of the Office of Public Buildings and Public Parks of the National Capitol, Records of the Commissioner of Public Buildings).
25. Curtis to Webster, May 20, 1851 (Navy Dept., Office of the Secretary of the Navy, Letters from Federal Executive Agents); Morgan to the Secretary of the Navy, Dec. 8, 1851, April 16, 1852 (Navy Dept., Mediterranean Squadron, Comm. C. W. Morgan, June 3, 1849–June 27, 1852).
26. *Travels,* p. 25; HG to Kennedy, Sept. 22, 1852; Washington *Daily National Intelligencer,* Sept. 2, 3, Nov. 11, 1853.
27. *Letters,* p. 232; Webster to HG, Nov. 15, 1852 (State Dept., Domestic Letters); W. Hunter to HG, July 9, 21, 1852 (State Dept., Domestic Letters); Everett to HG, Nov. 15, 1852 (letterbook); First Auditor's Report No. 109.184 (Feb. 7, 1853) (Records of the General Accounting Office).
28. Stringham to the Secretary of the Navy, March 16, 1853 (Navy Dept., Mediterranean Squadron, Comm. S. H. Stringham, May 1, 1852–July 1, 1855); Agreement between Binda and F. Malenchini and Co., Feb. 4, 1853 (copy, Treasury Dept., Miscellaneous Letters); Binda to the Secretary of the Navy, April 31, 1853 (Records of the Office of Public Buildings and Public Parks of the National Capitol, Records of the Commissioner of Public Buildings); Bill of Lading, Capt. G. Tar, *Atar Gull,* April 25, 1853; Binda to the Commanding Officer at Norfolk, April 30, 1853 (State Dept., Consular Letters).
29. Washington *Daily National Intelligencer,* Aug. 8, Sept. 3, 1853.

30. *Ibid.*, Nov. 14, 1853.
31. Records of the Office of Public Buildings and Public Parks of the National Capitol, Records of the Commissioner of Public Buildings.
32. Washington *Evening Star*, Aug. 19, 22; Washington *Daily National Intelligencer*, Aug. 22, Oct. 19; Washington *Evening Star*, Oct. 13, 1853.
33. Abstract of Expenditures for Freight & Transportation of Statuary (Records of the Office of Public Buildings and Public Parks of the National Capitol, Records of the Commissioner of Public Buildings).
34. Sept. 3, 1853.
35. Nov. 11, 16, 1853.
36. Nov. 18, 22, Dec. 12, 1853.
37. Copy, Art and Reference Library, Office of the Architect of the Capitol.
38. March 14, 1859 (Art and Reference Library, Office of the Architect of the Capitol).

Form as Function

1. Oct. 1831.
2. HG to Palfrey, Oct. 3, 1836.
3. Everett to HG, Jan. 28, 1841; Diary, Jan. 9, 1841.
4. *The United States Magazine and Democratic Review,* XIII (Aug. 1843), 205, 209, 206–210.
5. It is listed in *Auction Sale . . . May 7th and 8th 1895 . . . Catalogue of Miscellaneous Books . . . Together with the Remaining Portion of the Library of the Late Horatio Greenough*. Boston : C. F. Libbie.
6. For a brief account of him, see Emil Kaufman, *Architecture in the Age of Reason* (Cambridge, 1955).
7. For an account of them, see Emil Kaufman, *Three Revolutionary Architects, Boullée, Ledoux, and Lequeu,* in *Transactions of the American Philosophical Society,* n. s., XLII, pt. 3 (1952).

8. An account of this controversy is given by HG's nephew Henry G. Huntington in his *Florentine Notes* (London, 1884).
9. Sigfried Giedion, *Space, Time, and Architecture* (Cambridge, 1941), pp. 153–154.
10. HG to Allston, Oct. 1831.
11. Nov. 16, 1839.
12. *Vide infra,* pp. 269, 270, 279, 280, 288–290, 300, 301.
13. Emerson to HG, Nov. 1, 1852.
14. Richard Adams, in "Architecture and the Romantic Tradition : Coleridge to Wright," *American Quarterly,* IX (1957), 46–62, was first to point out the probability that the chief line of descent of the organic idea as applied to architecture in America was from HG to Emerson to Furness to Sullivan to Wright.

Part III

5

Florentine American : 1837-1851

Homage to the Goddess

1. HG to Allston, [Nov. 22, 1836].
2. Frances Appleton, Diary, Dec. 5, 11, 1836 (Longfellow House, Cambridge).
3. G. B. to Mrs. A. H. Shattuck, Dec. 1, 1836 (MHS); Elizabeth T. Thomas, Diary, Nov., Dec. 1836, *passim* (Maryland Historical Society); Cogswell to ——?——, Dec. 28, 1836 (photostat in copy of *Life of Joseph Green Cogswell as Sketched in his Letters* [Cambridge, 1874] [Harvard]).
4. *Letters,* 114; Appleton, Diary, Dec. 15, 27, 28, 1836; Gray to Nathan Appleton, Sept. 15, 1837 (MHS); *Letters,* p. 128.

5. Cogswell to Mrs. Francis, Jan. 13, 1837 (photostat in copy of *Life of Joseph Green Cogswell as Sketched in his Letters* [Harvard]).
6. *Letters,* p. 114.
7. HG to Hoffman, Sept. 21, 1838; Philadelphia *National Gazette and Literary Register,* May 4, 1839; *Letters,* p. 117. See also HG to Gilmor, April 1, 1839. Probably the work of HG's called "Nun" in the 1844 exhibition catalogue of the Pennsylvania Academy of the Fine Arts was one of his "Héloïses."
8. *Letters,* p. 114.
9. HG to Salisbury, Dec. 2, 1837, Feb. 23, 1838; Harriet Hosmer to Mrs. S. C. Hall, n. d. (Thomas Brumbaugh, Emory, Ga.).
10. *Letters,* pp. 114–116.
11. *Catalogue of the First Exhibition of Sculpture in the Athenaeum Gallery* (Boston, 1839), p. 7; Henry Greenough to Mr. Norton, March 21, 1860 (Boston Athenaeum).
12. Russell to Thomas Appleton, April 1, 1837 (National Archives, General Records, State Dept., Consular Letters Received); Thomas, Diary, Jan.–May 1837, *passim; Letters,* p. 115.
13. *Letters,* p. 117; G. W. Greene to H. W. Longfellow, Aug. 9, 1837 (Harvard).
14. Marriage Register, Church of the Holy Trinity, Florence (for access to the register I am indebted to William F. Coppinger, Florence); HG to Wilde, [Oct. 1837]; Stato Civile nel Commune di Firenze, Vol. 90, fol. 161, c. 2 (copy, author's collection).
15. Edward Everett to HG, Jan. 13, 1834.
16. Frances B. Greenough to Harriet B. Loring, Nov. 20, [1848]; commonplace book of Louisa G. Greenough (David Richardson, Washington); Frances B. Greenough to Harriet B. Loring, April 25, [1846]; to Francis Boott, [1847?]; Everett to Louisa G. Greenough, June 26, 1836 (Richardson); Suffolk

County Registry of Probate; Powers to Francis Alexander, Dec. 8, 1837 (Historical Society of Pennsylvania).

17. Oral reminiscences of Marguerite Wagnière Horton; HG to Gilmor, April 1, 1839; Calvert, "Greenough, the Sculptor," *Putnam's Magazine,* I (March 1853), 318; Greene, "Letters from Rome," *The Knickerbocker,* XV (June 1840), 488; Boston *Daily Advertiser,* May 15, 1892.
18. *Letters,* p. 117; Henry Brevoort to HG, Jan. 28, 1838; *Letters,* pp. 124–125, 119, 126.
19. *Letters,* pp. 125, 123; HG to Greene, Sept. 15, 1839; to Powers, July 4, 1838; Powers to Francis Alexander, Dec. 8, 1837; *Letters,* pp. 127–128. The Brocchi house is presently Nos. 15–17 Borgo Pinti, occupied by the Oblate dell' Assunzione.
20. *Letters,* p. 127; HG to Green, Sept. 15, 1839.
21. Dec. 27, 1836 (MHS). The drawing is mentioned in the entry for Dec. 30.
22. *The Letters of Charlotte Brinckerhoff Bronson* ([Cambridge], 1928), III, 408, 424.
23. Apollo Association Exhibition Catalogue, 1839; Hubard to Powers, Sept. 30, 1839 (Valentine Museum, Richmond, Va.).
24. Louisa Greenough to Powers, Aug. 18, 1839; Hubard to Powers, Sept. 30, 1839; HG to Warren, March 1, 1839; *Letters,* pp. 128–129.
25. Frances B. Greenough to Harriet B. Loring, Jan. 10, [1846]; *Letters,* p. 130; Boston Athenaeum Exhibition Catalogue, 1842; HG to John Greenough, [c summer 1839]; N. B. Shurtleff, *Memorial of the Inauguration of the Statue of Franklin* (Boston, 1857), p. 379; John Greenough to Bancroft, Nov. 24, 1845 (National Archives, General Records, State Dept., Applications and Recommendations for Office).
26. John Greenough to Bancroft, Nov. 24, 1845.
27. HG to Greene, Sept. 15, 1839; Edward L. Pierce, *Memoir and Letters of Charles Sumner* (Boston, 1878–1893), II, 116, 111.

28. Everett, Diary, Nov. 23, 1840. See also Nov. 1840–Sept. 1841, *passim.*
29. *Letters,* p. 128.
30. HG to Paulding, Dec. 14, 1839.
31. *Letters,* pp. 118, 119, 124, 129, 121; *Recollections of Francis Boott for his Grandson F. B. D.* (Boston, 1912), p. 51; HG to Warren, March 1, 1839; Everett, Diary, Nov 17, 1840; HG to Capponi [between Sept. and Dec. 1841]; Louisa G. Greenough to the Trustees of the Boston Athenaeum, 1890 (Boston Athenaeum); to Powers, April 4 [1863 or 1864].
32. *Letters,* p. 116; Everett to HG, Feb. 20, 1852; Everett, Diary, Feb. 20, 21, 28, 1852.
33. J. A. Lowell to the Trustees of the Athenaeum Feb. 14, 1842 (Boston Athenaeum).
34. Cooper to HG, June 31, 1838; HG to Allston, Feb. 18, 1838; *Letters,* p. 130; *Niles National Register,* March 21, 1840.
35. Letters of Mrs. E. E. Salisbury, Nov. 22, 1838, Jan. 14, 1839 (Woolsey Family Papers, Yale); HG to Salisbury, Jan 3, 30, 1838.
36. HG to Allston, Feb. 18, 1838; to Salisbury, April 28, 1839; Pierce, II, 112, 111.
37. HG to Salisbury, April 28, 1839; Jan. 3, 30, 1838.
38. George Gibbs, *The Gibbs Family of Rhode Island* (N. Y., 1938), p. 107.
39. *Letters,* pp. 122, 130, 152.
40. HG to Allston, Sept. 19, 1839.
41. Elizabeth G. Powers to her mother, May 14, 1840.

A New American School

1. Tuckerman, p. 50; undated ms. in Morse Papers, Vol. XLVIII (Library of Congress); HG to Allston, Feb. 18, 1838; Everett, Diary, Nov. 8, 1840; HG to Powers, [May 3, 1851]; to Forsyth, Feb. 8, 1840; "Remarks on American Art," *The United States Magazine and Democratic Review,* XIII (July 1843), 48; *Travels,* p. 17; to Sumner, Oct. 24 ,1840.

2. Powers to Louisa G. Greenough, May 19, 1853; *Letters*, p. 126.
3. Powers to Benjamin T. Reilly, Jan. 16, 1839 (Brumbaugh); Joseph Mozier to Powers, Dec. 22, n.y.; *Letters*, p. 124; Harriet Hosmer, "The Process of Sculpture," *The Atlantic Monthly*, XIV (Dec. 1864), 734–737.
4. HG to Greene, Nov. 1, 1838.
5. HG to Fenzi, July 16, 1839, [summer 1839].
6. *Letters*, pp. 170, 224; Calvert, "Greenough, the Sculptor," p. 320; Powers to Calvert, May 25, 1853; Calvert to Powers, June 22, 1853.
7. HG to Powers, [between Feb. 20 and March 4, 1839]; *Letters*, p. 126; HG to Powers, [Aug. 1838]; Louisa Greenough to Powers, June 13, [1857]; Elizabeth G. Powers to her mother, July 12, 1841, March 3, 1842.
8. *Six Months in Italy* (Boston, 1877), p. 115.
9. Washington *Daily National Intelligencer;* Hawthorne, *Passages from the French and Italian Note-Books* (Boston, c 1871), I, 268; Kellogg papers, Indiana Historical Society, Indianapolis (information furnished by Mrs. Margaret Schaeffer); Frances B. Greenough to Charlotte G. Parker, Aug. 8, [1847]; to Elizabeth B. Greenough, March 12, [1848]; *Letters of Charles Eliot Norton* (Boston, 1913), I, 92.
10. HG to Sumner, July 12, 1840.
11. Hawthorne, I, 140.

In the Palace of a Bonaparte

1. HG to Allston, Feb. 18, 1838; see also HG to Salisbury, Jan. 30, 1838; *Letters*, p. 129; HG to Gilmor, April 1, 1839.
2. HG to Greene, Aug. 18, 1840; John Maquay to L. Bourbon Del Monte, Aug. 26, 1853; Del Monte to the Minister of Finance, Commerce, and Public Works, Aug. 31, 1853; Minister of Public Instruction to the President of the Academy of Fine Arts, Sept. 5, 1853 (last three letters in the Academy of Fine Arts, Florence). It stood for many years in

the Directors' Room, was moved to the Gallery of Modern Art in Palazzo Pitti about 1930, and apparently was destroyed during World War II along with other works by nationals of countries with which Italy was then at war, by order of Mussolini (information secured with the help of Mrs. Clara L. Dentler, Florence).

3. HG to Cogswell, Oct. 13, 1840.
4. HG to Sumner, July 12, 1840; transcription in the hand of Louisa G. Greenough of an undated, unsigned article in Italian (Henry G. Nickerson, Dedham, Mass.); *Letters,* p. 135. Reviczky retired to a monastery and died in 1862; his daughter Ada became a nun in Vienna; his only other child, a son, died without issue in 1886.
5. Everett, Diary, July 3, 1841; *Letters,* p. 152; Calvert, *Scenes and Thoughts in Europe* (N. Y., 1855), I, 142; *Letters,* pp. 122–123, 152, 134; HG to Capponi, [c May 1841]; *Letters,* pp. 134, 138.
6. Everett, Diary, Jan. 11, 1839.
7. Pierce, III, 116; Everett to HG, May 20, 1839, Jan. 28, 1841; Everett, Diary, Jan. 9, 1841.
8. HG to Greene, Nov. 1, 1838; to Paulding, Dec. 14, 1839; to Greene, March 29, July 15, 1839; to Cooper, postmarked Oct. 8, 1839; to Sumner, Nov. 16, 1839.
9. HG to Capponi, [c Christmas, 1839].
10. Bill of Lading, Capt. G. Tar, *Atar Gull,* April 25, 1853 (National Archives, Records of the Office of Public Buildings and Public Parks of the National Capitol, Records of the Commissioner of Public Buildings).
11. *Auction Sale . . . Dec. 12th and 13th, 1890 . . . Fine Books . . . Including Portion of the Library of the Late Horatio Greenough* . . . Boston : C. F. Libbie; *Auction Sale . . . May 7th, and 8th, 1895 . . . Catalogue of Miscellaneous Books . . . Together with the Remaining Portion of the Library of the Late Horatio Greenough. . . .* Boston : C. F. Libbie.
12. They were exhibited at the Boston Athenaeum in 1854. See

also *Auction Sale . . . May 16th, and 17th, 1895 . . . Catalogue of Rare Etchings . . . from the Estates of the Late Horatio Greenough . . . and the Late William Clarence Burrage. . . .* Boston : C. F. Libbie.

13. Everett, Diary, Nov. 8, 1840.
14. HG to Capponi, May 1, 1840, [c May 1841], [between Sept. and Dec. 1841]; *The Correspondence of William Hickling Prescott, 1833–1847* (Boston, 1925), p. 133.
15. Everett, Diary, Nov. 20, Dec. 5, 1840; Everett to Webster, July 25, 1841 (letterbook); *Auction Sale . . . 1890; Letters,* p. 134; Mouravieff-Apostol to HG, June 25, 1844.
16. *Letters,* p. 227.
17. Everett, Diary, Feb. 24, 1841; *Letters,* p. 132; HG to Sumner, Oct. 24, 1840; Everett, Diary, June 9, 1841; HG to Sumner, Nov. 16, 1839; Stephens to Powers, March 26, 1841; Pierce, III, 184; *Letters,* p. 136; Frances Trollope, *A Visit to Italy* (London, 1842), I, 174–175; Everett, Diary, March 27, 1841; Wilde to Powers, Aug. 24, 1844 (author's collection).
18. *Letters,* pp. 135, 139, 170.
19. Everett, Diary, Jan. 9, 1841.
20. HG to Sumner, Oct. 24, 1840; to Wilde, [Sept. 1840]; to Niccolini, Sept. 30, 1840; HG's diplomas from both Academies (author's collection).
21. Everett, Diary, May 10, 1841; Mouravieff-Apostol to HG, June 25, 1844; Hillard, Journal, Nov. 22, 27, 1847 (MHS); Calvert, "Greenough, the Sculptor," p. 318; *Letters,* p. 200; Louisa G. Greenough to Elizabeth G. Powers, Oct. 1, 1843.
22. Everett to HG, Aug. 4, 1840, to Louisa G. Greenough, Sept. 29, 1840 (letterbook); Miss Anna E. Urquhart to Powers, Feb. 24, 1842; Everett to HG, Feb. 7, 1842; Louisa G. Greenough's commonplace book (David Richardson, Washington).
23. Louisa G. Greenough to Elizabeth G. Powers, July 8, 1842.
24. HG to Powers, [after Aug. 25, 1842]; HG to Ward, Nov. 1, 1842; Capponi to Lamartine, June 13, n.y. (Richardson).

The Green Land and the Old Battle

1. *Letters,* p. 140.
2. *Ibid.,* p. 141.
3. HG to Patterson, Nov. 27; Patterson to HG, Dec. 28; HG to Patterson, Dec. 30, 1842. Patterson also recommended HG to Secretary of the Treasury John C. Spencer to design the medallion of Washington in the Presidential Series, but nothing came of this matter (Patterson to Spencer, May 19, 1843 [National Archives, General Records, Records of the U.S. Mint at Philadelphia, General Correspondence]). For locating the HG-Patterson correspondence, I am indebted to Mrs. Georgia S. Chamberlain, Alexandria, Va.
4. *Letters,* pp. 141–142, 145–151; Adams, Diary, Dec. 10, 14, 23, 1842, Jan. 3, 14, March 28, April 6, 1843 (MHS); HG to Sumner, Nov. 16, 1839.
5. *Letters,* pp. 149, 151.
6. *Ibid.,* p. 149.
7. HG to Folsom, June 2, 1843.
8. XIII (July 1843), 46–48.
9. HG to Spencer, July 3, 1843 (National Archives, Dept. of the Treasury, Miscellaneous Letters); Cooper to HG, June 25, 1843; HG to Folsom, July 8, 1843.
10. *Letters,* p. 153.
11. HG to Dana, Sept. 21, 1843; *Letters,* p. 154.
12. Sept. 21, 1843.
13. June 11, 1844.
14. Sept. 23, 1844.

The Water Cure

1. *Letters,* p. 155; Laura Wagnière-Huntington, *From Dawn to Dusk* (Vevey, Switzerland, [1929?]), p. 12.
2. HG to O'Sullivan (?), May 26, 1845.
3. Frances B. Greenough to Charlotte G. Parker, April 15, [1847].

4. Balbirnie, *The Philosophy of the Water Cure* (N. Y., 1846), p. 28; Wilson, *The Principles and Practice of the Water Cure* (London, 1854), pp. xvii, 21.
5. Everett, Diary, Aug. 21, Sept. 10, 12, 1843; Everett to HG, Aug. 25, 28, 1843, n. d. [1843?]; *Letters,* pp. 219, 161.
6. Louisa G. Greenough to Elizabeth G. Powers, Oct. 1, 1843.
7. *Letters,* p. 170; Boston *Transcript,* July 26, 1844.
8. *Letters,* pp. 169–170.
9. Crawford to Powers, April 30, 1844.
10. Everett to HG, Feb. 26, 1844; *Letters,* p. 170; *Letters and Journals of Samuel Gridley Howe* (Boston, c 1909), II, 143; Cogdell to Powers, April 30, Sept. 15, 1845.
11. *Letters,* p. 169.
12. Frances B. to Elizabeth B. Greenough, May 21, [1848].
13. *Letters,* p. 172.
14. *Ibid.,* pp. 188–199; Murray, p. 463; DeForest, *European Acquaintance* (N. Y., 1858), p. 70; *Letters,* p. 197.
15. Mouravieff-Apostol to HG, June 25, 1844.
16. Frances B. Greenough to Charlotte G. Parker, June 30, [1846]; *Letters,* pp. 177–180; Robert Wickliffe to Powers, Dec. 24, 1844.
17. HG to Winthrop, Aug. 1, 1844; to Waterston, March 25, 1845; to O'Sullivan (?), May 26, 1845.
18. HG to Powers, Nov. 17, 1844, May 13, 1845; to Waterston, March 25, 1845.
19. HG to Powers, Nov. 17, 1844; to Waterston, March 25, 1845.
20. HG to Powers, May 13, 1845; Louisa Greenough to Powers, June 18, 1845.
21. HG to Powers, July 30, 1845; Louisa G. Greenough to Elizabeth G. Powers, Aug. 1845.
22. A folded sheet, evidently once containing printed matter with a decorative border which has left a faint imprint on it, endorsed in Louisa G. Greenough's hand "Sent me by Count Olgar on my boy's birth—after which his bust no longer continued to improve," is in the author's collection.

23. HG to Powers, July 30, 1845.
24. March 25, 1845.
25. Ms. in the possession of Nickerson. In the printed version ("A Sketch," *The Crayon,* I (April 18, 1855), 243–244), part of this passage is inaccurately transcribed.
26. Tuckerman, p. 51.
27. "Etchings with a Chisel," *The United States Magazine and Democratic Review,* XIII (July 1843), 119, 120. "Ebarites" on p. 120 is apparently a misprint for "Charites."
28. Ms. in the possession of Nickerson.
29. HG to Winthrop, Aug. 1, 1844; to Waterston, March 25, 1845.
30. May 26, 1845.
31. July 7, 1845.
32. Tuckerman, pp. 33–34.
33. *Letters,* p. 202; Exhibition Catalogue of the National Academy of Design, 1848.
34. General details in the rest of this section about the Henry Greenoughs abroad come from Frances' and Henry's letters to relatives in America and from Frances' journal, 1845–1851 (Miss Alice Thorndike, Manchester, Mass.) The quotation in this paragraph comes from Frances to Harriet B. Loring, Dec. 14, [1845].
35. To Harriet B. Loring, Nov. 20, [1848].
36. To Harriet B. Loring, April 25, [1846]; Jan. 29, [1847].
37. Frances B. Greenough to Charlotte G. Parker, June 30, [1846]; to Francis Boott, [summer 1846]; to Mary B. Goodrich, Aug. 30, [1846].
38. Henry to Elizabeth B. Greenough, Sept. 3, 1846.
39. *Letters,* pp. 199–201.

Risorgimento

1. Boston *Transcript,* March 19, 1847.
2. John Locke, Letter from Florence, May 7, 1847, Savannah *Daily Republican,* June 18, 1847; photograph of a version of

the Castor and Pollux relief not preserved, in the author's collection; *Letters,* pp. 199–200; Jarves, *The Art-Idea* (N. Y., 1864), p. 260.

3. N. Y. *Tribune,* Nov. 21, 1849; Locke; *Life, Letters, and Journals of George Ticknor* (Boston, 1876), II, 241–242.
4. Author's collection.
5. *Letters,* p. 206; Tuckerman, p. 56. There are statues of Giusti at Florence and Monsummano (his birthplace) and a bust of him at Pescia by other sculptors. For assistance in searching for information about HG's sculpture in tribute to him, I am indebted to Prof. Rolando Anzilotti of the University of Pisa.
6. Louisa G. Greenough to E. N. Perkins, July 21, 1890 (Boston Athenaeum).
7. Archivio Notarile (Florence), Prot. XIII, no. 61, rep. 61 (Aug. 31, 1847), Prot. 37, no. 20, rep. 7 (Jan. 23, 1849) (Compra e Vendita; Fede pro Decima, Fede pro Voltura, [with map]); Il Cancelliere (Florence), 1850, Nos. 57, 58, 1853, No. 241; Henry to Elizabeth B. Greenough, Feb. 25, 1848; Frances B. to Elizabeth B. Greenough, March 12, [1848].
8. N. Y. *Tribune,* Nov. 21, 1849; Tuckerman, p. 36.
9. Everett to HG, July 17, Sept. 10, 1849 (letterbook); Ticknor, II, 242.
10. *The Home Journal,* Aug. 31, 1850; *Letters,* p. 224; Tuckerman, p. 56.
11. *Letters,* p. 226.
12. Author's collection.
13. *Letters,* p. 223.
14. HG to Bryant, May 7, 1851.
15. P. 57.
16. *Letters,* p. 229.
17. Frances B. Greenough to Charlotte G. Parker, April 15, [1847]; *Letters,* pp. 203–204; Frances B. Greenough to Harriet B. Loring, Feb. 27, [1848], Oct. 3, [1847].

18. Frances B. Greenough to Harriet B. Loring, Aug. 17, [1847]; to Elizabeth B. Greenough, Oct. 21, [1848]; to Harriet B. Loring, Oct. 14, [1848]; Henry to Frances B. Greenough, Sept. 11, 1849; Frances B. Greenough, Journal, Oct. 9, 1848.
19. Frances B. Greenough to Harriet B. Loring, Feb. 27, [1848]; to Elizabeth B. Greenough, March 12, May 21, [1848]; to Harriet B. Loring, July 23, [1848]; HG to Powers, [c July 25, 1848]; Frances B. Greenough, Journal, Aug. 6, 1848.
20. Frances B. Greenough to Harriet B. Loring, Oct. 14, [1848]; to Charlotte G. Parker, Dec 3, [1848]; Henry to Frances B. Greenough, Nov. 8, 1848; Frances B. Greenough to Harriet B. Loring, Nov. 13, Dec. 17, [1848].
21. Frances B. Greenough to Harriet B. Loring, Dec. 17, [1848]; to Charlotte G. Parker, Dec. 3, [1848]; to Harriet B. Loring, Feb. 11, [1849], Dec. 17, [1848]; Journal, Feb. 17, March 19, 1849; Henry to Frances B. Greenough, postmarked July 8, postmarked Sept. 3, Sept. 11, 1849.
22. HG to the Prefect of Florence, Jan. 9, 1851.
23. Henry to Elizabeth B. Greenough, Dec. 11, 1849.
24. Frances B. Greenough to Harriet B. Loring, Nov. 8, [1847], n. d. [1848], April 28, [1850]; *Bulletin of the American Art-Union,* May 1851, p. 61; *Letters,* p. 219.
25. L. C. Scott, *The Life and Letters of Christopher Pearse Cranch* (Boston, 1917), pp. 150 ff.
26. Margaret Fuller Ossoli to Calvert, May 10, 1850 (Harvard); *Memoirs of Margaret Fuller Ossoli* (Boston, 1852), II, 226–227; Margaret Fuller Ossoli to Lewis Cass, Oct. 8, 1849 (Harvard).
27. Frances B. Greenough, Journal, Nov. 12, 1845.
28. Everett to HG, May 21, 1849.
29. Powers papers, Florence; information furnished by Mrs. Clara L. Dentler, Florence.
30. Florence *Patria,* Oct. 19, 1847 (quoted by Guiliana Artom-Treves, *The Golden Ring* [London, 1956], p. 152).

31. Powers to Miner Kellogg, Dec. 6, 1848.
32. Powers to ——?——, Feb. 28, 1849 (clipping from a New Orleans newspaper in the Historical and Philosophical Society of Cincinnati).
33. Frances B. Greenough to Harriet B. Loring, April 14, [1849].
34. *Letters,* p. 233; Powers to Binda, July 6, 1849; to Mrs. James Austin, June 13, 1849; *Almanacco Toscano,* 1851, p. 326.
35. Jan. 9, 1851.
36. *Letters,* p. 216.
37. Sept. 26, 1850.
38. Jan. 12, 1853.
39. Dec. 11, 1849.
40. *Letters,* p. 227; HG to Norton, [c Nov. or Dec. 1850]; *Life of Joseph Green Cogswell as Sketched in his Letters,* pp. 256–257; DeForest, p. 5.
41. John Forster, *Walter Savage Landor* (Boston, 1869), p. 473; *Letters,* p. 236.
42. *Letters,* pp. 221, 226; Bill of Lading, Capt. G. Tar, *Atar Gull,* April 25, 1853 (National Archives, Records of the Office of Public Buildings and Public Parks of the National Capitol, Records of the Commissioner of Public Buildings); passenger list of the *America* (National Archives, Legislative and Fiscal Records Branch, Fiscal Section); *Letters,* p. 235.
43. *Letters,* pp. 233–234.
44. *Ibid.,* pp. 235–236.

6

Yankee Philosopher : 1851-1852

1

1. Samuel Longfellow, *Life of Henry Wadsworth Longfellow* (Boston, 1891), II, 217, 230.

2. Nov. 4, 1851.
3. Boston *Transcript,* Nov. 4, 5, 1851; Edward Everett, Diary, Jan. 26, 1852.
4. HG to Sumner, March 30, 1852; *Letters,* pp. 236–237; HG to Griswold, Nov. 19, 1851.
5. The quotations from *Æsthetics at Washington* in this section are from *Travels,* pp. 16, 18, 20, 33, 37, 46, 47, Copies of the pamphlet are in the Charleston (S.C.) Library Society, the Buffalo Public Library, Harvard University, the Library of Congress, and the New York Public Library.
6. HG to Emerson, Dec. 28, 1851. All the letters exchanged between HG and Emerson at this time, together with a letter from Emerson to Henry Greenough relative to HG, have been printed in their entirety in the author's "Ralph Waldo Emerson and Horatio Greenough," *Harvard Library Quarterly,* XII (Winter 1958), 91–116.
7. *The Letters of Ralph Waldo Emerson,* ed. Ralph L. Rusk (N. Y. 1939), IV, 271–272.
8. *Journals of Ralph Waldo Emerson,* ed. Edward Waldo Emerson and Waldo Emerson Forbes (Boston, 1909–1914), IV, 38, 88, 108–109, 483; V, 203, 205; VII, 199–200; VIII, 104, 272.
9. *The Writings of Henry David Thoreau* (Boston, 1906), IX, 181.
10. *Putnam's Magazine,* XI (Feb. 1868), opp. p. 137.
11. *Letters,* p. 237; *Memorial of James Fenimore Cooper* (N. Y., 1852), pp. 11–12; Boston *Transcript,* Dec. 15, 1852; HG to Griswold, Nov. 19, 1851.
12. HG to Bryant, Feb. 5, 1852. The letter to Bryant subsequently quoted in this paragraph is this one.
13. *Travels,* p. 174.
14. HG to Pell, [April] 17, [1852].
15. HG to Griswold, Nov. 19, 1851; to Bryant, Feb. 5, 1852.
16. Ms. notes at the Valentine Museum, Richmond, Va. I am

indebted to Mrs. Louise F. Catterall for a transcription of them.

17. This image recurs in HG's essay "The Stonecutter's Creed," printed in *Travels* and, under the title "An Artist's Creed," in Tuckerman. William Rounseville Alger, who found it in the latter volume, adapted it in his *Critical History of the Doctrine of a Future Life* (Philadelphia, 1864), in a passage in which he urged that the spider be imitated by man in search of proof of the soul's immortality. Inspired by the passage from Alger, Walt Whitman wrote "A Noiseless Patient Spider." (See William Sloane Kennedy, "The Germ Idea of Whitman's 'Noiseless Patient Spider' Poem," *Conservator,* XIV (Jan. 1914), 173.) I am indebted to Prof. F. DeWolfe Miller of the University of Tennessee for this reference.
18. HG to Bryant, Feb. 5, 1852; to Longfellow, Feb. 21, 1852; Longfellow, Journal, Feb. 6, 1852 (Harvard); Samuel Longfellow, II, 229–230; Everett, Diary, Feb. 21, 1852; Everett to HG, Feb. 20, 1852; HG to Dana, Feb. 23, 1852; *The Home Journal,* April 3, 10, 1852.
19. The chief account of this project is [James Lee], *The Equestrian Statue of Washington* (N. Y., 1864).
20. Tuckerman to Louisa G. Greenough, July 23, 1856 (David Richardson, Washington).
21. *Letters,* p. 238.
22. HG to Bancroft, May 7, 1852.
23. HG to Greene, July 27, 1852. *Hearnes' Brooklyn City Directory* (1852–53) gives his address as 115 Atlantic.
24. Gould to Hiram Powers, May 15, 1852.
25. Tuckerman to Louisa G. Greenough, July 23, 1856 (Richardson).
26. *Letters,* p. 238; *The Home Journal,* July 31, 1852; *Gleason's Pictorial Drawing-Room Companion,* VI (June 24, 1854), 388.

27. George Calvert, "Greenough, the Sculptor," *Putnam's Magazine,* I (March 1853), 319; *Letters,* pp. 240, 239.
28. *Letters,* p. 240.
29. *Ibid.,* p. 239; Longfellow, Journal, *passim;* Boston *Transscript,* Sept. 8, 1852; Suffolk County Registry of Probate (Boston), No. 38180; Tuckerman, p. 25.
30. Tuckerman, pp. 38–39.
31. May 20, 1852.
32. *The Home Journal,* June 19, 1852.
33. Tuckerman, p. 48.
34. N. Y. *Evening Post,* Aug. 7, 1852.
35. *Journals of . . . Emerson,* VIII, 318–319; Emerson to Henry Greenough, Sept. 15, 1863 (Richardson).
36. *The Letters of . . . Emerson,* IV, 306.
37. Louisa G. Greenough to Powers, April 2, 1863; *Letters,* p. 238. Two copies of the daguerreotype are in the author's collection.

2

1. One in the Library of Congress and one in the Charleston Library Society. A facsimile edition was issued by Scholars' Facsimiles & Reprints, Gainesville, Fla., in 1958.
2. The quotations from *Travels* in this section are, in order, from pp. 222, 197, vi–vii, 172, 187–188, 190, 199, 201, 203, 204, 202, 212, 73, 62, 63, 65, 68, 74–75, 80, 55, 60.
3. *Letters,* p. 238.
4. Sept. 6, 1852.
5. *The Letters of . . . Emerson,* IV, 312.
6. Sept. 11, 1852.
7. Sept. 25, Oct. 21, 1852.
8. *Journals of . . . Emerson,* VIII, 331–333; MS Journal *GO* (1852), pp. 212–217 (Harvard).
9. Nov. 1, 1852.
10. HG to Emerson, Nov. 4, 1852; Emerson to HG, Nov. 11, 1852.

11. Nov. 10, 1852.
12. Edward L. Pierce, *Memoir and Letters of Charles Sumner* (Boston, 1878–1893), III, 322.
13. *Catalogue of the Library of the late Henry T. Tuckerman, Esq., N. Y. . . . June 10–11–12–13, 1872*. Boston : Leavitt; Tuckerman to Powers, July 30, 1854.
14. Tuckerman, p. [60].
15. Louisa G. Greenough to Mrs. Sarah Whitman, Dec. 21, 1853 (Brown). The next quotation is from this letter.
16. Tuckerman, pp. 162, 164, 168–169, 188, 190–191.
17. N. Y. *Evening Post,* Aug. 13, 1853; N. Y. *Herald,* Aug. 13, 1853; [John Bigelow], "Nuces Literariae," N. Y. *Evening Post,* Aug. 22, 1853; *Letters of Charles Eliot Norton* (Boston, 1913), I, 91–92.
18. ["The Chinese make a plaything . . ."], *The Crayon,* I (Feb. 7, 1855), 89.

3

1. Tuckerman, pp. 40–41.
2. Dec. 20, 1852 (Harvard). The next quotation and all others from Dana in this section are from this letter.
3. Louisa G. Greenough to Elizabeth G. Powers, July 8, 1853; McLean Asylum (Somerville, Mass.) Cases, 1852–54, p. 211.
4. Tuckerman, pp. 43–44.
5. Emerson to HG, Nov. 17, 1852; *Prose Remains of Arthur Hugh Clough* (London, 1888), p. 192.
6. *The Journals of Bronson Alcott* (Boston, 1938), p. 263; F. B. Sanborn and William T. Harris, *A. Bronson Alcott* (Boston, 1893), II, 477.
7. Boston *Transcript,* Nov. 22–24, 27, 1852; Frances B. Greenough, Journal, Nov. [24], 1852; Sanborn and Harris, II, 263.
8. McLean Asylum Cases, 1852–54, p. 211. The chief facts in this and the next paragraph, unless otherwise noted, come from this record.
9. Sanborn and Harris, II, 263.

10. Frances B. Greenough, Journal. Henry's return with HG is also recorded here.
11. Henry's certificate, National Archives, Records of the General Accounting Office, Report of the First Auditor, No. 109. 184 (Feb. 7, 1853).
12. Tuckerman, p. 42.
13. *Ibid.,* pp. 41–42.
14. Ms. Journal.
15. Suffolk County Registry of Probate (Boston), No. 38180.
16. April 5, 1853.
17. Six letters from Louisa to Mrs. Whitman, bearing various dates in 1853, all relating to this matter, are at Brown.
18. Edward McAleer, "New Letters from Mrs. Browning to Isa Blagden," *Publications of the Modern Language Association,* LXVI (1951), 598.
19. N. Y. *Evening Post,* Dec. 20, 1852; Newport *Mercury,* Dec. 24, 1852; Tuckerman, pp. 244–245, 235.
20. Samuel Longfellow, II, 244; *Letters of . . . Norton,* I, 92; Emerson to Henry Greenough, Sept. 15, 1863; *The Correspondence of Thomas Carlyle and Ralph Waldo Emerson* (London, 1883), II, 219; *Journals of . . . Emerson,* VIII, 390–391.
21. See for example, MS Journal *VS* (1853), p. 296 (Harvard); *Journals,* VIII, 552; IX, 155; X, 234, 283, 357; MS Journal *NY* (1868), pp. 43, 94–97, 160 (Harvard); MS "Art and Nature," p. 1 (Harvard); Washington *Chronicle,* Jan. 17, 1872.
22. Louisa G. Greenough to Emerson, March 18, 1869 (Harvard).
23. (N. Y.), pp. 261–262.

Index

ABBREVIATIONS

BA: Boston Athenaeum

BMFA: Museum of Fine Arts, Boston

BPL: Boston Public Library

HG: Horatio Greenough

HSP: Historical Society of Pennsylvania

LC: Library of Congress

Letters: Letters of Horatio Greenough, to his Brother Henry, ed. Frances B. Greenough (Boston, 1887)

MHS: Massachusetts Historical Society

NA: National Archives

NYHS: New-York Historical Society

NYPL: New York Public Library

Travels: Horatio Greenough, *The Travels, Observations, and Experience of a Yankee Stonecutter* (N. Y., 1852)

Wright: Author's collection

Letters written by HG are entered under the names of the addressees. Locations of the known mss. of all letters cited, in the text and the notes, are given in parentheses. Page references are given only for letters quoted or referred to in the text. Dates are given only when ms. letters to the same person are in different locations. Letters of which no texts are available are indexed under names of addressees but not entered as "HG to."

If the only reference to a person or a character is in connection with sculpture of him by HG, the name is entered only under "sculpture by HG"; otherwise it is also entered alphabetically.

The purely bibliographical information in the notes is not indexed, only that which is of the general nature of the text.